Guillem Balagué is an award-winning football author, journalist and presenter who works regularly for BBC TV, BBC Radio 5 Live, ITV, LaLiga TV and th[illegible] network CBS. In his previous role at Sk[illegible] fixture of their Spanish footb[illegible], known for his regular ap[illegible] vista de LaLiga', his pundi[illegible] or anything relating to the [illegible] his own YouTube channel, 1[illegible] media, his own podcast (Pure Footb[illegible] Masterclasses in journalism at UCFB Universit[illegible] in Wembley (London) and the Etihad stadium in Manchester.

He wrote the bestselling *A Season on the Brink*, an insider's account of Liverpool's 2004–05 Champions' League winning campaign, recently updated. In November 2012, he published the first international biography of Pep Guardiola, based on conversations with him, shortlisted for Football Book of the Year, as were his following four books. The following year, he published *Messi: The Definitive Biography*, the only authorised biography of the Argentinian star. As well as two ebooks (diaries of the 2012 European Championships and the 2014 World Cup), he published the *Official History of FC Barcelona* in the autumn of 2014. In November 2015, he wrote *Cristiano Ronaldo: the Biography* which won the Football Book of the Year Award at the British Sports Book Awards and the Best Football Book of 2016 in Poland. His latest books *Brave New World – Inside Pochettino's Spurs* and *Maradona* were *Sunday Times* bestsellers in the UK. He is also chairman of Biggleswade United.

ALSO BY GUILLEM BALAGUÉ

Pep Guardiola
Messi
Cristiano Ronaldo
Brave New World
Maradona

A SEASON ON THE BRINK

A Portrait of Rafael Benítez's Liverpool

•

GUILLEM BALAGUÉ

SEVEN DIALS

First published in Great Britain in 2005 by Weidenfeld & Nicolson.
This revised edition published in 2025 by Seven Dials,
an imprint of The Orion Publishing Group Ltd
Carmelite House, 50 Victoria Embankment
London EC4Y 0DZ

An Hachette UK Company

The authorised representative in the EEA is Hachette Ireland,
8 Castlecourt Centre, Dublin 15, D15 XTP3,
Ireland (email: info@hbgi.ie)

1 3 5 7 9 10 8 6 4 2

A CIP catalogue record for this book is available from the British Library.

ISBN (Mass Market Paperback) 978 1 3996 2666 8
ISBN (eBook) 978 1 4091 3814 3
ISBN (Audio) 978 1 3996 2739 9

Printed in Great Britain by Clays Ltd, Elcograf S.p.A.

MIX
Paper | Supporting responsible forestry
FSC® C104740

www.orionbooks.co.uk

To my parents, Guillermo and Maria Oliva,
and to my grandma for buying me the sports papers
before I could understand them.

To George, who was the first one
to tell me about the Kop.

CONTENTS

FOREWORD
By Rafael Benítez

Twenty years after that memorable night in Istanbul, what remains with me above everything else is just how much it meant to so many people. To this day I am still approached by fans who tell me, 'That was the most important night of my life.'

I always reply, 'Don't say that in front of your wife, she'll kill you.' Recently, one of the fans told me that was never going to happen because, in addition to it being the most important day in his life, it was also the most important day in the lives of his wife and children too. It was something very special for many people, for a whole generation and also for those who would go on to enjoy the evolution of the club. The other day, during a game at Anfield, a fan said to me, 'We know what you did and how difficult it was.' That season and that success represented a golden era for Liverpool and it was achieved against the odds. A success that nobody expected. Maybe that gives it an even deeper, meaningful feeling.

When I arrived at Liverpool, I was told that the plan was to be competitive within three years. They didn't say to me, 'We have to win.' Back then, the club did not have the financial power to compete with the likes of Chelsea, Arsenal or Manchester United. Later, when they changed ownership, there was even a period when the club came perilously close to going into administration. That was what we held in our hands. Up until the change of ownership, my relationship with the management was fantastic. Everyone was positive right from the very start. The Chairman, David Moores, was very supportive and even though I argued with the CEO, Rick Parry, over the speed of signings, my dynamism combined with his experience and more measured, phlegmatic British approach ensured that we worked well together. All the support and help from above ensured we got that unexpected reward, the first Champions League or European Cup win in 21 years.

Many people talk about winning that competition as if it were a matter of luck, but we didn't win it by luck. We won it because of the effort, commitment and determination of the predominantly young squad. We came from behind against Olympiacos in the last game of the group stage, where we scored the three goals we needed in the second half thanks to the combination of the young and more experienced players in our side. And Steven Gerrard, of course. In the knockout stages, we beat Dimitar Berbatov and Andriy Voronin's Bayer Leverkusen, and then we faced Fabio Capello's Juventus, who had just eliminated Real Madrid. A great team, as good or even better than the AC Milan side we would go on to face in the final, with players like Buffon, Cannavaro, Thuram, Nedvěd, Ibrahimović, and Del Piero in their line-up. With Xabi Alonso back in the team after a three-month absence because of an injury, we changed the system to play a 5-3-1-1 formation, with Igor Biščan, Antonio Núñez, Luis García and Milan Baroš up front and with Xabi placed close to our three centre-backs to counteract the fact that they were playing with two forwards and an offensive midfielder.

Our unexpected success saw us drawn in the semi-finals against a high-spending Chelsea, who were at that time dominating the Premier League, and we emerged victorious over two legs thanks to our great competitiveness and attention to detail. The fact that Chelsea were 33 points ahead of us in the Premier League counted for nothing and only seemed to serve as an extra motivation for our fans during the return leg at Anfield, after a 0-0 result at Stamford Bridge. What an electric atmosphere we were surrounded by! Luis García's famous 'ghost' goal that ultimately put us into the final, if disallowed, could have been instead a penalty and seen Petr Čech sent off – something people always forget to mention – which would have made for a very different game.

In the final, we found ourselves up against a very strong AC Milan side with Dida in goal. Cafu, Stam, Nesta, Maldini at the back; Seedorf, Pirlo, Gattuso in midfield and Kaká in front of them, just behind Crespo and Shevchenko. We started by conceding a goal . . . then another . . . and another. But our fans never stopped singing. We fought back, refusing to give in, and dragged ourselves level. The match went to penalties – a heart-stopping encounter, the kind you never forget. What a game that was. Even now, I'm still in awe of what happened that night. I've watched the final a couple of times, but not as many times as people might think. At the end of the day, it is still very much in your head. Having said that . . . What is interesting is that, when you see it, you remember some details in a different way. We all have a selective memory, sometimes you keep in your mind what you want to keep. Overall, I always felt we lacked control in the first half, but in the second, we improved. We managed the game better, and by extra time, we were even dictating play. In fact, with Cissé's pace, I truly felt we could have won it on the counterattack. That was my instinct on the night in Istanbul and I kept saying that years after. Now, looking back at the footage, you can see that while clear chances were rare, once we were level, we had a grip on the game. But to be honest, in the end, there wasn't much separating the two sides.

The other day, a Liverpool fan asked me, 'Why didn't you start with Vladimír Šmicer?' Well, when you have Steven Gerrard and Xabi Alonso, nobody can say that's a mistake. And if you choose Harry Kewell, a very talented player, and Luis García, you're adding even more creativity. In games like that, you need talent, players who can create moments, open up opportunities, and give you more options. At the time, my main striker was Milan Baroš, and while he worked hard, he wasn't a 30-goal-a-season forward. We had to make tactical changes at half-time and, to be honest, not many things went wrong after we corrected the space that Kaká was enjoying in the middle of the park with the appearance of Didi Hamann.

Nothing that happened was just luck. Of course, luck always plays a part, but this was about constant work and preparation.

The coaching staff had meticulously planned for every scenario, including penalties, which we had practiced extensively beforehand. For the generation that lived through that time, what happened in Istanbul is something they will never forget. Even for those that admitted to me they left the stadium at half-time. Or especially them! We won, a memorable victory but, just as importantly, our triumph served to transform the mentality of the club and the people. The levels of expectation rose dramatically. If we could win it once, then why shouldn't we win it again? That same season, even though we didn't achieve the necessary consistency in the Premier League because of the distraction of being in the Champions League and reaching the final, we also achieved another level, an extra layer of competitiveness. Winning took us to the European Super Cup against CSKA Moscow, which we also won. Then we faced the following season with a lot of confidence and won the FA Cup. And we won it with hard work, by studying our rival, by improving our players, and with the support of our loyal fans who felt very close to us.

Let me tell you in detail the work we did. It would help you understand why we started winning titles. Since we had arrived, we changed everything. I was a manager, but I took training every day. We spent the time on the field, looking for improvements, correcting, doing exercises. We changed the diet, the physical control tests, made detailed anthropometry studies (the scientific study of the measurements and proportions of the human body), looked long and hard at the type of training, the methodology. We prepared ourselves 80 per cent of the time with the ball. It was never just using the ball for fun, but rather with clear objectives and an organization behind it. One Friday in the first season, before our debut match against Tottenham, which was going to take place early on the Saturday afternoon, I asked the players after a light training session to do ten 300-metre runs at 80 per cent effort, and then the same back. Josemi looked at me in disbelief before saying, 'ten runs?' And then they set about doing it until I stopped them.

'Where are you going? Don't you see that today is Friday, that we have a match the next day, that we have just finished training . . .

How are we going to do ten runs?' I realised that as praiseworthy as it was to have players who wanted to follow instructions, it was also important that they should understand the reason for each action, the motive behind every exercise. If a player was going to press a full-back, he had to know when and how to go about it. For example, you can't press the full-back if he's 20 metres away and has the ball at his feet. You must do it when the pass comes from 20 metres away and the full-back doesn't have the ball, because that gives you time to get there. Explaining to players precisely why they should press at any given moment is a fundamental part of the learning process, how to close ranks. And all that information was relatively new to many of them.

That tactical rigor was always part of our methodology. But beyond that, order, discipline, motivation, and the full commitment of the players helped us compensate for our limited budget. It was about maximizing every detail and deepening our understanding of the game. Many players I spoke to long after they had left told me it was our vision and meticulous attention to detail that made the difference. Things they had never even considered before, like body positioning before making a run, or scanning the pitch before receiving the ball, suddenly became second nature. It was those seemingly minor details that elevated their game. What most players want above all is to play and enjoy it. If they can do that whilst also absorbing what they need to, those habits become part of their DNA, they improve almost without realizing it. I remember Jamie Carragher once saying that our improvement came from the constant repetition of everything we did. It meant that every player instinctively knew their role, functioning on autopilot, not just deliberate actions, but automatic reactions, like brushing your teeth or changing gears in a car. And then, when the game changes, you have a Plan B or C ready to go. That's how players evolve.

Lucas Leiva was a case in point. On the pitch, he would arrive where he needed to be, rush his next decision and commit a foul, time after time. I would say to him, 'Get there, arrive. And delay!' And I would keep on saying it to him, keep on repeating it until it was implanted firmly in his head and became a natural course of action. It was all about creating automatisms. Eventually, I would say, 'Get there . . .' and he would quickly reply, 'Arrive and delay!' I was with him recently and we laughed a lot remembering the insistence. We made footballers think until better reactions became part of their DNA. At first, players absorb information like a sponge, but there comes a point where they hit saturation, which is their way of saying, 'Enough.' That's when they've peaked, reaching their maximum efficiency. And that's when you need new, better players. It's why constant analysis is essential – understanding what you have, what you need, what's available, and who you can bring in without disrupting the balance and harmony of the squad. At Liverpool we didn't have much room for manoeuvre. I will explain later.

As a coaching group we looked at everything that was necessary in order to improve and gain an advantage. Concentrating on building the cohesion of the group was one such aspect we looked at and I asked a university professor to prepare group cohesion exercises for me that could be applied to football. If you are not in a dressing room, it is difficult to fully understand the work that is done on the seemingly minor details. For example, I see Unai Emery's Aston Villa, and I see a team that is organized and pays serious attention to each play; be it a foul, a throw-in, or whatever, everyone knows what they have to do, and it reminds me of what we did at Liverpool. But what happens when you have so much learning and information crammed into your locker? We had 300 plus exercises in the database, 20 per cent of which we would usually use and, perhaps, seven per cent we would use more than the others. This is interesting because, in the end, experience and knowledge guide you in choosing the right exercises. You have a vast amount of information at your disposal, but ultimately, you also rely on instinct – which is nothing more than accumulated knowledge refined over time. That instinct is what leads you to the best conclusions, the ones that best serve your objectives. Then on the pitch you know that you have at your disposal players like Mascherano, Xabi Alonso, Lucas Leiva, Jamie Carragher, who manage the rest of the team because they are clever enough to better understand what is required, put it into action and then transmit it to their teammates.

Arsene Wenger always told me, 'It is so difficult to play against your team!' We made it very complicated for our opponents to find gaps because our players would always help each other, press at the right moment, work hard without the ball. And we did it better and better, and that allowed us to compete against better teams. And beat them! That's how we had won the league with Valencia, for example. My technical team and I took care of every detail, and we were highly valued. However, when you stop winning, those same details that you took the utmost care to maintain can become a problem – a stick to beat you with – because it can be said that they put too much pressure on the players. In the end, the entourage can end up blaming the very thing that led it to victory in the first place. I am in favour of giving freedom to players who understand football, who know what to do. But there are others who need orders, and to obey them to get the most out of them. Each player has certain abilities and they must be exploited to the maximum.

At the beginning, I had three assistants: Pako Ayestarán, Paco Herrera and José Manuel Ochotorena. We all spoke English… badly! In fact, I was the one who spoke it best; can you imagine? But we gradually came to understand the players, the directors, the fans and together we learned the language, the culture and eventually the mentality. At the beginning it was difficult, because English players are very emotionally involved, particularly somewhere like Anfield. That deep connection was something I always looked for, but equally important was the need to be able to control what was happening on the pitch. In Merseyside derbies, I would remind Steven Gerrard about the need to stay calm. And then in the first play he would go diving in to make a memorable tackle and the crowd would go crazy. We quickly had to take on board that approach to the game, realise that it was part of English football culture, learn from it and incorporate it into our game. We worked hard and got close to the people, we treated the staff well, and we managed to make the project feel like a collaboration between all who loved

Liverpool, the fans and the professionals. We collaborated with charities, for example, and that information spread throughout the city, and little by little, people began to appreciate us, not just because of results, but also for the way we became involved in the community. And it was done with a totally honest belief that you have to put roots where you are, no matter where you come from.

When I arrived, I was probably not aware of the value that people from Merseyside give to footballing achievements and the way to achieve them. I very soon discovered it. I remember a banner that read: 'Rafa has been the best invention since the potato came to England.' Very funny! People appreciate your involvement, the success and how it was achieved. When I go to Valencia or Extremadura, they also welcome me with affection and in Newcastle or Naples I also sense that love from the fans. But here, in this part of England, it is something very special. Just yesterday I was at a game at Anfield and it was crazy. And although young people don't know me as much now, people from that generation still recognise me. We became more integrated into the world we inhabited, into Liverpool's culture and into the club's mentality, even to the point of strengthening contact with former players. At a certain point, we brought Kenny Dalglish back into the club because we needed someone who could offer something extra to the team during my final years at the club. We thought that with the help of Kenny we could regain institutional presence as well as improve relations with the footballing authorities. We needed to fight more battles than on the pitch. The club was no longer doing the things we had done at the beginning, when we had fewer resources. Those things that are less visible and that made us more competitive at the beginning, were no longer being done.

In England, we had some rivals, people unwilling, or unable, to recognise our achievements against clubs like Chelsea, Manchester United, Arsenal, Tottenham. If you beat them often, you are not going to make many friends. But there are a lot of people who value and recognise what we did, more I would say than even in Spain, where they always question you. Here you are a legend, and that remains. And I am eternally grateful for it. But it became clear that slowly but surely many relationships that had been good at the start of my presence in the Premier League, later on became strained. José Mourinho and I shared secrets and admired each other. But, suddenly, as we started to take points away from Chelsea or knock them out of important competitions, our relationship waned. On 1 January 2005, on the steps of Anfield, after the game against Chelsea, Mourinho told me that he wanted to sign Steven Gerrard. The conversation, a meeting between colleagues, was relaxed, respectful, but from then on, we started to become rivals and ended up being enemies. I think we faced each other 16 times, and we knocked them out of the Champions League a couple of times. And although they were superior in the league, on those occasions where we could compete against them head-to-head, in two-legged matches, where a mistake could cost anyone dear, we always gave as good as we got.

When I was developing as a coach, I went to see Sir Alex Ferguson train. Steve McClaren, who was his assistant, looked after us very well, although I barely spoke to Ferguson. I crossed paths with Sir Alex at the Paris final between Barcelona and Arsenal in May 2006. As winners the previous year, UEFA had invited my wife and me to attend. He was also there with his wife. As he got off the minibus that takes you to the stadium, behind some barriers that acted as a corridor, Arsenal fans appeared and started to insult him. I stood in front of him, trying to discreetly protect him, and then we sat down and watched the game together. Then, on the way to Nyon for the UEFA meeting, I sat with him on the plane, and everything was fine. But of course, when you start to become a real rival, the tension begins. The rivalry extended off the pitch. We both stood for different things, we were ambassadors for different clubs, with a different philosophy of life and football. I was very aware that I represented our fans wherever I went. I remember that when I arrived at a managers' meeting – when we had already begun to have our disagreements – they sat us next to each other at a very long table. I went to another manager and asked him if he wouldn't mind changing places with me, which he kindly did. I am polite, but I'm not a hypocrite, certainly not at that level. Now, I have a respectful relationship with him, he was a great manager, no doubt about that.

My now famous press conference, where I cited a series of 'facts' that were purely objective and where I criticised Ferguson's excessive influence, was misinterpreted. Nobody questioned the content, only the timing and the manner. But the content was absolutely objective and clear. Liverpool, Chelsea and Arsenal had four more Saturday morning games than Manchester United after European and international competitions, and away from home, while they played at home at a time that allowed them more rest. I remember a game that Manchester United played at home on a Sunday, against Aston Villa, whilst we had to play away at the likes of Sunderland, Newcastle, or Portsmouth at 12.30 in the afternoon. And those details conditioned our planning. For example, before Sunderland, Mascherano and Lucas Leiva went straight to the game because they had been with their national teams in South America. You have to think very carefully about whether or not to include them both in the starting eleven, because at that point you don't have the guarantee that one, or both of them are fully fit. In the end, there were many small factors that complicated our path. Our pre-match preparation was radically affected for no fewer than four matches, equal to 12 points, and nobody saw fit to question it. Just over two months later we faced them in the league at Old Trafford where I remember seeing a kid with his dad carrying a banner that said 'Rafa, cracking up!' We beat them 4–1.

After that press conference, on a cold and icy day in Stoke, we drew in a game which saw Gerrard strike the post. We drew a couple of games more and United had games in-hand to play because they had gone to the Club World Cup. Since they won those games and we drew, they caught up to us. It has been said by some that the press conference had a detrimental effect on our team's performances. But if that were the case, how do you explain the fact that we won ten and drew one, at home to Arsenal, of our last eleven games of the season? In fact, we only lost a couple of games after that press conference. Against Tottenham, in Harry Redknapp's first game, in a match where Xabi Alonso had a couple of chances that didn't end up in the net. We were superior and even Redknapp came up to me at the end of the game and said the result was 'difficult to explain.' We also lost against a Middlesbrough side who would end that season being relegated, thanks to an own goal. It was a game we should have won. We were doing well, but so were United, occasionally settling matters very late on in the proceedings. 'Games last until United score,' Liverpool fans would joke, but we were challenging the giant that is Manchester United for the league title. Pitting ourselves against a side that had such a good squad that they could afford to leave £20 million players on the bench, the sort of money that we would only pay for a player that would be guaranteed a place in our starting XI.

We became the disruptor of the league and that is also where the connection with the fans came from. And I firmly believe that part of our success is due to that. It happened to me at Valencia, at Napoli and also at Newcastle. When you have a committed group, players without big egos, but rather more focused on hard work and sacrifice, it is easier to get the best out of them. Managing stars who are not involved with the group is always difficult, especially if the environment does not support the coach, and the star who is not very committed to the group is protected. A big difference is made when you have a leader, both on and off the pitch, like Steven Gerrard who is the first to roll up his sleeves, and set an example. If the best player in the team also happens to be the one who plays anywhere he is needed, runs furthest, works hardest and never fails to show up, then the rest have nowhere to hide and no choice other than to follow his example. That group mentality creates a culture of commitment and effort that makes you grow more as a group. We were always more successful when the group was united. The value of the team as a whole always exceeds individual excellence.

That was the groundwork we did, but to compete constantly you need more. But we had a gross budget of £20 million when I signed, so I had to sell to increase the money available. The signing of Djibril Cissé had already been made that summer by the time I landed, and he cost £14 million. So, £20 million minus £14 million, imagine. You had to sell in order to spend and sign well. Or sign players at a very small cost with the hope that you can get something out of them. In fact, the following year the Chairman invested money out of his own pocket. It was £15 million, but then it had to be returned. It was a challenge, and that is why every decision to buy or sell was important. Each operation had to be carefully thought out because we had no room for error. And, of course, you don't usually sell the bad ones, but you have to sell the good ones (Xabi Alonso, for example) to be able to increase the budget. It is not easy to maintain that balance when every decision is key. Some players, like Jermain Pennant or Peter Crouch, ended up costing us more money because as soon as we showed interest, their clubs raised the price – something that often happened to a team like ours. We needed a substitute to Fernando Torres, so we did not play him constantly. We went for David Ngog, a talented young player. The price? £1.5 million. We wanted Aaron Ramsey, who was 17-years-old at the time, and was going to cost us £1.5 million in transfer fees, plus £1.5 million in bonuses. Cardiff, who at that time were still in the FA Cup did not particularly fancy losing their star player – their Steven Gerrard, if you like – and asked Liverpool to wait. The reward for our integrity? Arsenal steamed in ahead of us, provided a private plane for him and his family to meet Arsène Wenger, Arsenal handed over £5 million and stole him from under our noses.

We also tried some speculative deals with sporting director Eduardo Macià to bring in 17-to-18-year-old burgeoning talents from around the world for around £200,000 with the hopes that at least one of them could develop into a top flight player. But the harsh reality was that on an economic level we could not compete with the biggest clubs. When you reach your budget limit, you can't afford to make mistakes. If things don't go to plan for whatever reason, your chances of growing are seriously hampered. If, for example, a big signing like Alberto Aquilani has a bad ankle, you have to adjust accordingly and there simply isn't enough time. You can't replace him easily, unlike the richest clubs who make a mistake and can sign three full-backs, and solve the problem. It's a tricky balance, and the difference in resources means that some clubs can sustain their level for longer, whilst others can't. When you're driving your car flat out you might be able to stay at 150 kilometres an hour for a while, but you'll have to be careful. Others, with a superior engine, can go 150 kilometres an hour at half throttle. That's what happened to us in the Premier League.

I have often met with players from that Istanbul final. Some are coaches and have called me to talk about coaching methods. Djimi Traoré came to see me train at Newcastle. I have kept in touch with John Arne Riise and with Didi Hamann as well. On one occasion, Didi made arrangements to be considered by Bayern Munich. He knew the sporting director, we had a meeting, the change of coach was imminent, but due to one of those mysteries of football, in the end it didn't happen. With Carragher, I collaborate with charities. The other day I spent a few hours signing more than 500 shirts that will have the signatures of all those who were in Istanbul. I have already done it a couple of times for different organisations. I keep in touch with Gerrard from time to time by messaging too. I met Mascherano at the last Champions League final in London and we talk about players regularly. I also speak with Fernando Torres every now and then, and we chat about his experience as a coach, he is doing very well. I met Lucas Leiva in Liverpool recently, where we chatted about Brazilian football, and I exchange messages with Fabio Aurelio and Neil Mellor, too. I've congratulated Xabi on his success, but we don't have regular contact. I've crossed paths with Luis García and Vladimír Šmicer at some games, and I occasionally see others, like Jerzy Dudek, at Legends matches. I think Steve Finnan is still upset with me for taking him off early in the second half of the final. I ran into Sami Hyypiä the other day, and I know Djibril Cissé wants me to join a Legends match he's organizing.

It's natural for clubs to evolve, but sometimes past achievements don't receive the recognition they deserve. I've heard that at the training ground, reminders of that era are few, though I understand this is changing under the new owners. On a recent visit to Anfield, I noticed the fifth Champions League trophy placed somewhat discreetly. Celebrating recent successes is important, but it feels even more meaningful when they're framed within the club's rich history. The way the 2004–2005 season developed and how it ended, will never change. It will remain there for good, burned into the hearts and souls of everyone. Nobody can take that away from us. There would be other stages where we win more, play better, but that year belongs to all of us, to the fans who experienced it and to those of us who worked at the club. Forever.

Everything is connected, we have all helped Liverpool grow.

INTRODUCTION

On a balmy day in July 2004, thirty-five years after he had first arrived at Liverpool FC and eleven since he had become one of their coaches, Sammy Lee got to Melwood for the last time as a member of the club. He had come to collect his belongings. I went to help him. He drove us into the training ground after winding down the car window and signing a couple of autographs for the teenage signature-hunters that wait for anybody with any connection to Liverpool FC to come in or out.

'Hi, Sammy, have you seen the new coach? Is he going to sign Aimar? Baraja? Is Owen going? Is Rafa a nice guy? Is he gonna win the league for us?' It felt like one hundred questions cascading down on him, in record time. Who said kids are not curious these days? Every query followed hot on the heels of the previous one, nobody was waiting for answers, and Sammy was left open-mouthed in his seat. Nobody, though, asked the question that would haunt Sammy every day for the next twelve months: 'Why are you leaving?'

The previous night, we had shared a few beers and reminisced in a pub that was like a thousand others in Liverpool: the same flowery carpet, the same awkward smiles from the barmaid in response to increasingly poor jokes, the same fireplace that is never lit. You could sense that Sammy wanted to prolong the night, chatting and drinking, because he was hours away from severing the umbilical cord that had tied him to Liverpool FC for all those years. It was not going to be easy.

During the evening he did his utmost to explain his precise motives for leaving Liverpool, but he didn't quite convince me. I simply couldn't understand his logic. Later, I discovered that until he was named as assistant to Sam Allardyce at Bolton Wanderers the following summer, Sammy had been struggling with the same doubts that had left me confused on that warm July evening. Not even he had been able to figure out why he had left. The nearest he came to a valid reason was that he had made a brave decision that had come from deep inside his footballing psyche and ambition. He knew he needed to make personal progress in the game, prompted by the stark realisation that he was roughly the same age as the new Liverpool boss, Rafa Benítez – both of them being in their mid-forties. Sammy needed to shape his future.

That night, we had been in the company of his son Matthew, Bernie (the club's driver) and some of Sammy's oldest friends. It was the first time I had seen him surrounded by normality – not framed by a stadium or a TV camera, nor next to the likes of Sami Hyypia, Phil Thompson and Gérard Houllier. Three years earlier, at the old Melwood training ground, I had shared lunch with Houllier and Sammy, who had pointed out the new facilities that were being built at the time. The stylish staff offices were to become Houllier's nerve centre: he wanted his presence, his watchful eye, to be felt by everybody. Now, they belonged to Benítez. 'Look, this is the gaffer's office; he's not in today,' said Sammy. 'You can see all the training taking place from his window. But we'll enter by the back door and say "Hi" to the secretary.' He acted as if he'd forgotten that this was the last time he could wander freely into the building. But, of course, Sammy Lee hadn't really forgotten at all.

As he showed me around his pride was obvious. There was a 'good morning' for everyone, a comment about every corner, even though the building boasted almost no history. His short figure moved nervously from corridors to rooms, trying to make sure I was watching everything, being introduced to everyone, ensuring I missed nothing. He was in the process of quitting the club where he had grown up, where he had developed as a footballer and as a man. I was half-expecting him to say at some point, 'I'll show you this and then I'll leave this club for ever, if that's OK with you.' Ten months later he admitted, 'I put on a good show. I was turning my back on a place I never, ever wanted to leave. I cried and my family cried, but such is life.'

Deep in the bowels of Melwood, Graham, one of the kit men, was leaning by a door. John, his colleague, was sitting inside the room. Sammy left me with them while he continued his farewell tour of the staff. Graham and John just shook their heads in puzzlement, aware that his departure from the club was much more than the end of a personal era. It also signalled the beginning of a new age in the history of Liverpool FC, which brought new fears as well as the promise of better times. As he said his goodbyes, Sammy tried to calm his evident trepidation with a nervous: 'Everything's going to turn out fine – no problem.' He fended off any deeper questions by enquiring about families, summer-holiday plans and, of course, the weather.

Naturally, my conversation with the kit men swiftly turned to all those worries that were nagging at Sammy. Above all, the greatest fear was about language problems: 'The new people seem very nice but they don't speak very much English, do they?' Well Rafa did, of course. And he had at least made himself popular with his efforts to make himself understood during the brief time since his arrival as Liverpool's new manager. Even at that early stage he was Rafa rather than Rafael. Everyone at the club had already decided that this was a down-to-earth bloke whose 'normal' attitude was very welcome after years of tension in the corridors of Melwood under Houllier. However, there were numerous other doubts, of the kind that can debilitate a football club if answers are not found early enough: 'How will *we* make ourselves understood to *them*?' 'Will Rafa change and turn out to be as paranoid [a word used commonly around the club to describe Houllier's latter years as boss] and difficult as the Frenchman?' 'Will he surround himself with as many of his own men as Houllier had?'

The kit men needed someone to set their minds at rest. And quickly. 'We have to go to the States for a tour but don't know when he wants the kit ready, or even what he wants in the bags. We don't even know whether we'll be kept on or kicked out.'

On the floor above us, Sammy had finished his painful duty. Now he finally reassured himself, 'OK, that's it, everything is in order. Time to grab the bull by the horns and move on.' He started to take his belongings out of drawers and put them in two small cardboard boxes. There was no ceremony as he transferred his history to the boot of his car. It was all over quickly and quietly, as is usual with him.

Back in the kit room, Sammy, animated again, told us that Paco Herrera and his wife Josefina had just arrived at Melwood and were on their first tour of inspection. It would be fair to say that Paco walked around the training ground that day as Benítez's assistant manager, although a few months later his role became much more ambiguous. On that first day, he was a Spaniard in awe. Liverpool FC carries that kind of historical weight for those involved in football.

Sammy sought out Paco and introduced us in what remained of his Spanish from his playing days at Osasuna, somewhat surprising himself with his fluency. '*No hablo bien, no hablo bien, perdona*' (I don't speak well, I don't speak well, sorry!), he was saying in almost perfect Spanish.

Then, before we realised it had happened, Sammy was in his car and driving away from Melwood, away from his beloved club.

Left with my fellow Spaniards, I offered to show Paco and his wife around the city. I had lived in Liverpool between 1991 and 1997. The place had developed greatly since I'd left, but I still knew it like the back of my hand, right down to its darkest streets and alleyways. Walking to Paco's car, I had the sensation that Sammy had gently but deliberately passed the baton to a new generation of coaches who were on the point of beginning the biggest revolution since Bill Shankly departed in 1974. That much seemed clear. But I had no idea that ten months later they would win the Champions League after twenty-one barren years on a balmy Istanbul night that seemed to encapsulate a turbulent year in the life of Liverpool Football Club. Chief executive Rick Parry called it 'a perfect microcosm of the season, with all the ups, downs and unexpected twists and turns'.

The path from that bittersweet day in July 2004 to the triumphant return from Istanbul with the 'cup with big ears' is the story of how Rafa Benítez imposed himself on a club that had stagnated. Against many expectations, he proved himself to be perfectly in tune with the ethos and line of succession established at Anfield by Shankly in 1959. Meanwhile, Liverpool (the fans, the city and the club) regenerated Rafa's own love of football and his dreams of what he could achieve in his professional career.

Along the way, Rafa, Paco, Xabi Alonso, Luis García and the rest of the new inhabitants of Anfield discovered what it means to belong to Liverpool and to pull on the red shirt.

(1)

RAFA'S ARRIVAL

Rafa, We *Have* to Go to Liverpool

The first time Rafa Benítez's name was mentioned in Liverpool FC's upper echelons was after a UEFA Cup tie against Marseille. It was the middle of March 2004 and the French team had just sent Liverpool crashing out of Europe. The strong rumour was that if Gérard Houllier didn't improve things rapidly, then Benítez was top of the list to replace him. The road ahead already looked bleak for the French coach, given that the best he could realistically aspire to was a mere fourth place in the Premiership. But that at least would give Liverpool a shot in the qualifying rounds for the next Champions League.

Houllier's reign had peaked in 2001, when Liverpool won five trophies in six months and finished third in the Premiership. 'The next step had to be winning the title,' the Frenchman's then assistant and now Sky Sports pundit Phil Thompson admits. But Houllier's big-money signings had not improved the team's performance (El Hadji Diouf in 2002 for £11 million; Harry Kewell in 2003 for £5 million), while other players ghosted through the club almost unnoticed (like goalkeeper Patrice Luzi Bernardi, who played a mere thirteen minutes with the first team, and midfielder Alou Diarra who never debuted at all). Matters finally reached the point where 'you are either sacked or you come to a friendly agreement', as Thompson delicately phrases it. Although the final decision on Houllier's future was taken only after the season was over, not even a better run in the UEFA Cup could have saved the manager. 'It was time for a change,' admits Jamie Carragher. Phil Thompson agrees: 'To quote what people said, we had gone as far as we could. We couldn't go that extra mile to win the Holy Grail – the Premiership. If we couldn't do it, we had to get someone who could.'

Chief executive Rick Parry understood that the upheaval had to be postponed until the summer, but he had been quietly planning for the change ever since that Marseille game. 'We took it a step at a time until the end of the season, because we still had objectives to play for,' he recalls. 'It was very important to finish fourth and we didn't want attention to be distracted from that. Then we had to decide, in a measured way, what to do about Gérard Houllier.'

The season had been a rollercoaster ride in terms of the team's performance – at one point the side had slipped to ninth position, and even the long-suffering and loyal Kop started a booing campaign. David Moores, the club's stoic chairman, then made public his feelings that nothing less than fourth place would be acceptable. That represented the first step towards a change of regime.

After two bad defeats, losing 4–2 to Arsenal at Highbury and 0–1 to Charlton at Anfield, Liverpool raised their game to secure three epic victories (including a sweet 0–1 triumph at Old Trafford thanks to Danny Murphy's penalty) and two draws to grab the final Champions League spot. Anfield bid good riddance to a tough season with the optimistic chant: 'Champions League here we come.'

Nine days after the end of the season and six years after he had arrived at Anfield, Houllier stepped down. Or, more accurately, he was pushed. Liverpool had finished thirty points behind the champions, Arsenal, which was simply unacceptable. He departed on Monday 24 May, and by 16 June it was confirmed that Rafa Benítez would be Liverpool's new coach. 'Obviously we were aware of Rafa's achievements,' says Parry. That's an understatement. Valencia, more than any other team during the final two years of the Houllier era, had taken Liverpool apart. Their superiority over the Reds was more acute than even that of Arsenal or Manchester

United. 'They played extremely well against us three times,' Parry remembers, 'twice in the Champions League and once pre-season. Our players had come off the pitch saying, "That is a well-organised team." In truth, we had not played against many better teams than Rafa's Valencia, and that is something you keep in mind.' Another understatement: those at the top of the Liverpool hierarchy knew that Benítez *had* to be their man.

The first game at which the Spaniard met his future team was his very first in charge of Valencia, in the Amsterdam Tournament during the summer of 2001. Liverpool, still coming back down to earth after their dramatic UEFA Cup final victory over Alavés, beat Valencia with a single Jari Litmanen goal. But the Spanish side, though short of fitness and physical power, gave a good account of themselves. A year later, the coach showed what he could do with talented players and a little time. In the first match of the Champions League group stage, Benítez was making his debut in the primary European club competition and Valencia defeated Liverpool 2–0 in the Mestalla Stadium with a magnificent display of football. Both the English and Spanish media compared his team to the famous Liverpool sides of the 1980s. His first visit as a manager to Anfield yeilded a solitary Rufete goal and a 0–1 victory, but Liverpool were flattered by the scoreline. Valencia qualified from the group. Houllier's team did not.

The friendly match between the two sides at Anfield in August 2003 was used by the Valencia board to try to take the heat out of the increasingly bitter confrontations between Jesus García Pitarch, their director of football, and Benítez, who was publicly complaining about Pitarch's interference in transfer deals. This dispute turned out to be the beginning of the end for Benítez at Valencia. Despite the tension behind the scenes, Rafa's Valencia won 0–2, and the Kop honoured their visitors with a generous ovation, a display of sportsmanship that pleasantly surprised Benítez. 'These supporters are different, aren't they?' he said that night. So, amid a deteriorating relationship between the boardroom and the coach, but with terrific football on the pitch, Valencia began the most successful season in their eighty-five-year history. And their last with Rafa Benítez at the helm.

Ten months later, the English press was full of rumours about José Mourinho, Alan Curbishley and Martin O'Neill as potential replacements for Houllier at Anfield. But O'Neill was never seriously considered, and Mourinho ruined his chances with the way he celebrated Costinha's goal against Manchester United at Old Trafford in the Champions League: his leaping along the touchline was very un-Liverpool. Curbishley was a stronger candidate, but even he was just a back-up in case things didn't come to fruition with Benítez.

But, of course, by this stage Benítez had had more than enough of the office politics at Valencia, even though he'd just won them both La Liga and the UEFA Cup. However, he still had one year left in his contract at the Spanish club, and he was prepared to see it out, but he felt his work was not being recognised by the directors, who refused to sign the players he asked for, or, worse still, bought others he did not want. He asked for a right-back and a well-known striker, suggesting Brazilian World Cup-winner Cafú, Alessandro Birindelli and Giovanni Elber. Instead he got a left-winger, the Uruguayan Nestor Fabián Canobbio, and a young, virtually unknown forward, Ricardo Oliveira. When he was presented with Canobbio, Benítez unusually lost his cool. 'If I was stubborn about this, then Canobbio simply would not get a game with Valencia,' he told a shocked press conference at the club's training ground one day. 'I asked the club for a sofa and they brought me a lampshade – and that can't be right,' he added poetically. Before this public outburst, he had made his disappointment known to the Valencia directors in several of their regular, heated meetings. In one, he told them, 'Previously, if I made a pit stop, you'd change a wheel for me. Now, I don't even get anywhere near the pit stop because you won't let me drive in.'

The renegotiation of his contract had begun in early 2004, when Valencia's league performances were faltering. Managing director

Manuel Llorente seemed in no hurry to finalise matters, and his stance didn't change even when the season was coming to a climax and Valencia were in with a chance of snatching the title off Real Madrid. 'My ideal scenario was to continue the work I had started at Valencia,' explains Benítez. 'But the managing director said to me, "If I give you two more years on your contract and then you lose three matches, it is going to be my problem!" If that was how much respect my three years of work had earned, then it seemed obvious to me that they had little interest in my staying. The worst thing was that he said all this to me on a late Seville evening the day before my team went out and reclaimed La Liga. I wanted to stay, but it was not to be because a guy with this attitude was always going to sack me sooner or later. He couldn't wait to axe me. I think he felt that I was in his way and he wanted freedom to spin his little web around the club without a strong-minded coach in the way. Personally, I was just waiting for them to sort out my situation properly. But that individual just didn't want things resolved, so, of course, I was left with no choice but to lodge a legal claim against the club and to explain in public the reasons for my departure. I did not leave either in search of better wages or because I was unhappy at the club. It says a lot that when they were due to negotiate my new contract, the person who was supposed to be in charge of that particular task didn't even come to the meeting, and around the same time he was speaking to other coaches.'

At the end of the 2004 season, Benítez accused Llorente of stalling contract talks and of reneging on a planned meeting with Rafa's agent Manolo García Quilón. He also knew that Valencia had tried to sign the former Mallorca coach Gregorio Manzano, another client of Quilón, the previous year. Furthermore, in March 2004, Llorente had sounded out César Ferrando, who was successfully improving with his tactical work a poor squad at Albacete. And a week before Benítez announced his departure, the general director had called Claudio Ranieri. Rafa felt hurt and, probably for the first time in his public life, he could not hold his tongue. Llorente, Rafa said on TV 'is a man with no friends who stays in the shadows waiting to stab you in the back'. In another interview, he lamented, 'It appears that I'm valued more outside the club than I am at Valencia itself.' Unable to cope with any more dents to his pride, he told Quilón at the end of May that he wanted to leave.

Meanwhile, after many years of in-fighting between the club's biggest shareholders, peace had finally been restored to the Valencia board. The new majority shareholder and soon-to-be president was Juan Bautista Soler. His top priority was to renegotiate Benítez's contract. But it was already too late. On Monday 31 May Benítez's home was the venue for a meeting between the coach, his agent and key members of the Valencia board. As the directors arrived, Benítez, with his hand still closing the front door behind them, told Soler and Llorente that they were wasting their time. 'Won't you stay, even for more money?' asked the anxious new man in charge. Benítez was offered a two-year contract extension on the spot, plus the chance of attaining the position of director of football. But the coach was not convinced. The very next morning, he held a press conference and announced that he was leaving Valenica. Tears soon began to stream down his face, so much so that he couldn't finish reading his statement. The sentence he omitted was: 'I have two daughters, one born in Valencia, and both of whom are *falleras* [lovers of Valencia's spectacular spring firework festival], and that is why the club and the city will always be in my thoughts and in my heart.'

'I've always said that Benítez is made of stone and doesn't show feelings or pain – but the first time I saw him cry was in Valencia on that day of the press conference,' says Pako Ayestarán. As Rafa mentioned in the statement, the 'damage to his state of mind and personal well-being' that the Spanish club had caused him in the previous year and a half had effectively forced him to pursue his career elsewhere. He decided very swiftly where his future would be. That same day, Rick Parry confirmed in Liverpool that 'There will be an announcement about the new coach in two weeks.'

Benítez asked Valencia to rescind his contract in an amicable fashion. The club, still in shock about the situation they had created, initially accepted such a solution and agreed to settle the matter out of court. But Llorente, the main reason for Benítez's decision to quit the club, convinced the board to sue him for breach of contract, plus damage done to the sporting, economic and corporate health of the club. The figure the board concocted was €3 million, a sum which has no basis in any clause contained in the coach's employment contract. 'Don't be stupid,' Benítez had warned Llorente when he first heard of the threat. The coach knew that the law was on his side and that the club was obliged to compensate *him* under the labour laws of the country as long as he had followed due process.

So, backed into a corner by the stubborn attitude of the club, he counter-sued and took Valencia to court in order to guarantee his rightful compensation. He was finally awarded €2.4 million (Pako Ayestarán received €600,000). The club's lawsuit against Benítez is still unresolved, but he believes they have no chance of winning. 'Instead of going back to Valencia for a tribute to the achievements of my team, I'm having to go back there to resolve a court case,' he points out bitterly. In fact, he has not returned to the city since the summer of his departure.

Despite his disillusion with the club with which he achieved so much during his three-year reign, Benítez has not totally severed his ties. He calls his old contacts on an almost daily basis to find out the latest news and gossip. And he regularly reads the Spanish sports papers (sometimes in the small hours, when the first editions are published on the internet), so he witnessed all the ups and downs at Valencia in 2004–05. He understood that the return of Claudio Ranieri, who had coached the team before Rafa himself, had been designed to pacify the supporters. For his part, Ranieri says, 'I know how these things go, and from the beginning I accepted as normal the very long shadow left by Benítez. To overcome that was always going to be my major challenge.' Clearly the board felt he was not up to the challenge and swiftly sacked him after a run of poor results.

Benítez saw it as a betrayal of trust that his former assistant coach, Antonio López, then took over. Their relationship had soured anyway in Rafa's last few months at the club, and especially when López bizarrely claimed that Benítez owed a great deal of his success to him. Soon after his appointment as coach, López lost all support inside and outside the dressing room, and he was sacked after only three months in charge. It's doubtful that Benítez shed any tears for him.

At the last match of the 2004–05 season, against Osasuna, Valencia fans voiced their feelings. In the first post-Benítez year, the club had finished seventh, twenty-six points behind La Liga champions Barcelona and they had only qualified for the competition that nobody wants to enter, the Intertoto Cup, which forces the players to end their summer holidays early. The supporters exchanged text messages that exhorted everyone to treat the Osasuna game as a chance to pay tribute to the Liverpool coach, who had lifted the European Cup the previous Wednesday: 'Sunday, match against Osasuna, homage to Benítez. Pass it on.' At the game there were banners everywhere congratulating their former hero.

Benítez had indeed cast a long shadow over Valencia. Quique Sánchez Flores, the ex-Getafe coach, took over the team at the start of the 2005–06 season, and in his first press conference announced, 'The style that we have to follow is that of Rafa Benítez.' The irony is not lost on the Liverpool manager. 'What pained me most over the last year was to see that all the work I started was failing to come to fruition because it was not followed through,' he complains. 'You have to look within the club for those reponsible. Some of them would like to have me airbrushed out of the old squad photos!' Certainly, on the website and in some club publications they *have* omitted his name and those of his staff, even though they orchestrated the most successful era in the club's history. 'At Valencia there is a biased flow of information because the media is controlled by a particular line of thought and opinion coming from the top of the club,' he explains. 'It means that the ordinary fans don't really know what's happening.' Only by understanding this can you put into context his efforts to fight against the hatchet-job done on him in Valencia.

Unaware of the nitty-gritty of the politics that were upsetting Rafa so much, but conscious of the problems that had made his job so difficult at Valencia, chairman David Moores and chief executive Rick Parry flew out to Spain shortly after they had announced Houllier's dismissal. 'Rafa came to my place in Spain, where Rick and I met him I was very impressed with the way he spoke,' the chairman remembers. 'We spent half a day with him and I was amazed by his knowledge of Liverpool FC. He told us that when he was growing up, Liverpool were the team that were winning everything, so he'd consider it a great honour if we took him on as our manager.'

Benítez reminded them that he was well acquainted with the demands of English club football, having developed his coaching skills with Tottenham Hotspur's under-19 side, worked with Manchester United's and Arsenal's first teams, and observed at close quarters the FA's development programme at Lilleshall. 'What was also remarkable was his obvious enthusiasm just for *talking* about football – tactics, players and so on. And from his personality you got an immediate sense that he was unassuming in the right way: there was no arrogance,' says Parry.

On the day of his public, emotional farewell, Benítez also handed in his letter of resignation to Valencia. He then had to work out his fifteen-day notice. During that period, from 1 to 16 June, Liverpool gave off-the-record briefings about the encouraging progress being made in negotiations with the new coach. Rumours spread quickly that Benítez was already in at Anfield, and would soon publicly reject three other offers which were on the table – from Spurs, Internazionale and (by far the most lucrative) a €4m per season deal with Besiktas in Turkey.

Liverpool had chosen their man in a bid to return to the style of leadership initiated by Bill Shankly. As one banner in Istanbul proclaimed a year later, the club 'dare not forget today that we are the heirs of that first revolution'. Benítez, like Shankly, is an unpretentious coach who does not agree with 'star systems'; he does not like to grab the headlines; and his motto is 'work, work, work'. Above all, he has the ruthless focus of a winner. It was important for the club to make sure that the rebuilding process that everyone knew was essential was given to somebody who understood the 'Liverpool way'. This man had a record of success, but he was still young (forty-four) and hungry.

During his first long conversation with Benítez, not so much an interview as a chat about football, Rick Parry could tell that the Spaniard was going to fit the bill. 'You can try to explain the "Liverpool way" to a head-hunter and ask him to go and find somebody, but it is really only by talking for hours that you realise whether you have the right person. With Rafa, we had that feeling almost right away,' Parry remembers. 'We sensed there was a clear and natural link to the past with him. The key is not to try to manufacture that link for the sake of it. There were lots of things in the past that were perhaps wrong, and you cling to them for the wrong reasons. It is important to hang on to the bits that were good, and that was a critically important part of Liverpool's sustained success in the past, irrespective of the personalities. What we saw in Rafa was modesty, calmness and above all his hunger for more. And perhaps Rafa saw something of the club in him. Maybe he realised that it was not "just another job".'

He certainly did. It was made clear from the start that Benítez would be given an incredible amount of responsibility as both coach and manager. This powerful dual role simply does not exist in Spain. He was also going to take charge of a sleeping giant with a degree of football history which very few clubs can boast. Liverpool possessed its own special magic. Moreover, he was offered a five-year contract which would bring him the support, the time and the faith that had been so cruelly denied to him at Valencia.

'I knew precisely what to do and which offer to pick,' explains Rafa. 'Perhaps on a day-to-day basis the greatness of the club is not plainly obvious, but we felt there was something special in the air right from the start. For example, when we have a minute's silence at Anfield, you cannot hear a single sound. They place a high value on tradition and they like to feel different. It is not just a football team, it is a sentiment. You are made to feel at home immediately. People here value the effort almost as much as the results, and the fans are very civil. They ask for your autograph very politely. If you are busy with someone, they will wait until you finish speaking. They will even offer you a beer. Sometimes your heart stops when you arrive at nine in the morning and you see a child waiting outside the training ground. You sign an autograph for him and have a picture taken with him. Then when you are leaving to go home, at whatever time it is, he'll still be there waiting for someone else to come out. It makes no difference whether it's raining or it's cold.'

Benítez's choice of Liverpool was also prompted by some persistent lobbying from Pako Ayestarán, a constant presence by his side as 'physical trainer' since Rafa had first coached Osasuna in 1996. 'Rafa, we *have* to go to Liverpool,' Ayestarán frequently told his boss. 'Pako has always been a Liverpool fanatic,' explains Benítez. 'When he was eighteen he wrote to the club asking for a scarf and they sent him some complete team kits for him and his friends.' Ayestarán confirms, 'I'd been saying to Rafa for ages, "Let's go to Liverpool, let's go to Liverpool." I was suggesting that we had to try England, and if possible this great club in particular.'

Pako was born in 1963, three years after Benítez, and belonged to that generation of teenagers who had been hypnotised by the Liverpool team that won almost everything in the 1970s and 1980s. Obviously, kids always want to support the winning team and the one they see playing most often on television, but there were other elements to Ayestarán's devotion, too. He was a born Real Sociedad fan, and one 1970s UEFA Cup tie produced his dream match: Real Sociedad versus Liverpool. The Reds' thumped the Basques 9–1 on aggregate, and Ayestarán, far from being bitter, was in awe. Playing for Liverpool at the time was John Toshack, who later went on to coach Real Sociedad. Later still, John Aldridge left Liverpool to become the first ever non-Basque to play for Real Sociedad. So, for two decades, Pako, just by supporting his local team, was reminded of Liverpool. And he never lost that admiration he'd felt as a youngster in the Basque Country. 'After leaving Extremadura in 1999, we went to England and Italy to see training sessions,' he recalls. 'We were in Manchester for a week and I kept insisting, "Let's go and see Liverpool – you'll see what it's like!" but he refused and we stayed at Manchester United's training ground for the entire week.' Nevertheless, this early visit to the world of the Premiership helped Benítez gain an insight into Liverpool's place in English footballing folklore. It was a depth of understanding that would impress Moores and Parry years later.

According to one Liverpool player, Ayestarán is not only the 'best coach I have ever had', but 'the man who takes charge of training, looks after the physical shape of the squad and also has a say in tactics'. During a match, while Benítez patrols the touchline, Ayestarán remains seated, taking notes. His job at that time is to spot any problems the opposing team are causing and work out how these can be overcome.

The long professional relationship with Ayestarán is one of the key elements in Benítez's success at Tenerife, Valencia and now Liverpool. Together they have accumulated experiences and information about training systems and tactics, 'and we are still open to anybody who can teach us new ways to do things', says Benítez. 'Pako is very dedicated but even more importantly he is very knowledgeable and always learning,' adds the Liverpool boss. 'Without doubt he is the best physical trainer there is, and now that he has become my assistant manager I rely on him for many of the jobs I used to do at Valencia. Given that I'm now the general manager as well as the coach, I have to delegate. The guys gather all sorts of information, but Pako is the one pulling it all together to give it shape and meaning.'

Some people have accused Benítez of favouring a scientific approach which can sacrifice player–coach relationships. There is certainly an element of truth in this. It is partly due to a personality that prefers to analyse rather than work on emotion, but is also a deliberate tactic to maintain a certain distance between himself and his players. Pako and Rafa play the good-cop, bad-cop game. As Pako takes on most of the coaching, he has a close relationship with the players, while Rafa gives the orders, and the bad and good news. He doesn't want any of his decisions to be disputed, so at some point he has to treat the players not as friends but as employees.

A couple of 'the guys' that Benítez mentioned are two more of his loyal Spanish assistants: José Manuel Ochotorena and Paco Herrera. Ochotorena, or 'Ochoto' for short, was a successful keeper at Valencia and Real Madrid and is now the goalkeeping coach of both Liverpool and the Spanish national side. Benítez's opinion is that Ochoto 'adds serenity to the analysis of situations'. Paco Herrera, now the reserve-team manager, is also a vital component in Liverpool's scouting operation. He has taken on the job of rebuilding what Benítez judged to be the club's insufficiently stocked database of potential signings. Furthermore, he analyses rivals, using cutting-edge technology to prepare videos of the strengths, weaknesses, successful tactics and flaws in opponents. This material then becomes the basis for Rafa's regular technical briefings. Herrera's multifaceted role has confused many commentators, who seem to expect backroom staff to be given one job and to stick to it. Rafa clarifies the situation eloquently, simply calling Herrera 'my adviser'. 'He is doing a very important job in the wings,' adds Benítez. 'He not only talks to agents and finds out about players, but chats to me about tactics and analyses games. Away from the playing and coaching side, Paco has given players, particularly the ones coming from Spain, the confidence and protection they sometimes require when either changing club or moving country. To some of the guys here, he is almost like a father figure.' Herrera, who was a professional in La Liga, has coached teams in the Spanish first and second divisions (Mérida, Badajoz, Extremadura) and his knowledge of European football, his reading of games and his coaching talent have been essential elements in Benítez's work.

Alex Miller, the chief scout under Houllier, helps Rafa and the team understand the demands of a domestic competition that takes time to master, as well as playing a paternal role with the English-speaking contingent. The Scotsman's story is one of survival. He is now the only coach remaining from the previous regime with his five years at the club (plus the seventeen he spent at Rangers) providing the experience Rafa needed. 'Alex is useful for me,' says Benítez. 'He is a very good coach who knows the players and the English Premiership. It's important to have him because he can tell me about the teams we will play.'

Sammy Lee probably could have done Miller's job, but he felt too much a part of the previous era and thought it was not fair to either the club or Houllier to attempt to continue with the new boss. 'As time goes by there must be someone with a little bit of history in the club,' says another Liverpool old boy, Phil Thompson. 'I think Rafa made a big mistake with Sammy Lee. There should have been a place for him.' But Rafa preferred to count on people he knew, so he brought them with him. He made it clear from the moment he arrived that Lee would not be part of the new decision-making team, and that was enough to convince Sammy to hand in his resignation. Rick Parry asked him to stay, and the club even invited him to come on the pre-season tour of America so he could get to know the new team before burning his bridges. Paco Herrera also tried to make him feel needed, but Sammy could not be persuaded to change his mind. Some supportive words from Rafa might have made the difference, but they were never uttered. Nor were they a little later for Michael Owen or later still for Steven Gerrard. Benítez the bad-cop again.

On that USA tour, Rafa soon realised he had a much bigger

job than he had imagined. In some cases the squad lacked basic knowledge and, more worryingly, even the enthusiasm to learn. But the new boss didn't allow himself to be deflected from his mission. He threw himself straight into the rebuilding process.

(2)

BEFORE THE KICK-OFF

(THE FANS)

My Wife Thinks I'm at Work but I'm in the 'Bul with Stevie and Rafa

For at least 10,000 of the 35,000 Liverpool fans who travelled to Istanbul, the journey began at John Lennon Airport. Eighty-two flights using nineteen different European airlines left Liverpool's runway over the three days building up to that day of days, with the last charter flight leaving Liverpool at 9.45 on the morning of the match – Wednesday 25 May. That was the busiest day in the airport's history. Naturally, they called it 'Operation Turkish Delight'.

Other intrepid fans had booked cheap package deals to Bulgarian seaside resorts and were willing to brave a bumpy twelve-hour journey over the border into Turkey. But that wasn't the only alternative. From all corners of the globe they came: from Cape Town via Athens; from Cologne, Amsterdam, Eindhoven, Sofia, Frankfurt, Paris, Düsseldorf, Brussels. The list went on and on. Those Liverpool fans who managed to reach any European city with an onward connection to Istanbul spent an average of £600 travelling to the Turkish capital. It took some five days to get there. Purpose of the visit: the UEFA Champions League Final.

Once they landed at Atatürk International Airport or the smaller Sabiha Gokcen, in the Asian half of the city, they headed straight to Taksim Square, the Red Army's HQ for the forty-eight hours leading up to the match. On that Wednesday, once the right bus had been located and boarded (which happened in most cases), the idea was to join those who had arrived earlier in the week and had spent their time organising the biggest party the city had ever witnessed. More than one Liverpudlian became very familiar with Efes, the local brew.

In the square, the Beatles Café, with pictures of the Fab Four and copies of the *Merseybeat* newspaper adorning the walls, and an Irish pub with the Portuguese name Fado were full for the whole day. From the trees, Scouse lads were singing, 'Treeboy, Treeboy' with Efes in hand, and every time the first notes of 'The Fields of Anfield Road' or Johnny Cash's 'Ring of Fire' were chanted, hundreds of Reds duly joined in. The sellers of fake Liverpool shirts were doing a roaring trade, even though some still bore the name of the exiled El Hadji Diouf, and some Reds exchanged scarves with the hugely outnumbered Milan supporters who had ventured into the square.

There was a noticeable sense of friendliness both here and around the city that contradicted the predictable media scare stories. The press had forgotten two crucial points. First, the travelling fans belonged to a new generation of supporters, nurtured in seated stadia for a game that had been turned into a family affair by politicians, Sky Sports, marketing men and history. Second, Turkey was desperate to send a positive message to the world, and especially to a sceptical European Union. The country wanted to be seen as modern, Western and sophisticated; as a place that could successfully organise the biggest events. Low-profile policing, impromptu chants of 'Istanbul, Istanbul, Istanbul' and a huge Liverpool flag unfurled in front of the Blue Mosque all helped to push Turkey's image to new heights.

Turkish children spent hours clapping along to 'You'll Never Walk Alone', while other locals cheered the fans on their way to the stadium as if it were the most exciting thing they had done in years. Hundreds of supporters breathed in the atmosphere. They had plenty of time to do so, too. Some of the drivers organised by travel agencies to take fans to the stadium were decidedly nervous of the motorway traffic and hugged the inside lane. 'Listen, mate, either you go faster or we're gonna throw you out of the window' was a threat made by some of the more impatient fans who feared they would miss the kick-off. Closer to the stadium, the traffic jams were horrendous. For some, the twenty-mile journey from the centre of town took over three hours. The coaches were forced to stop for calls of nature, and, more crucially, to purchase more drinks. 'One, two or three beers per head?' asked one travel company representative. 'Ten,' came the reply from the bus's passengers.

On top of a hill bereft of any other buildings, the Atatürk Stadium is, according to the UEFA website, 'fortunately not trapped in a heavily developed location'. There is plenty of potential for future extension or redevelopment, as an estate agent might put it. In other words, Atatürk Stadium is in the middle of a bleak, lunar landscape featuring piles of rubble, bricks and stones (potentially dangerous in the first Italian–English final since Heysel), and can be reached only by taxi or dedicated coaches. The two one-lane roads to and from the stadium had to cope with the arrival of 70,000 spectators. The second road had been completed just a few weeks before the final and the paint on its surface was still glistening on that May night.

The moment that the Atatürk could be glimpsed in the distance, fans abandoned their buses, which were haphazardly dumped a couple of miles away from the stadium, and foot-slogged it the remainder of the way. It was a mighty spectacle: like a huge trail of red ants. They passed yellow taxis, queuing in a long, static convoy, their occupants deliberating whether to join the infantry, too. Some cows patiently crossed the road to find some of the scattered green patches that decorated the hill. Fans left their crates of beer to scramble up the hillside and have their pictures taken with the nonchalant animals.

Although the infrastructure had patently been unable to cope with so many visitors, the day after the final UEFA released a self-congratulatory piece of propaganda that had probably been written weeks before: 'The issue which had been of most concern to the local authorities, in advance of the final, had been the traffic in the streets around the Atatürk Olympic Stadium, but once more it seems that on the big day Istanbul's organisational ability overcame another potential problem.' Was there another final in Istanbul that day? The gridlock that started at motorway exits four hours before the match led to more than a few fans missing the whole of the first half.

As for those who had arrived early to avoid the jam, they spent hours searching for food and drink at the stadium. Toilets were thin on the ground, too, and many of those that had been provided stopped functioning before the match had even begun. The Atatürk is, by the way, a 'Five-star ground', according to UEFA's classification system.

Nevertheless, outside the ground the atmosphere remained upbeat. At a concert featuring some of Liverpool's finest – the Coral, the Zutons and Cast – it was obvious that Liverpool fans outnumbered their Milanese rivals by about three to one. Neville Skelly took to the stage with the Mighty Wah! to sing 'You'll Never Walk Alone' in front of a large proportion of the 35,000 Reds. One of them got up on the stage to dance, waving his scarf in the air. Others decided that this was the greatest idea they'd ever seen. A Turkish policeman went after them and grabbed the microphone – not to give a local touch to the encore of 'Walk On' but to beg for the restoration of a little calm. Unfortunately, he was perhaps a little over-dramatic to be taken seriously: 'Please! Get off the stage. You are all going to die!' he beseeched the dancing Reds.

There was a three-hour queue for programmes. Or at least there was until a couple of Scouse entrepreneurs came up with a cunning plan to alleviate the congestion. One grabbed a box of programmes and started distributing them free-of-charge to the cheering fans. Meanwhile, the other cut through the back of the marquee to where they were being stored, and made off with the lot.

Entering the stadium, the segregation of supporters worked as planned, but other than that the organisation was very poor. At the first checkpoint, a few stewards lost patience with fans who didn't have tickets. Their solution to the problem was simple: give up, go home and let everyone through. Some ticket-machine scanners didn't work, and instead of just taking the stub the tickets were being ripped in half by stewards. At that stage, real tension started to fill the air for the first time. As the crowd inevitably became bottlenecked in the turnstile areas, nerves were becoming frayed. (For many Liverpool fans, the memory of Hillsborough is ever-present.) But the flexibility of the Turks and the good humour of the Red Army meant that there was not a single arrest and the atmosphere gradually lightened.

Inside the Atatürk, the pitch seemed miles away from the stands, and the huge proportions of the ground meant that the fans' anthems were lost on the wind. But you could have been inside Anfield. The Italians had returned 2,000 unsold tickets, and the night before the match the local Turks had none left to sell, so there would be no neutral area. The Milan fans were occupying one of the ends; the remainder was red.

The Italians practised their choreography, coordinated displays of coloured cards that formed a giant mosaic. Although it is a spectacle, it pales in comparison with the electric spontaneity of the Kopites and their uncoordinated flags and banners. Some of them are simply brilliant: 'For those of you watching in blue and white, this is what a European Cup looks like' is one of Jamie Carragher's favourite stadium memories. Ingenuity and wit were everywhere: 'My Wife Thinks I'm at Work but I'm in the 'Bul with Stevie and Rafa'; 'Moses Said Come Forth – Rafa said, "We'll win the Cup instead"'; and 'Has anyone seen the Special One?' The Liverpool fans didn't go to Istanbul to *watch* a final; they went to *participate* in it.

Finally, everything was in order and almost everybody was in place to start the game. The pre-match spectacle organised on the pitch by the Turkish football authorities, pretty and colourful as it was, gave the impression that everything was structured towards the television audience. The vast majority of the fans simply wanted to sing their songs, and it was an anticlimax when the organisers demanded that attention be focused towards something so tame. The show featured dozens of youngsters running around the pitch forming shapes, and a bizarrely dressed woman with an umbrella who wandered around aimlessly.

In Anfield, fans, fed up with the way football is being taken away from them, like to remind the world that real football happens in stadiums, not on TV, and that all the noise should come from the stands. So, with a militant stance, the supporters duly boycotted, for the whole season, the UEFA anthem that precedes all Champions League matches (and tends to coincide with the beginning of the live broadcasts). Instead, they regaled the television audience with raucous renditions of 'You'll Never Walk Alone'. Anfield is the only stadium in Europe that has decided that the 'official' anthem represents some of the worst things about modern football and has tried to do something about it.

Back in Liverpool, minutes before kick-off, the entire city had stopped. The streets were deserted and all the pubs were full. Twenty thousand hats and flags commemorating the occasion were sold – the sense of expectation was greater than it had been before any of the five finals Liverpool had contested in its 'previous' life. People knew that in May 1985, the month of Heysel, twenty years of meticulous planning had collapsed literally overnight, and that when the club had finally returned to European competition, the team sent out to try to recapture former glories couldn't hold a candle to the one which had dominated the European Cup for nearly a decade. Liverpool had had to start from scratch. Three Champions League campaigns later, they were again gracing the biggest stage in club football. Some have labelled it the 'second coming'.

Certainly, a new generation of Kopites, tired of listening to the old stories, was discovering new territory. Their sentiments were similar to those felt in the first European Cup Final in Rome, also played on 25 May, twenty-eight years earlier. The wait had been interminable. Defeats and humiliations had come so regularly that they didn't even hurt any more. There is a saying at Anfield: 'Winning is a good habit but losing is a harder habit to change'. This time the citizens of Liverpool genuinely felt that their time had come again, and they all went home or out to the pubs to witness it.

The match had also captured the imagination of the world. In the Italian city of Siena, Mafalda, the daughter of assistant coach Paco Herrera, sat down with her friends to watch the match. She explained to some of the girls that this was the final of a football competition and one of the teams was 'almost Spanish'. 'How many players are there in a team and what do they have to do with the ball?' she was asked.

In Badajoz, near the Portuguese border, Paco's neighbours met in the streets to greet each other before retiring to their sofas to watch the game. Even the wives, Josefina's friends, joined their husbands on this occasion. If the match went on to fulfil a series of requirements (goals, good football, impeccable behaviour on and off the pitch) there would be new generation of converts, hypnotised by the Beautiful Game.

Their feelings were echoed throughout Spain. At Xabi Alonso's childhood club Antiguoko, 200 kids were settling down to watch the match on giant screens wearing Liverpool kits. Irish pubs were full. People were looking again at the special reports on the final in the national sports newspapers. Spain was ready to watch one of its teams. There was more to this than the mere presence of Spanish players and coaches – the magic of the club, the lack of Spanish teams involved thus far, their victory against Chelsea, the aura of a final that involved such a historical pairing in an era of underdogs like Greece, Portugal, Monaco and Porto. Six and a half million Spaniards were glued to their television sets that night. They were nearly all supporting Liverpool.

Just as at the stadium, though, some missed out. Fernando Alonso, the new Formula 1 sensation, was in a taxi around kick-off time and couldn't persuade the driver to let him take over at the wheel. To his despair he missed the first half. Middlesbrough and

Holland's Bolo Zenden, already on Rafa's 'wanted' list for the next season, was on holiday in the Netherlands and watched the first half in his hotel bedroom. At half time he decamped to a local, but the tiny TV set was obscured by two other customers and he missed the rest of the match.

Two Merseyrail ticket inspectors were about to commit a crime which, a couple of weeks later, they paid for with their jobs: they listened to the match through a dodgy mini-TV with no picture. One of the two is an Evertonian.

In the bedroom of a luxury Chicago hotel, the technical staff of the English national team sat around their television set. Sammy Lee was the most nervous and the most optimistic. There was no logic to it, but Sammy had faith: Liverpool were going to win, he told anyone who'd listen. Joe Cole, also in Chicago with the national team, went shopping because he couldn't bear to watch the final.

Former Reds striker John Toshack was on his way to the stadium, where he was due to commentate on the match for BBC Radio Five Live, when, oddly, his taxi began to go down streets which didn't look anything like the motorway. Suddenly, disconcertingly, the taxi driver stopped at a bar and jumped out of the cab. He came back, full of enthusiasm and excitement, bringing his brother, the bar owner and a throng of other friends. All became clear when he eagerly pointed out the Welshman, whom he'd recognised as the ex-Besiktas coach.

Michael Owen had been invited by ITV to be a panellist on their coverage of the final just as he'd been in the semi-final. But the striker decided it had been such a hassle to convince his club to let him accept the invitation that he preferred to watch it at home. Ironically, Owen had started his own season with Liverpool, sitting on the bench in the Champions League qualifying round against Graz AK, to avoid being cup tied for Real Madrid. He had talked with Jamie Carragher during the week about the final, and an hour before kick-off sent him a good-luck text message – and another to Stevie Gerrard. ITV instead recruited Steve McManaman, who had spent the night before singing Liverpool songs with Robbie Fowler in the bar of the Radisson Hotel in Istanbul.

Gerry Marsden (of the Pacemakers fame and the most famous singer of 'You'll Never Walk Alone') asked for the match to be recorded because, at kick-off, he was in Ireland recording a TV special.

Before taking his seat in Liverpool's Radio City commentary box, John Aldridge had time to share a hug with me, and admitted, 'My legs are jelly. I've never been this nervous in my life!' By the time the players were coming through the tunnel with the referee, Aldridge was even more shaky, microphone in hand. Another striker from an earlier Liverpool era, Michael Robinson, half-formally, half-jokingly apologised to the audience of Canal Plus in Spain, where he is the leading football pundit, because that night he had no intention of trying to be objective. '*No puedo ocultar que soy un Red*' (*I can't hide the fact that I'm a Red*), he told his massive audience.

At the Liverpool end, while the players formed a huddle around Gerrard seconds before kick-off, fans were asking similar questions to the ones pundits were airing in their live broadcasts. Why was Harry Kewell in the starting line-up? Why was Didi Hamann on the bench? What was Benítez's game plan? Nobody could have realised that the Spanish coach was still racked with doubts about his decisions less than two hours before the referee blew his whistle for the first time.

(3)

BEFORE THE KICK-OFF

(THE TEAM)

Should I put Baroš or Cissé in the Line-up?

In the days before the final, the good omens were mounting. Coming up with a new one became one of the most common games in the rough pubs of London Road and in the noisy haunts of Mathew Street. In 1978, the year of Liverpool's second European Cup victory, just as in 2005, a Pope called John Paul had died. Then, as now, Wales had won a glorious rugby Grand Slam. In both years, the winner of the English League had beaten Liverpool in the final of the League Cup: Nottingham Forest in 1978 and Chelsea this season.

Then there were the coincidences between 1981, the year of Liverpool's third European Cup, and 2005. In 1981, Prince Charles married Diana Spencer; in 2005, he got hitched to Camilla Parker Bowles. *Coronation Street*'s Ken and Deirdre also got married in both years. And in 1981 Norwich City and Crystal Palace were both relegated, just as they were in 2005. Most amazingly, in both 1980–81 and 2004–05 Liverpool won only seventeen league games and ended up in fifth place. Finally, Liverpool had won all four of their European Cups wearing red in the final, each time against a team in white. Those would be the colours for Liverpool and Milan in Istanbul, too, after Liverpool won the toss about who should wear their 'home' strip.

Montse, Rafa's wife, had a premonition that Liverpool were going to win the Champions League (and Rafa promised her a new wristwatch if it happened, his usual present after any big victory). But mention an omen to Benítez and he'll produce one of his trademark short bursts of mock laughter that translate as 'Stop wasting my time' and/or 'That was *almost* funny.' As if to emphasise Rafa's trust in routine rather than 'fate', his team prepared during the week before the final exactly as they did before any match. To Benítez, the key factor in the build-up was how to control, and lessen, the tension. Between the last domestic game, against Aston Villa, and the Istanbul final there were ten long days. He had to keep his players calm in that time. 'The best competitor is the one who manages to be relaxed before a match, becomes tense during a match and relaxes after a match,' says Pako Ayestarán, Benítez's loyal assistant over the last nine years. Unfortunately, not many players have the mental and emotional self-control to manage that. Some 'live' the game too soon in the build-up. By the time the whistle blows, they are filled with tension and can make mistakes as a consequence. Steven Gerrard is prone to such stress. 'It was hard to relax in the build-up to the final. I was thinking about it twenty-four hours a day,' he admits. Ayestarán says, 'Gerrard is a player who suffers from an excess of tension, perhaps because he knows that the time has passed without him achieving what he had expected to achieve in his hometown club. What that means is that Steve goes looking for results instead of waiting for them to come to him as a consequence of his daily work.'

According to Benítez, it's important not simply to 'go out to win' but to 'go out *prepared* to win', which means players have to put in the same level of work on a daily basis. Anything else is unacceptable. One of the Spaniard's most unexpected surprises on first arriving on Merseyside was the number of his inherited players who did not understand the philosophy that 'things only happen if you make them happen'.

The Liverpool squad arrived in Turkey two days before the final. Benítez had one of his fittest squads of the season at his disposal. The team had also carefully prepared for the match at Melwood with analysis of their opponents, plans for dead-ball situations both for and against, technical talks and strategic tactics. By the time they arrived in Istanbul, the players knew almost everything about Milan and what they had to do to beat them. They *should* have felt relaxed and in control.

However, in the training session at the Atatürk the day before the match, Benítez and his team were on the edge: hurling themselves into tackles, sprinting after every ball, running themselves into the ground. Gerrard, talking before the trip to Turkey, knew exactly why the session was so frantic: 'The manager has told us he is not announcing the team until the day of the game, so I'm sure the remaining training sessions will be really intense. Everyone will be pushing for places.' Djimi Traore agreed: 'On that session, it was the first time you could feel the extra tension.' The technical team had to take immediate action to stop the players burning themselves out. They reckoned that the match was going to be tight, so wanted their men to stay calm, relaxed and to preserve their energy for the big night.

Back at the team hotel, some of the players sat in the lounge for a chat before going to bed. Some retold Steve McManaman's tale about the night before Real Madrid's 2000 Champions League final victory against Valencia – an easy 3–0 win – as the best example of tension release in recent memory: the players had drunk beer and got massages from the physio at one in the morning! It was the same tactic that Jack Charlton had employed on the eve of Ireland versus Romania in the 1990 World Cup, when he had roused his team from their slumber in order to take them for a few pints of Guinness. Rafa had no intention of getting his team drunk, but he had to figure out something to relax them. 'I could see the players were full of hunger and eagerness so we knew that we had to lower the tension because it was still twenty-four hours before kick-off,' he remembers. 'Their anxiety was palpable; we had to calm them down. So we had a chat with them and reminded them that we were not favourites – and that we had to just enjoy the moment.'

The oldest group of friends in the squad (Hyypia, Carragher, Gerrard, Hamann) met after dinner in one of their rooms and talked for well over an hour about what sort of match they could expect. They all knew it was going to be a very tight one. Also, they all obviously expected to play. Xabi Alonso spent some time with friends in the hotel, in a corner overlooking an unmemorable garden. The rest of the team simply went to bed and slept. 'There are some who need to be hyped up, but I'm not like that,' admitted Carragher. 'I look forward to playing in big games, doing the job I'm supposed to do, making sure whoever I'm playing alongside gets the help they need and getting on with it. So I slept well the night before the Champions League final.'

Before going to bed, Rafa spent some time with Rick Parry, Liverpool's chief executive, discussing the game plan, but also talking about signings for next season. Benítez knew that the final was not the be all and end all – life would go on, win or lose.

Wednesday 25 May dawned with the promise of a clear sky for the rest of the day and a pleasant spring temperature. Despite the lateness of the scheduled kick-off, 9.45 p.m. local time, the preparation was only slightly different to what the team might expect before a midweek league or a home Champions League match: a stroll, a technical chat, food, siesta, pre-match briefing and, ninety minutes before the kick-off, arrival at the stadium. However, Pako Ayestarán, aware that since their arrival on Monday they had spent many hours in the hotel, suggested that around midday they should go for a walk and do some shopping in Istanbul. But the squad, given the alternative of ten-pin bowling just across the road, eagerly opted for that option. 'I think Pako was disappointed,' Carragher remembers. 'But we just wanted to enjoy ourselves, have a laugh and a joke. At that point, there had been so much build-up to the game and we had had to wait ten days after our [domestic] season had finished. We just wanted to get on with it.' The tension eased down a notch or two.

Benítez felt the weight of Liverpool's history bearing down on him, but attempted to use it to his advantage. 'In one of the meetings which took place in the hotel, we watched a "motivation" video showing various Liverpool victories: all the goals from the Champions League and various victories from other years,' he recalls. The four-minute video helped the players to focus very closely on the task ahead.

Some of them, including Jamie Carragher, had already been musing that their coach's achievements might surpass some of Liverpool's previous triumphs, because the four European Cups had all been won by a team at the height of its powers. By comparison, Benítez had been knee-deep in the essential job of reconstruction since the previous summer. On the other hand, the European Cup victories could be interpreted as the peaks in an era of planned, perpetual success. What was happening in Istanbul was different. It was the beginning of something fresh ... and some of the footballers who were going to play their part in the final knew that their future was destined to be far from Anfield.

While the players had lunch at the hotel, Chris Bascombe, the Liverpool FC correspondent of the Liverpool *Echo* and a man who understands better than most the inside workings of the club, was writing the last few words of his article for the late edition of the paper. He believed that this trip to Istanbul had not started in August with the qualifying game against Graz AK, but twenty-one years earlier:

> Liverpool's followers have had more to endure than enjoy since 1984 [the team's penultimate appearance in the final of the competition, when they won on penalties after a 1–1 draw against Roma in Rome]. The two tragedies which have defined a generation, the cup humiliations, the laughable signings, the false promises from a series of failed Messiahs, the arrival of Paul Stewart and Torben Piechnik and, perhaps the killer blow, the sight of Manchester United captains lifting trophies which once had 'Property of Liverpool FC' stamped on them. Winning the European Cup tonight is as much about cleansing the club's soul after two decades of grubbiness as it is about reviving it.

Benítez neither ignored the past nor disregarded the future. He understood clearly that his team was only a distant cousin of the great Liverpool sides which they had watched on that motivational video. Yet he also sensed a unique opportunity to write himself and his team into Liverpool history.

Of course, one crucial aspect of Benítez's role in the final was the team that he picked. The players knew that their boss would remain tight-lipped until an hour before the match, after a brief walk on the turf. This had been his tactic during three successful years at Valencia and he'd continued the practice throughout his first season on Merseyside. Finally, though, he sat them down and gave them the news. Dudek was in goal. The defenders virtually picked themselves: Finnan, Carragher, Hyypia and Traore. In the midfield, Luis García would be on the right, Xabi Alonso and Gerrard in the centre, and Riise on the left. Upfront were Kewell and Baroš. On the bench: Carson, Josemi, Nuñez, Biscan, Smicer and Didi Hamann.

On a number of occasions during the season, Benítez's players had been surprised by some of his late team selection announcements. And he had just stunned them again: Kewell was in, although he had not played a full game for Liverpool since the previous December. Which meant Hamann was out, although he had more big-match experience than anyone else in the team. Earlier in the preparations for the final, Benítez had decided that Liverpool had to attack Milan and shock them, rather than sit back and let the Italians come on to them, the tactic they'd used so successfully against both Juventus and Chelsea. Kewell, if he was fit, had to be the best option in light of that strategy. 'Kewell had to keep possession of the ball for us. He's blessed with a great shot from distance, he's very difficult to cope with one-on-one and he's pretty decent in the air, too.' Benítez assesses now. 'He's a very rare player and someone who can work well anywhere across the attacking third of the pitch.' But while nobody questioned his ability, many did doubt his commitment. And Benítez himself had often voiced his concerns about the winger's constant injuries. But Rafa overcame his reservations and went for Kewell because of his potential firepower.

Didi Hamann took the blow with his usual professionalism, even though he felt he had proved his worth in matches where experience and tactical awareness were essential – in both ties against Bayer Leverkusen and against Chelsea at Anfield, for instance. 'I didn't expect not to be in the team,' the midfielder admits. 'I only found out one hour before the match. It was hard to take, but I had to keep focus, take it on the chin, as they say.'

One of Didi's team-mates, Jamie Carragher, had been taken aback by the German's omission. 'I talked to Stevie [Gerrard] the day of the final and we thought that the first goal would have a massive impact on the match. We had reached the final because of our defensive strength and didn't think it was going to be any different against Milan. Normally it's just so difficult to score against an Italian team. We had been playing 4-5-1, with Hamann in front of the centre backs and Stevie in an advanced role between midfield and the striker, and it was a big surprise to everyone that the boss changed it to 4-4-2. He felt he had to go and win the game: we couldn't sit back, we had to be a bit bolder.'

The strategy was aimed at exploiting Milan's possible weak link: their ageing back four (average age: thirty-three) – particularly after viewing the defensive weaknesses they had displayed against a dynamic, pacy PSV Eindhoven in the semi-final. The key was to 'press' high up the field, maintain the pressure on the defence and keep the game at a very high tempo.

The inclusion of Kewell was not the only surprise. Milan Baroš was certainly better regarded by commentators outside the club than by some of those within Anfield, while Djibril Cissé had just made a stunning comeback after a lengthy lay-off through injury. But Benítez finally plumped for the Czech striker just minutes before he announced it to the team.

Baroš had presumed he was not going to play. He had not received any vibes from Benítez about his possible inclusion, and that could mean only one thing – the boss was going to choose Cissé. Baroš even mentioned his conviction to some friends. But while Rafa had clearly been favouring Cissé during the last training session at the Atatürk on Tuesday, there was another crucial factor to consider. Liverpool had already agreed to sell Baroš to Valencia after weeks of negotiations and the Czech was aware of it. Benítez therefore had to ask himself several questions. 'If I use Baroš from the start, will his mind be on Valencia? But the transfer is not yet finalised, so if Baroš is not my first choice, will Valencia back out of the deal? If I use him as a sub, will he come out and give it his all or will he be so pissed off that we'll get nothing from him? If I play Cissé only in the last minutes, will *he* be psychologically prepared?' The conclusion, more or less, was: 'If I use Baroš from the kick-off, it will be a vote of confidence even though he knows he's not going to be around next season. Then, if I need Cissé later, he'll give me all he's got, too, to prove he's back to his best. He will accept the decision.' So, with typical cool calculation, the Liverpool coach ditched his original plan and put Baroš in the starting line-up at the last minute.

Then the players warmed up, and some allowed themselves to savour the atmosphere. 'Just think how lucky I am: I'm going to play in the Champions League final,' Xabi Alonso remembers musing while he was stretching. 'From that moment onwards, I just completely lost myself in the game and nothing but the game.' Back in the locker room, the players withdrew into their own worlds and started the personal rituals which make them feel comfortable. 'You know that if someone sees one of the guys doing something out of the ordinary by breaking with his usual habits, he will immediately be told that he must do the same thing as always,' reveals Alonso. But some of the English players see the continentals' rituals (crossing themselves, kissing a ring, always putting on the right boot before the left one) as unnecessary gestures – even if they follow them religiously, they still sometimes lose! So for them, a firm handshake before leaving for the pitch is enough.

The locker room was filled with the smell of liniment, the hard tapping of boots, some shouting (but not much), lots of movement. Defenders talked among themselves while they pulled on their boots, while Rafa, with his usual matter-of-fact approach, spent the hour between his tactical talk and the walk onto the turf going one by one to each of his line-up to remind him of his role. Then he gave each man a gentle pat on the back. While he talked, Benítez would try to catch their eye to glean an indication of their state of mind. The players, still preparing themselves, would generally avoid direct eye contact. They accept the chat from the boss because it tends to happen before every match, but at that point they know exactly what is expected of them. Twenty minutes before kick-off, they are simply a team preparing for battle. Sometimes even the boss feels superfluous to this ceremony.

There were no final words to the group as a whole from the gaffer, but there was a warning from Luis García: 'Whatever you do, don't touch the cup!' It's an unwritten rule of football that only the winners have the right to touch the trophy. When the two teams and the referee came out, UEFA had heartlessly conjured up another test for the players: the European Cup was right in the middle of their route out onto the pitch. 'Never mind touching it, I didn't even want to look at it,' Alonso recalls. Two Milan players were not so circumspect, and touched the cup as they were passing it – Italian Gattuso and Brazilian Kaká. Did they feel, like the Italian press has suggested, they were doing a gesture equivalent to the very Catholic kiss of the Virgin's feet so common in their cultures? 'They won't be touching it for a while now,' Xabi Alonso laughs.

The referee, the Spaniard Mejuto González, had promised himself that he would enjoy everything surrounding his first Champions League final, 'even the smell of the grass. The official has to be part of the spectacle, not alien to it, another element of the whole party. That is why I loved UEFA's decision to include a kid dressed as a referee to take to the pitch with us, as they do with the teams.'

Others, mainly in the Liverpool camp, felt that González was a little overawed by everything which had been said before the game about the potential for bias in having a Spaniard refereeing a Liverpool match. His behaviour was radically different to that which he'd shown at Anfield in the game against Olympiakos. Right up to the end of this historic night in Istanbul he stayed well clear of Benítez and Liverpool's staff: he barely exchanged a couple of hellos with the coach and his technical team throughout the match.

The players lined up and the official anthem was played (as usual, the travelling Kop launched into 'You'll Never Walk Alone' at that point). A cameraman panned along the teams, and, as he had done all season, when the camera reached him Jerzy Dudek winked his right eye. A couple of minutes later, Stevie Gerrard initiated the huddle and waited for his team-mates to bow their heads before finally doing so himself. The skipper shouted, peppering his harangue with some swear words that not everybody understood: 'This is an unique opportunity. Do *not* let it go. You don't want to regret this for the rest of your life.'

Pako Ayestarán, who was seated on the bench next to Benítez, recalls thinking what a great experience the game was going to be. Benítez, however, was able to detach himself from the emotion and focus on the job in hand: 'I had a moment, during the brief walk to the bench, to taste the atmosphere but almost immediately I tried to remind myself of my mission in the match and what it was I had in my repertoire. I reached the overwhelming conclusion that I had to convey some calm to the players.' So Rafa walked to his bench as nonchalantly as he could, as if he were about to watch a practice match at Melwood.

(4)

THE CLUB BENÍTEZ INHERITED

We Want to Go Back to the Seventies and Eighties

'It all started with Traore giving the ball away when we should never have lost possession,' Rafa recalls with a level of detail which gives an idea of his extraordinary footballing memory as well as his almost obsessive analysis of his team's performances. 'It was immediately after the kick-off and we were playing very short, tight passes when the norm in these situations is to get the ball long. Then, as Kaká pushed down the right wing, the referee blew for a foul by Traore which wasn't really a foul. But the key point is that we should never have put ourselves in that situation because we should never have gifted possession of the ball. Then, to add insult to injury, we conceded a goal from the free kick. As Pirlo sent the ball into the box we had two rows of defenders lined up to zone-mark opposition players, but the second line was too deep and should have moved out a few metres. If you watch the goal again, you'll see that the ball basically drops right at Maldini's feet. Everything just went badly for us.'

Only fifty seconds into the Champions League final in Istanbul, Paolo Maldini hooked home a volley from twelve yards after Andrea Pirlo's clever free kick. It was the fastest goal in fifty European Cup/Champions League finals and hit Liverpool as if they'd had a bucket of cold water poured over their heads. Benítez, totally focused, remained detached from the emotional and historic connotations of the game. He viewed the goal and its speedy arrival as a further indication that his team was a long way from being fully formed, a long way from fulfilling his own image of what a football team should be. But, in a more practical sense, the goal became just one more obstacle for him to overcome that night.

'In that sort of match and against opposition of Milan's quality, a mistake is automatically a goal conceded,' concedes Traore. 'That was precisely what happened to us and all that I had running through my mind was: "Oh my God!" For Xabi Alonso, it was more a case of trying to keep up his optimism, despite the realisation of how difficult it normally is to score against an Italian team. He consoled himself with the slender belief that 'an early goal is better than one which hits you as a sucker punch really late on'.

Sitting on the right-hand side of the crowded bench, Paco Herrera and José Manuel Ochotorena optimistically saw the glass half full. The Milan staff would have been surprised to hear Paco say: 'This is going to work in our favour.' The whole coaching staff had felt that the team had been weighed down by pressure and anticipation leading up to the final. Now there was nothing to be tense about, nothing to anticipate. The players could shake off the pressure and get back into the game. The nerves of the young team would have been run much more ragged had they been clinging to a 0–0 draw against a seasoned, talented and experienced team like Milan deep into the match. Italian teams are renowned for relishing such situations and usually end up scoring when it is most damaging to the opponents.

By contrast, up in the VIP box, Rick Parry knew Benítez's tactical plan inside out and understood that it had already gone out of the window. 'It was devastating,' admits the Anfield chief executive. Pako Ayestarán adds: 'The players were not relaxed when they went out on to the pitch. OK, they did believe that they could win, but they certainly carried an excess of tension on their shoulders. We had identified it in the previous couple of days but it had not been alleviated. Also, this final had arrived too soon for us to have constructed a team which was able to play at the same level and with the same conviction, whether it happened to be losing or winning at any given time.'

His assessment echoed Benítez's own thoughts during the first few minutes of the final. Rafa had tried to make Liverpool resemble his old Valencia or José Mourinho's Chelsea: he wanted a team so confident that regardless of whether they were winning or losing, the shape, rhythm and consistency of their play would remain unchanged. 'Bloody hell! Let them score so we can go home and enjoy ourselves,' Sevilla centre-back Pablo Alfaro had said half-jokingly during a match against Rafa's Valencia. They were simply relentless. And they loved the football they played. Benítez had built a team with total self-belief that was able to react to any circumstance during a match. For them, the satisfaction of completing the week's work (producing good pressure, executing offensive tactics as planned, scoring a goal from a dead-ball situation that they'd practised in training) was almost as welcome as the actual result on the weekend. As Ayestarán puts it, 'We made them believe the key was not only *thinking* of winning, but *being ready* to win. Valencia were capable of losing but of saying to themselves, "OK, no problem, we know how to turn this around." We haven't achieved that with Liverpool, yet.'

Prior to Istanbul, the technical staff had, of course, studied Milan in detail. 'We may or may not win, but the key is that we know *how* to defeat them,' Ayestarán had insisted a week before arriving in Turkey. But that start, the dramatic Maldini goal, caught everyone off-guard. 'We never got into the game in the first half,' Didi Hamann, watching from the bench, admits. 'It did not help to get an early goal. We were losing against one of the best teams in Europe, if not the best. We had planned to counterattack and, with a goal behind so early, we had to change tactics, we had to take the initiative.'

Carragher saw problems earlier on too. 'Obviously you're sick you've conceded a goal so early, but I thought we were going to get back into it. But soon after, they just kept picking us off on the break, and Kaká was causing us a lot of problems.'

Livepool's response to the Maldini goal was almost immediate: Sami Hyypia powered in a bullet header from a Steven Gerrard cross which Dida grasped. But, as Carragher noted, Kaká was already starting to drift around freely, exposing the limits of the offside trap Benítez had prepared. Shevchenko and Hernán Crespo moved wide, targeting Liverpool's fragile full-backs and receiving passes from Pirlo, who was finding it easy to put his team mates in behind the defence. Without Hamann protecting the centre-backs, and with Gerrard revealing some alarming defensive shortcomings, Milan looked comfortable. In the fourteenth minute, Luis García had to clear a Hernán Crespo header off the line.

Rafa bided his time. He was waiting for his team to settle after the early knockback before making some tactical changes, but he was already standing up, screaming and demanding more from the central partnership of Xabi Alonso and Gerrard, as well as reminding players that retaining the ball was essential. A couple of times he punched the air in disgust when possession was lost thoughtlessly. 'Our whole idea had been to press Milan high up the pitch and try to take advantage of their lack of pace at the back. That early goal forced us into a total change of tactics,' he admits.

His challenge in Istanbul was the same as it had been all season: to produce a priceless jewel from a group of rough diamonds. 'This job is really a dream,' says Benítez. 'In Spain, when you imagine the Premiership, you always have Liverpool in your head. For the Spanish, it has always been their favourite English team, irrespective of our arrival here. Also, for a professional like myself, Liverpool is the most important club in England. But I still wasn't kidding myself. I knew precisely what kind of team I was about to take control of. But I am a fighter.

'When my guys and I started, the club not only told us the dos and don'ts of being Liverpool's manager, explaining the traditional philosophy which had been followed throughout the club's history, but also underlined the expectation that we must win a trophy within the first three years. The first thing I did was trawl for every scrap of information from everyone who was already at the club. I talked to everybody from the lifetime staff to Gérard Houllier, the existing technical staff right down to the very last person who worked at Melwood. I wanted to get to know people but also to draw out their opinions on every player, the workings of the club and how Melwood functioned.

'My biggest surprise at the start was the level of cooperation which people gave me. I'm talking about Phil Thompson, for example – someone who knew he was not going to be part of the club any more. I met him after he had had a chat with Rick Parry and he did not let me speak! "Look, Rafa, I understand what is going on. You don't need to say anything. I am off!" I almost had to interrupt him because I wanted to talk to him the same way I had done to Gérard Houllier. Then he surprised me again. He was willing to talk about subjects that departing regimes tend not to wish to discuss – about which players had the wrong attitude and which were important. Many of the decisions we took regarding the squad had to do with that chat. Phil showed me clearly that he loved the club above anything else.' Then Benítez, thorough as always, spent many nights watching DVDs of the team's performances during the previous season.

During his initial dialogue with the new coach, Rick Parry did not try to sell Benítez 'the perfect club'; quite the contrary. 'We told him he had some challenges,' says Parry. 'When he started training, he probably thought, "OK, perhaps there is more to do here than I imagined," but we always try to be fair. He had always been very positive in his outlook; he doesn't worry about things that he can't influence. So many managers get upset about things and do it through the press. In contrast, Rafa will say, "Can we fix it? No? OK, so we carry on. Let's worry about the things we *can* change and not waste time on the things we can't."' Admittedly, Rafa was told he had a better squad than later turned out to be the case, but the chief executive and the chairman had been sincere in their assessment.

Like many Liverpool fans, they thought they had a good team that was badly managed. In fact, they had a poor squad that was badly managed. 'I think Houllier left a very mediocre group of players,' says the *Echo*'s Chris Bascombe. 'The foundations of the club were in a very poor state. People talk about the new training ground and the great academy, but that's not the manager's job. I don't see why Houllier takes credit for that. That would have happened whoever was in charge. Liverpool always intended to build an academy and to rebuild the training ground. Houllier just happened to be there when it happened. It is not his legacy. His job was to create a solid team and he left a very poor team. The best players inherited by Rafa were Steven Gerrard, Michael Owen (who left immediately) and Jamie Carragher, who had all developed through the youth system. The rest of the squad included some good footballers, but if you made a list of who you wanted for your fantasy Premiership team, it probably wouldn't include any of the rest. If Rafa had forty million quid, he wouldn't have signed Djibril Cissé, with all due respect!'

The club seemed to have a blurred vision of its own future. One of Houllier's last comments as Liverpool manager was: 'We talk about going back to the sixties and seventies. Not with me!' Yet that was exactly what Liverpool needed to do. 'He was talking about the professional conduct of players in those years, but the sixties and seventies were more about dignified men, humble men from a very closed environment, in a small city, playing for a small club that becomes the biggest in Europe,' says Bascombe. 'Six years at Liverpool and Houllier still gave no indication that he understood the point. There was an unbelievable paranoia clouding the judgements he was making. And, of course, Rafa comes in and says, 'We *do* want to go back to the sixties and seventies and eighties. Maybe we cannot do it straight away, we won't promise anything, we will go match by match, but that is the way.' So Houllier was right. "Not with me," he said. Nope, with Benítez!'

The signing of the Spaniard, who, along with José Mourinho, was one of the two most coveted coaches of that summer, showed the club still burned with ambition. But the new boss had to lead a club that was still confused about Houllier's 'five- or six-year plans'. Benítez surely realised that the departure of the backroom staff (Lee and Thompson, along with Joe Corrigan and Christian Damiano) also meant the end of the boot-room dynasty, and consequently the biggest revolution in forty years at Anfield. Nevertheless, undaunted, and with the help of people he trusted, he addressed urgent problems instantly and bravely.

However, his first meeting with the whole squad hardly resulted in a call to battle. 'It wasn't stirring stuff,' he admits, 'because I always emphasise precisely the same themes: "We have to work professionally, show respect to our colleagues, the team and the technical staff. Every single day we have to try to give everything we can to our work in order to give our absolute best."' Benítez never has been, and never will be, a man for inspirational speeches, in spite of what many have chosen to believe happened in the locker room at half time in Istanbul.

The organisation and infrastructure he inherited were more than adequate – several training pitches, covered areas with artificial grass, a high-class gym, medical facilities, pool, no end of machines to measure players' fitness, and so on. After all, the new Melwood was only three years old. However, it was underused and lacked the kind of people who could develop it. It was all there, but the club did not know exactly what to do with it.

Midway through July, with about half the squad back at work and the internationals who had played in Euro 2004 about to return shortly, Benítez took some crucial decisions concerning the needs of the team, which players he valued and where the squad required strengthening. Houllier had just brought Djibril Cissé from Auxerre for £12 million, and Rafa accepted the deal as it was done and dusted, but reports of his interest in the French striker when he was the Valencia boss were greatly exaggerated. Benítez was also paying close attention to Milan Baroš, who had won the golden boot at the European Championships that summer, and wondered if he could find a place for him in his system. Obviously the new boss valued the commitment and prowess of Carragher and Gerrard, and he quickly decided to let El Hadji Diouf go, but he reserved judgement on the rest.

In his role as manager, he organised a small restructuring but immediately started delegating several crucial responsibilities to Herrera and Ayestarán. The Spanish management team was shocked at some of the dietary regimes in force at Melwood – frozen food given to the players for lunch; beans routinely eaten one and a half hours before the match – and implemented changes from the outset. 'The players eat at the club every day and must eat well,' emphasised Benítez. 'The diet is very varied but we have tried to introduce more Mediterranean ingredients.' This was not a trivial matter for a man who likes to oversee every single aspect of his club. In his first success as coach with Extremadura, he forbade players from chewing gum because it gave the club a bad image. At Valencia, the press reported that he had 'banned' ice-cream and paella. In fact, he is not the killjoy that the media described. The players *could* eat ice-cream – just as long as it wasn't made with full-cream milk. And paella was also allowed, but he simply wanted some of the local players to eat something *else*, too. Nevertheless, his demands led to clashes with several players, among them Miguel Angel Angulo. Benítez also objected to his team drinking beer after matches, and following one game he found Angulo enjoying a bottle in the bar. 'Did you ask for my permission to do that?' demanded the coach. The footballer just glared at him. The next day, Benítez approached Angulo before training and in front of his team-mates warned him: 'This is the way we do things here under my regime. If you don't like it, then I don't want you here any more!' Angulo did what was necessary to stay at Valencia, but, like several of his colleagues, he never warmed to Benítez. Some at the club still refer to their former boss as 'God' – and it's not a compliment. Under the influence of the Argentinian players, he was also nicknamed 'Diego', after Maradona. Both of these jibes refer to the boss's omnipotence: he knows everything. 'He is even in possession of the right way to open a Coca-Cola and if he sees you opening one, he would stop you and tell you the right way to do it,' a former and anonymous player of Benítez says jokingly. By contrast, at Liverpool Benítez was highly respected from the moment he landed on Merseyside. He's one of the few at Melwood who *doesn't* have a nickname.

The pre-season tour to America and Canada at the end of July, in which Liverpool played Celtic (5–1 victory), Porto (0–0) and Roma (2–1 to the Reds), was viewed as vital in the team-building process and a perfect time to implement changes. During the last two years of his regime, Houllier had been 'more a president than a manager or a coach', as Chris Bascombe describes it. Benítez's real passion was coaching and he immersed himself in it from day one. Later he would feel that his managerial responsibilities dragged him away from the training pitch much more often than he would like.

There was certainly enthusiasm in the squad, an eagerness to return to playing and training, getting their feet to the ball again. And suddenly there was a coach who was prepared to stop and explain techniques to the players. 'Houllier kept saying that at last the players had a great training complex to spend the day in,' Bascombe remembers. 'Trouble is, under him, the players wanted to go home as soon as they could. They started to hang around a lot more under Benítez. You can go to Melwood at three o'clock (they finish training at twelve) and you will still see players around. They'll be doing something ... maybe watching the telly, playing pool. It's an environment where people want to be before they start training again.'

In short, Liverpool players had stopped enjoying themselves. Steven Gerrard, at the press conferrence in the summer of 2004 when he confirmed he was staying, looked miserable. Was it that bad to be playing for Liverpool? With the new regime, it soon became fun to train again. The new staff had little tactics to increase the sense of camaraderie. For instance, instead of everybody eating when they wanted and then disappearing (something which is commonplace in English clubs), everyone was ordered to sit together at the table and share mealtimes. While some resented this at first, soon everyone could appreciate its value in developing team spirit. And morale had to be kept high because the workload was much greater than in past seasons. After the warm-up exercises, Ayestarán demanded that the players work on possession and tactical work before finishing with a thirty-minute jog followed by sprints. At Extremadura Pako was nicknamed 'the Pest' because he used to work the squad to exhaustion. 'The new manager and Pako would do a lot more tactical work, a lot more stuff on set pieces,' says Carragher. 'The manager is known as someone who never stops talking about football, and you can see that in the way that we train. We cover in training virtually everything you are going to do in a game, something we didn't do before.'

The new staff inherited two goalkeepers, both of whom had question marks hanging over their heads: Chris Kirkland because of his constant injuries, and Jerzy Dudek because of his supposedly fragile state of mind. The Kop seemed to put Dudek's every movement under the microscope, and as a result he always played under a great deal of pressure. Both keepers were accustomed to a different rhythm of training and were used to doing so in isolation from the rest of the squad. At first, they could not understand why they were suddenly being involved in some of the tactical preparation with their team-mates instead of being left to their own devices. When they were ordered to take part in constant repetitions of specific match-based situations, they both responded with blatant indifference. However, as will become clear later, Dudek's astonishing double save against Shevchenko in the Istanbul final owed much to what he had been made to repeat over and over again with goalkeeping coach José Ochotorena.

In general, though, the squad was responsive, and in time welcomed the changes and valued the planning and seriousness Benítez had introduced. Nothing was improvised. Individualised work programmes were used and the tempo hardly ever dropped, not even after a good result. In contrast to the majority of Premiership teams,

Liverpool never gave the squad three consecutive days off. Pako and the rest of the staff believe that such a lay-off breaks the rhythm of preparations and means you need longer to regain your form. Finally, there was a planned route forward instead of always reacting to circumstances.

Bolstered by Steven Gerrard's choice to reject Chelsea's advances, decisions about the squad were gathering pace. On 17 August Real Sociedad issued a statement stating that twenty-two-year-old Xabi Alonso was about to sign for Liverpool. Real Sociedad were in desperate need of cash, and Xabi was their prize asset. It was almost inconceivable that a talented youngster like him, linked during the year with both Real Madrid and Barcelona, could be enticed abroad, but his departure was the start of a new Spanish import trend. La Liga was losing its financial clout, and the Premiership was going to take full advantage.

Almost as soon as he arrived, the refrain 'Xabi is class' was being chanted by the Kop. The midfielder, in spite of his youth, performed like a veteran both on and off the pitch. At Real Sociedad, runners up in La Liga in 2002, he was the brains of the team when barely into his twenties. His team-mates all looked up to him; he never hid; he was the coach on the pitch. That, along with his unerringly accurate passing and uncanny understanding of the tempo of the game, was precisely why Rafa targeted him. And he got him for possibly the bargain of the decade: £10.7 million. He became the third Red Spaniard, after the £2 million capture of Josemi from Málaga and the arrival of Antonio Nuñez, valued at around £2 million in the deal that took Michael Owen to Real Madrid.

At this time, Luis García was getting ready for a new season with an unusually optimistic Barcelona (Samuel Eto'o had just arrived and Ronaldinho looked hungry). García had just spent his first year as a first-team player back at the club that had nurtured him after loan deals with Valladolid, Tenerife and Atlético Madrid. However, 'Rafa asked me if I was willing to change my surroundings; that he had thought of a special role in the side for me; that the adventure was going to be interesting, attractive; that he needed competitive people like me. He knows me very well from our time at Tenerife, and I have a relationship with him way beyond the professional. I had to come.' Barcelona were happy to let him go for the right price – £6m. He made his debut on 29 August at Bolton (a 1–0 defeat), where he had a perfectly legitimate goal disallowed.

Other choices were taken concerning players deemed insufficiently talented or potentially troublesome for the new regime. So Bruno Cheyrou (Marseille), Alou Diarra (Lens), Carl Medjani (Lorient), Anthony Le Tallec (St Etienne), Gregory Vignal (Rangers) and, as mentioned, El Hadji Diouf (Bolton) all had to go. As a result, most of the French players bought by Houllier were on their way out and four Spaniards had arrived.

Benítez's preference for La Liga players stemmed from his desire to take advantage of the cheaper Spanish market, but also because he wished to sign those he knew well. With his Spanish buys, Rafa had effectively emptied the club's coffers. He'd even got a little into the red, but the sale of Danny Murphy to Charlton helped balance the books. The decision to get rid of the midfielder brought in £2.5 million, but perhaps more importantly it served to shake up the rest of the English contingent at Liverpool. Benítez had seen the English players sitting on their own at lunch in Melwood, despite having been warned that this was not the way things worked under him. They had to integrate themselves with the newcomers.

Jamie Carragher admits it was an uncertain start and did not know quite how to react when right-back Josemi was signed: 'You always look at it from a selfish point of view and wonder if the manager will take to you. Will he maybe try to bring in some other players from Valencia? Even though he's coming for the good of the team and the good of the club, to start with you worry about yourself, to be honest. It didn't look too good for me when he bought a right-back as his first signing. That's where I'd played the year before, so the pre-season was a bit worrying.'

Throughout that time Michael Owen had been even more

concerned. He had travelled to America but was left on the bench in Benítez's official debut, the Graz AK Champions League qualifier on 10 August. Six days later he moved to Real Madrid. 'I was very happy with Michael and I wanted him to stay. The problem was he only had a year left on his contract,' the new Liverpool manager said at the time. But in his mind he had been clear from the outset that Owen had to be sold. The club was on a tight budget, and the coach did not want the own-goal of another McManaman – who had left on a free transfer at the end of his contract a few years before.

Benítez had met the three Liverpool England internationals at their European Championships training-camp hotel in Portugal, and the way he treated each of them had given clear clues about their respective futures. He praised Carragher's attitude on the pitch and told him that he was going to be very important for the team. He told Gerrard, the focus of most of the conversation, that he knew there was a great offer on the table from Chelsea, but asked the midfielder to give him time to turn Liverpool around. He promised that Gerrard would soon have colleagues in midfield who possessed talent equal to his own. (Nevertheless, at that point, Gerrard still thought he was going to Chelsea. The full story is given in chapter 8.) In comparison, Michael Owen felt almost like a hindrance. His situation was rarely mentioned and Benítez seemed frosty towards him. Owen genuinely felt it was a personal animosity. But he was wrong. Benítez had nothing against the young striker: he had simply made a decision and was not going to renege on it. The club needed money and Owen could provide it. In spite of what the press claimed, it was nothing to do with Owen not 'fitting in'. The backroom staff backed the coach in this, his first difficult decision. It was certainly a risk, but it brought in £8 million and so eased the arrival of Xabi Alonso and Luis García.

David Moores and Rick Parry accepted the departure of Owen despite their emotional attachment to the player. Jamie Carragher phlegmatically saw it as part and parcel of normal life in a big club. Only Steven Gerrard broke ranks: he felt that without Owen he would feel more isolated, and even mentioned publicly that he wished one of his best friends hadn't left. With Owen and Danny Murphy now gone, and confused by the relative coldness of his new coach in comparison to Houllier, the skipper began to doubt if staying had been the best decision he'd ever made.

The deal that took Owen to Madrid brought Antonio Nuñez to Anfield. 'I don't want him ever to go, as he could become a bit of a cult figure here. Obviously he's not that good, but he's a trier, and with Igor Biscan gone there is definitely room for another cult figure!' was the tongue-in-cheek view of *The Liverpool Way* fanzine editor, Dave Usher. Unfortunately, Nuñez was blighted by injury throughout the first half of the season, and even when he was fit he rarely lived up to his billing. After just one stop–start season, Benítez told him he didn't feature in his plans for 2005–06, and he was sold to Celta Vigo.

Back in August 2004, with the squad in place, the next step was to work day-in day-out to improve what Rafa had inherited. But due to injuries, some signings who did not fit in well and the imbalance of a squad better prepared to compete in Europe, a pattern of away defeats (for instance, 1–0 to Bolton and Chelsea) was set early in the season which Benítez couldn't break for the rest of it. Were these defeats the result of having a limited squad? Or, as some were suggesting, were they due to a coach who was finding out at first hand how tough the Premiership can be?

(5)

THE MANAGER LIVERPOOL APPOINTED

I Learned Not to Trust People

As Benítez's Liverpool progressed in Europe and Valencia slipped ever further down La Liga, the streets of the city which had been Rafa's home for three years filled with rumours. According to one, early on in Claudio Ranieri's reign, Amadeo Carboni asked his new coach what would be the best way to defend. Ranieri answered: 'Just like you did last year.' To which the puzzled player responded: 'But we had *five* ways of defending last year, depending on the opponent and the situation.' Ranieri's alleged solution was: 'Just use whichever one you feel like, then.' Whatever the truth of the story, it certainly defines Benítez's work.

Rafa had left behind a team very similar to those he grew up admiring. 'My reference points are Johann Cruyff and his Barcelona "Dream Team", plus John Toshack's Real Madrid, and, of course, Arrigo Sacchi's Milan. Their hard work, with or without the ball, is the only path to follow, but it is almost impossible to copy because of the fantastic quality of their players. Their success does, though, underline the importance of "the team". In the past, Liverpool's teams hunted like a pack and the team was the star. Now we have to get as close as possible to that mentality. In any case, it is easy to impose your ideas here in England, because the manager has complete freedom to construct, coach and impose his will on his team.'

He mainly makes his mark in training or during his tactical

preparations, when he rehearses each and every situation which is likely to arise during matches in order to work through their pitfalls and possibilities. His objectives are to teach the players, to improve their level of understanding and ability to react properly, and eventually to enable them to take control of their own destinies and seek their own solutions when under pressure in a match. 'I am a physical education teacher, I have worked in schools,' remembers Benítez. 'You soon learn that if you tell people to do a thing they will do it at once. Whereas if you teach them how to do something, they will do it all the time. It will be automatic then, it will last a whole career. I don't have any special secret other than that. It all comes down to work and time on the training field, and having players who are intelligent enough to understand. Time is short, but if the players understand what I am after, they learn quickly.'

For example, the controversial zonal defence, which hardly any English team uses and which failed to stop Maldini's goal in Istanbul, had been rehearsed week after week. Benítez positioned the players where he wanted them to be, walked them through the tactic and explained the dos and don'ts of the system. Although learning the ropes has cost Liverpool two or three goals, the team is now starting to adopt the defensive shape which the Anfield boss demands of them.

Benítez is meticulous and his quiet charm hides an anorakish obsession to detail. He has more than 1,500 tapes in his parents' house and already around 300 of players and matches at Melwood. He can talk for hours about the game, can spend 22 consecutive hours working for the club, as he did before the Chelsea Champions League semifinal, and, of course, is a devotee of the two more tactical games, chess and *mus*, the Spanish equivalent of bridge.

Rafa himself gives a measurement of how meticulous he is, even in preparations when he was 18. 'I was a player-manager for the university side. We played a final in Seville of a tournament and the players of all the other teams went to parties in the evening and I said to my players we needed to go to the hotel to be ready for the next game. We went home at one o'clock, the other teams were partying until six o'clock in the morning.'

'Benítez works on the team, shape and tactics every single day – defensively and offensively,' explains Stevie Gerrard. 'Houllier only used to do that sort of stuff two or three times a week. But Benítez is really keen on working on the small details – so training sessions are very long. He wants every player to know their job before they go out. He's extremely tactically oriented. Before the Milan game, we worked on how to beat them and how to defend against them, how to build our attacks and what their weaknesses and strengths were. We worked on all of that every single available day.'

Throughout 2004–05, the Liverpool squad made progressive leaps in quality as the players acquired new knowledge. Small but important details would be highlighted repeatedly until suddenly their importance became clear to the players. 'Some of the guys have been surprised by the strategic work we always undertake in the last two days before any given match,' admits Paco Herrera. 'Every week there are new variations to tactics depending on what kind of rival we are going to face.' One week it will be how to attack, and how to defend corners. Then the next training session will focus on different ways of coping with the same set play, depending on the rival's particular players.

'More than anything, he's been giving us ideas,' Carragher admits. 'It's all very well a manager telling you to do this or that, but, rather than just saying, "get in the box" or "get crosses in", he's been showing us how to make the space to get crosses in and how to make the runs, giving us ideas about things we've maybe not thought about before.'

Some teams still watch full matches to look for strengths and weaknesses, but at Liverpool they work differently: every movement on the pitch is recorded and the information processed. Every week the players are shown a selection of their own successes and failures, and those of the players they are about to face. It's a system that seems to work. 'Things have improved here and I am learning so much,' says John Arne Riise. 'I feel more confident whichever position I play in.'

'We call it the Integral Method,' explains Benítez. 'Coaches used to apply the football theory, practice and physical preparation only with movement. They did not include the ball in any of those phases of training. But we feel it is very important that we do.' Notice that Rafa hardly ever says, 'I'; it is nearly always 'we'. He is well aware that Pako and the rest of 'the guys' all have crucial parts to play and he is indebted to them, especially Ayestarán. Some time ago, Rafa's right-hand man had to decide whether he wanted to stay within his comfort zone at Osasuna of Pamplona (near his Basque home and his family, at a modest club with no pressure) or move 1,000 km to Extremadura to develop professionally beside a coach he'd got to know during a training course run by the Spanish FA. He barely hesitated. 'It was clear that we espoused the same methods,' says Pako. 'Benítez is a ceaseless worker, but he is very analytical and above all he has a massive knowledge and understanding of football. Naturally, I chose to go with Rafa! We've often reflected on everything we have achieved from that moment until now. I always remind him that when success begins to accord you status and "importance", that can start to strip away some of what has been good about your philosophy and your work. We must never forget that triumphs are a result of huge amounts of work and a deep analysis of every situation.' This philosophy is why Pako will never allow himself or Benítez to take their foot off the pedal. 'The difference between Rafa and many other coaches is that some of them teach footballers how to play because it earns them money. Others, like Rafa, do it because they love to teach, and the players notice the difference,' he explains. 'In Valencia, the squad told us we were "very demanding", but now many of the players realise what a great coach they had in Rafa. The truth is it's very difficult to be super-demanding of your players and still preserve a "comfortable" relationship with them. I'd love to be more laid-back with them and still achieve the same level of professionalism and success, but I don't have the formula for that. I'm not sure it exists.'

Unlike in Spain, where he was at the training ground from 10 a.m. to 2 or 3 p.m., Benítez arrives at Melwood at 8.30 a.m. every day and often doesn't leave until eight at night. As was said before, the extra workload is the consequence of managing and coaching a club at the same time. Now myriad tasks have to be performed each day. 'In my life away from football I'm not a particularly serious guy. On the contrary – I like a laugh and a joke now and again,' reveals the notoriously sombre Benítez. 'But in my work I must be serious. I follow this demanding timetable because I have so much work every day: almost every minute of the day is occupied. The club needed, and still needs, a big push forward and that demands that I concentrate on several different areas of the development. In the beginning I was so busy that I couldn't take as many of the training sessions as I wanted to, but now I spend a good deal of time out on the pitches leading the tactical work and sorting out little details. Here, managers tend to attend training only once or twice a week, but I do not have that kind of attitude. I assume full responsibility for my position in terms of all the tasks that entails, but I value being on the training ground very highly.'

Perhaps Rafa's biggest initial surprise as coach of Liverpool was when he saw Rick Parry and David Moores attending the tactical talk before the matches, sitting alongside the players and the coaching staff. But he soon realised that this was a time-honoured tradition, and it did not undermine his authority one jot.

In his role as manager, Benítez meets with agents and then reports back to the chief executive. After all, it's Parry who has control of the purse strings. The two men have a healthy relationship, and the manager understands the need to balance the books, but there have been a few tense moments, most notably during the conflict with Steven Gerrard in 2005, when the coach demanded speedier decision-making. He also plans media access with the public relations people and is consulted on everything from the training timetables to the design of the facilities. He is already instituting improvements at Melwood: he has bought new equipment for the gyms and is proud of his own headquarters. From his office, Rafa can see all three of the major training pitches, where the first team is normally put through its paces. This is his nerve-centre, bursting with videotapes, documentation, a computer, a TV and usually a couple of Spanish sports papers. The newspapers are one of the few links with the country he's left behind. In contrast to José Mourinho at Chelsea, he did not want a translator in the club. There are classes for those whose English is not up to speed, and the coaching staff demand that newcomers make the biggest effort possible to acclimatise themselves quickly by learning the language.

There are more clues to Benítez's personality on the office walls. The only picture of himself is from the front cover of the club magazine which was published when he arrived. It is framed, but is not even hung, rather just casually hidden away on a shelf full of videos. In contrast, Houllier, almost like a head of state, had numerous pictures of himself standing next to some of football's biggest personalities and prizes. Next to the desk there used to be one with World Cup-winning coach Aimé Jacquet and Houllier holding the trophy, as well as others that reminded him of team or personal successes, including manager of the month awards. On Benítez's desk are pictures of his two daughters.

If the boss of Liverpool does not keep his feet firmly on the ground, the continuous demonstrations of fan loyalty – or faith, devotion, madness, whatever you want to call it – could easily turn his head. Historically, every new manager at the club receives a huge amount of goodwill and respect even before he has produced the goods on the pitch and sometimes long after he deserves it. It's another Shankly legacy that goes some way to explaining why Houllier lasted so long. But Rafa already seems to have *earned* the Kop's respect. 'He is bringing hope back', 'He respects the club's traditions', 'He is down to earth' are all common appraisals of the new boss. Some simply say, 'He is our manager.' Tony Barrett of the Liverpool *Echo* agrees with all that, and thinks that another reason for the popular appeal of Rafa is his 'aura of mystery'. This has developed largely because of the careful and conscious way the Anfield boss uses his adopted language.

Benítez got a taste of what a hero he'd become when he and his coaching team decided to go and watch a match in an Irish pub in Germany. 'I was with Pako and Alex. We were playing Bayer Leverkusen the following night and the lads suggested that we go and watch the Chelsea–Barcelona game in a pub in the middle of Cologne. So we got into a taxi and got to the pub, still dressed in our tracksuits. The bar was jammed with Liverpool supporters and very quickly some of the guys around me looked astonished and said, "*Rafa?*" I put one finger up to my lips to ask them not to say anything. So much for that! They began to sing and chant, take photos, ask for autographs and some wanted to plant a kiss on the top of my head. One huge guy almost broke my hand when he shook it. Pako and Alex even had to protect me a little. We only stayed for fifteen minutes because we couldn't see the game, and it took us five minutes to work our way out of the pub. It was total madness.'

There have been other instances of the special relationship which has become firmly established between Benítez and the supporters. During his first Merseyside derby, the travelling fans chanted, 'Rafa Benítez!' for the entire first half, which drove the Goodison faithful crazy. Later in the season, the most memorable image during the build-up to the Carling Cup final came in the streets of Cardiff, with two supporters walking around with a giant gold-framed portrait of Benítez. People wanted to touch it and have their photos taken next to it; fans were bowing down, worshipping their leader. 'I felt like the Ayatollah,' says the cringing coach. 'I saw it from the team bus as we arrived at the stadium.' He is well aware that he must never allow the fans' devotion to swell his head, though: 'When you hear people called "the special one", "the new Shankly" and stuff like that, you have to keep serene and run away from those labels. It is all put about by the press, which continually needs to sell papers with bigger and bigger headlines. You have to look for the real satisfaction of a job well done.'

'Rafa is so responsible that he never lets people see whether these things are affecting him or not,' claims Paco Herrera. 'In fact, he never allows himself a moment's distraction.' Every single member of the club must have tried the 'Come-on, ease up, you are with friends!' technique at some point in order to see a more relaxed version of the Spaniard, but it has all been to no avail. Benítez remains focused on teamwork and keeping everything in perspective. He has had more than enough experience of professional football to be brutally aware that you can be up one day and a failure the next with everyone against you. 'Nobody I know had better call me "special",' he says. 'I remember that when I started training one of Real Madrid's youth teams, I had to run for twenty-five minutes in my tracksuit and carrying my kit. To get there on time, I would leave the institute where I was studying and run the five kilometres to the sports ground. I asked the club for expenses, less than the equivalent of five pounds per week, in order to cover the bus fare, and, although they had said yes to other people, they refused me. That kind of experience makes you.'

But Benítez is also shrewd enough, or possibly well enough advised, not to go too far in the other direction and spoil people's natural desire to express their devotion to him and the club. A few hours after beating Juventus at Anfield, he was driving home when he heard a couple of young supporters, draped in scarves and flags, chanting his name. 'We had stopped at traffic lights and my wife told me that I couldn't just ignore them, given that they were singing my name,' he explains. 'I did think the situation might be a little dangerous, but, in the end, I followed her advice and got out of the car to give them an autograph. I got back in the car and watched them walking off, singing even louder than before. I've never seen anything like it.'

'For me, all this brings great responsibility. I try to return the affection which I'm shown and thank them all for their passionate support of the club. Shankly was the ideological founder of Liverpool FC's modern era, and he utterly changed the club's mentality, making it ambitious and great. Paisley and Fagan then won the trophies. I've got a massive amount to achieve before I reach anything approaching the stature of any of these men.'

His awkwardness in moments of triumph indicates that Benítez is much more comfortable in the workaday surroundings of the Melwood training ground. His half-hearted hugs to staff and players, his terse handshakes after a memorable night, his wish to move on quickly instead of wallowing in adulation and congratulations (even from Alex Ferguson after the Istanbul win), his tactical debriefings (minutes after holding the European Cup for the first time, on his return to the changing room, he had to be reminded by Rick Parry of what the team had just achieved because Rafa was concentrating on the mistakes of the first half!) all hide a commendable respect for his colleagues at work. He feels they deserve as much recognition as himself, if not more. There's also the fact that he's extremely shy.

Benítez will always be grateful to Liverpool for engaging him as both manager and coach, because the combined role allows him to demonstrate his utter devotion to his sport. He never tires of football. This, after all, is someone who spent part of his honeymoon watching AC Milan ... as they trained! He never stops being a 'football-man'. David Hodgson, an exiled Scouser, went to watch Liverpool train in New Jersey in the summer of 2004. A tremendous thunderstorm had sent the players scurrying for cover, which left Rafa and Pako to clear up. Hodgson and a friend decided to lend them a hand. Benítez started passing them the balls, but then dropped the last one at his feet and started running towards the two friends. 'Being great defenders, me and my friend obviously set up a two-on-one situation against Rafa,' says Hodgson. 'He tried to dribble us, then a nutmeg came off for him. This continued for a couple of minutes until Rafa trotted off with a "Thanks, guys." It was surreal.' Little things like that nutmeg must be bittersweet for a man who was robbed of his chance of becoming a professional footballer. 'I was in the Madrid youth team, and, of course, I dreamed of making it big. But I got injured and that finished my career. Even if I had never been injured I would never had made it as a top Madrid player. Although I did possess some important qualities, I was definitely lacking others. However, I'm sure that I could have been a La Liga player for another club,' he says.

But even when he was a player, Rafa thought like a coach. He first gave tactical instructions when he was sixteen, and player/coach of a team in Villalba, where he used to go on holiday. 'I have always been drawn to coaching. When I was thirteen my father gave me a notebook as a present and I copied down line-ups – adding my own notes and keeping a chart of the top scorers. Even now I've still got loads of stuff in my house left over from that period in my development.' That early start in coaching and the injury which ended his playing career for good at just twenty-six helped shape his personality and his managerial life, which started at Real Madrid. After running a youth team for three years at the end of the 1980s and then the under-19s from 1990, Madrid appointed him B-team manager in 1993. It was a rapid promotion for a thirty-three-year-old who was still learning.

By then, he had completed his degree in physical education as well as a national football coaching course. He had also managed a gym in Madrid, where he met his future wife, Montse. Impressed by his training methods, Vicente del Bosque chose him as assistant manager to the first team halfway through the 1993–94 season. The Argentinian Jorge Valdano became head coach the next year, and Benítez returned to the B team. The demands of the new first-team boss, who wanted to see certain players in the B team, created tensions between two stubborn men who had very different football philosophies: Valdano is a great believer in creativity on the pitch; Benítez is an advocate of a more demanding work ethic based on team and tactics.

'With Madrid I learned the value of being calm. I learned this from Luis Molowny,' says Rafa of that period. 'He was a legendary club man in the same mould as del Bosque and the technical secretary at the time I was there. Before making any decision, he examined it so thoroughly. Now, whenever I am tempted to dive in with a rash word or decision, I always say to myself, "Molowny, Molowny . . ." It's my way of telling myself to keep calm. I use it, say, when a player gets injured or a problem crops up at the very last minute. You've got to be ready to deal calmly with every unexpected situation and not worry about things before they happen.'

The following summer, Valladolid gave Benítez the chance to be their manager in La Liga, but after just two wins in twenty-three games he was sacked. 'In Valladolid, I learned not to trust people – not everyone, but certain people.' He was promised certain things – a future at the club, for a start – but when things went wrong these were all forgotten. And he's never totally lost the scepticism he developed there. One consequence of this is his relationship with the English media: affable, open, entertaining but always distant and professional rather than friendly. Chris Bascombe, for one, has had to learn how to deal with that attitude. 'I would see and speak to Houllier every single day, but for perhaps only five minutes, in which I could ask him a couple of questions. Rafa is different. We chat for thirty minutes to an hour once a week and I get more out of him than I ever did with Houllier. Even if you know that it is a hard question, even if you know it is a struggle, he'll answer it eventually. But he may not give you the line that you want to hear. You'll look at the answer later and say to yourself, "Hold on. I don't know whether he answered that question." But he'll have said it with a smile on his face.'

In 1996, Benítez was appointed manager of second-division Osasuna, but after just one win in his first nine games he was soon out of work again. 'It was a great pity at Osasuna,' he admits, 'because I found that there were great people there and I also had a terrific relationship with the board. But sometimes circumstances can overwhelm certain people.'

So his first two solo jobs had both ended in sacking. Rafa firmly believes in learning from his failures. He was as well aware that his next step had to be the correct one, because one more setback could have scuppered his career. Fortunately, he did choose wisely, and in Extremadura (1997–1999) his winning streak started. His first year at this modest club in a town of only 40,000 people won promotion to the elite of La Liga, and the next season represented his first full one working at that exalted level. A poor start and an improved succession of scores after Christmas almost provided enough impulse to avoid relegation, the result expected by everybody involved due to the lack of financial power and even infrastructure of a club not ready to establish themselves at the top level. Finally, Extremadura were relegated only after losing a play-off with Rayo Vallecano.

'In Extremadura, despite the relegation in my second year, I learned that unity equals strength. There was a great atmosphere. People told me that in my first season we'd be unable to equal the promotion which they had had in previous years, but by sticking to our methods we proved them wrong.'

In the summer of 2000, following a sabbatical that took him to England, he managed second-division Tenerife. In just one season with the islanders (2000–01), Benítez won promotion on the last day of the season, dooming some much bigger clubs, like Atlético Madrid and Sporting Gijón, to another year in the second division. His work at the club opened the doors of Valencia to him. 'I learned at Tenerife that playing good football usually brings its own rewards,' he recalls. 'We played really well, particularly during the first half of the season. Young Luis García had a great year with us: I used his versatility to our advantage.'

Then, of course, came the job that made his name, gave Valencia the most successful period in the club's history, but ended in such acrimony. Nevertheless, 'I prefer to think positively about Valencia,' Benítez says now. 'I learned that the work of the team is much more important than having one or two stand-out stars. Achieving collective commitment to the same objective is fundamental to success.'

Now he's at Liverpool, but even during his first season rumours about his future started. Everyone knows that Real Madrid, despite their suspicion of Rafa's 'team without stars' philosophy, want him as their coach at some point in the future. During the negotiations over the transfer of Fernando Morientes, Florentino Pérez, the Chairman of Real Madrid, told Benítez, 'You do know that one day you'll be the coach of Madrid.' Benítez wisely did not respond. Then, when Valladolid knocked Real out of the Spanish Cup, Madrid publicly put Benítez's name into the frame by leaking to the Spanish press that he was one of two potential replacements for their current coach, Vanderlei Luxemburgo (the other being their former manager, Fabio Capello, now at Juventus). This time Rafa did not speak to *anyone* for two whole days. When he did finally address the subject, there was massive media attention concentrated on the press room at Anfield. Rafa had what he wanted – everybody's ear. Then he made it abundantly clear that he viewed his work with Liverpool as a long-term project, and said no one should doubt his commitment to seeing it through. The Liverpool press corps breathed a hefty sigh of relief.

(6)

SIGNS OF INEQUALITY

We Were Not Ready for the Premiership

In the eighteenth minute of the Champions League final, Milan launched another attack. Kaká ultimately headed wide after initiating the move in his own half. However, another Milan goal seemed inevitable: they were growing in confidence with every minute. The Italians were exposing Sami Hyypia's lack of pace, and were pulling him and Carragher out of position almost at will. Ancelotti had asked forwards Shevchenko and Crespo to play between the centre-backs and the full-backs, and his tactic was working beautifully. Gerrard and Xabi Alonso were having similar trouble stopping the four Milan midfielders (Seedorf, Kaká, Pirlo and Gatusso). And Liverpool also appeared fragile out wide: Djimi Traore still seemed particularly ill at ease. All in all, Milan were utterly in control wherever you looked.

Up front there was not much hope, either. Milan Baroš was running around diligently but he didn't look likely to produce an end product. Luis García was sniffing away for half chances, but when they came his way he did not show any killer instinct. John Arne Riise was not making much progress down the left, with Cafú and Gatusso, instead of trying to get the ball off him, cleverly preferring to corner the Norwegian and then forcing him to look for another route. Kewell had been anonymous in his role as the link man between the midfielders and Baroš. Then he felt something. His groin had torn; he'd have to go off.

*

It is tempting to draw parallels between those early minutes in Istanbul and the first half of Liverpool's season. Just as Liverpool seemed tactically and technically inferior to Milan, the first two months of the season proved to be depressing. Solid performances in European games, especially at Anfield, were routinely followed by dreadful away defeats in the Premiership.

The European campaign had begun with an edgy, narrow victory over Graz AK in the Champions League third qualifying round – just 2–1 on aggregate. Two away goals from Stevie Gerrard allowed an awful 0–1 defeat at Anfield to count as mere embarrassment rather than an utter disaster. Before that game, Benítez had suggested that his team was only firing at 60 per cent. Clearly he had high hopes that these were just teething problems and eventually this group of players would improve. However, after the Champions League final, he acknowledged that it was no longer a case of turning the squad into better players; he needed *new* players in the squad: 'Introducing new players, new ideas and new ways of working takes time. There is room for improvement in the squad,' he admitted in his Turkish hotel. By then, he had already identified at least four of the players that would later join Liverpool: striker Peter Crouch, midfielders Bolo Zenden and Mark González, and keeper José Manuel Reina.

After the Graz scare, Champions League Group A kicked off with Anfield welcoming Monaco, the previous season's defeated finalists. The evening produced a convincing 2–0 win and a composed team performance which left Benítez satisfied. 'It was a good game. The players were very motivated and came up against a team whose style let us play. One thing about Liverpool is that we always noticed fans' heightened enthusiasm before and during Champions League matches. It goes without saying that that had a motivating effect on the players as a result.' Gérard Houllier was in the stands to applaud Djibril Cissé's first European goal for Liverpool and Milan Baroš wrapping up the points six minutes before the end.

But the optimism was short-lived. The new coaching staff were about to face a defining moment of the season – that would challenge many of their preconceptions about the Premiership, and make them realise that their earlier analysis of the players they had inherited and some of those they had signed was fundamentally flawed. From that point on, Benítez and his assistants understood they had more to do than they ever could have imagined. 'In the match against Manchester United [the fifth match of the domestic season, which Liverpool lost 2–1 at Old Trafford on 20 September] they gave us a lesson both on and off the pitch,' admits Pako Ayesterán. United showed us what it meant to be mentally focused on winning during the game, even before the kick-off. Their concentration and their level of aggression were far above that of our team. I think that was when we realised that Liverpool simply didn't possess all the necessary components to have a successful league season.'

Luis García still grimaces at the memory of the moment when he first received the ball with his back to goal. Rio Ferdinand instantly clattered into him from behind and the Spaniard recalls, 'I was sent flying about a metre in the air!' As the United defender bent down and offered a helping hand, he muttered with grim satisfaction: 'Welcome to the Premiership.' The players, and the coaching staff, were discovering that adapting to life in England was going to come at a cost.

In the next Champions League encounter, against Olympiakos in Greece, Liverpool produced another terrible performance and slumped to a 1–0 defeat. Benítez doesn't try to mask his disappointment when reliving the experience. 'We did not play well. We had no confidence, we never won a fifty–fifty challenge all night, and our problem again was failing to retain the ball, as was so often the case in that season, so we couldn't build our moves from the back. We were made to pay for that failure. Their goal was perfect, it flew into the top corner, but we contributed to it by committing a couple of basic errors. It was typical of the performances all season away from home.'

Liverpool's first away win of the season finally came against Fulham in their fifth away game. They hardly made it easy for themselves: they were 2–0 down at half time. If Alex Ferguson had been Liverpool's boss, they no doubt would have received the hairdryer treatment. But that's just not Benítez's style, and especially not in this early part of his reign at Anfield. 'During the break I thought that the key was to motivate the players,' he says, 'but on this occasion I needed the help of my staff. I didn't feel my English was fluent enough, so I called on Alex Miller to help get the messages across. There was a tactical change, too: Salif Diao off and Xabi on. The team needed his distribution. We recover control with him. And we scored an early goal in the second half. That match crossed my mind in Istanbul. When you claw that first goal back after half time, your spirits and confidence are lifted. Suddenly the players wanted the ball.' In spite of having Josemi sent off in the second half, the Reds stormed to a 2–4 victory.

It was a highlight, but during those first few months, Benítez often stood on the touchline in a state of near despair. Djibril Cissé seemed to be doing lots of basic things wrong. Rafa had to explain the correct way for him to angle his run in order to beat the offside trap, for instance. Josemi had played well against Bolton away, but then seemed to lose his way and made costly mistakes against Fulham, Olympiakos and Bolton at Anfield. The Kop started making him some sort of cult figure.

Then there was enthusiastic Luis García. 'On the day of my debut at Anfield, I wanted to show everyone how good I was, but nothing that I tried came off – although the fans applauded me anyway,' he explains. 'If that had happened in Spain, by the third time I'd tried something which didn't come off the crowd would be jeering and whistling. At the end of the match the boss came to me and said: 'Listen, son, this is not *Oliver and Benji*.' Benítez was referring to a Japanese fantasy football cartoon which is hugely popular in Spain, and catalogues the exploits of two footballers who make Roy of the Rovers look heavy-footed and distinctly lacking in ambition where scissor-kicks are concerned. A few months later he might have used a more familiar Scouse expression: 'Calm down, lad.' At this time, though, Benítez was becoming frustrated that his English was not fluent enough for him to do his job properly. He even felt the deficiency was affecting his decision-making and the behaviour of the team. 'I still have problems with Gerrard and Carragher,' he admits now, 'but I see that they are understanding me more and more. At delicate times when there is a lot of tension you need to make very specific points and there is no time for elaborate explanations. Bit by bit you notice that not having a full grasp of the language prevents you from using all your own coaching resources.

'If you change one letter in English you can change the whole meaning. One morning I saw a player in training taking a free kick and I said, 'Be careful with the wine.' He was worried, of course, but I only meant to say "wind"! I hadn't spoken English for several years before coming to Liverpool and I've had no time for lessons all year. I couldn't even improve my language by listening to the car radio because I'm always on the phone. My main source of English practice comes from listening to Beatles CDs.'

But the Beatles hid their accents in their songs, so nothing had prepared Benítez for the full-on Scouse of Jamie Carragher. 'The boss has told me that he often doesn't understand me when I speak, so I have to slow down when I'm trying to get a point across to him,' he admits.

'Quite often through the season the boss would admit to me that he feels frustrated. He's explained that sometimes he feels angry with the players at half time but can't permit himself to show it because he hasn't got the words he would use in Spanish. You can see that he always thinks really hard about what he is saying rather than simply letting it flow. If he was speaking his mother tongue, then the message might come straight from the heart, but now he has to guard against miscommunication by choosing his words carefully.'

As the season went on it was clear that the other Scouser in the team, Steven Gerrard, was growing more confident, and he would occasionally pipe up with some suggestions of his own at half time. Benítez would generally respond to these with a terse, 'Yes, yes,' in order to get on with what he himself was saying. Gerrard should perhaps now be made aware that his manager didn't understand a single word of what he was saying on most of those occasions.

Once the disappointing pattern of away defeats had set in, Benítez introduced a series of tactical changes aimed at forcing the team's style of play to tie in more closely with his own ideals. 'Rafa has always been extremely clear about the fact that his team should have two wide midfielders who are very dangerous in one-on-ones against defenders but who also work hard for the team,' explains Paco Herrera. 'Vicente at Valencia, is a perfect example. Wingers win you matches and we didn't really have that type of player, which was a problem all season. Smicer spent a long time injured; as did Kewell.'

On the other hand, the technical staff were surprised to learn that in England the strikers tend to play only as strikers: they make lots of runs but then stay high up the field without any involvement in the defensive work of the team. The backroom staff found it impossible to incorporate Baroš and Cissé in Rafa's collective idea of the team, so they soon abandoned the English standard of twin centre-forwards and, given the lack of width, decided to make some other tactical alterations in a bid to try to find an alternative that worked. 'We were a much harder-working team with a line of four midfielders and four defenders,' explains Herrera. 'We gave freedom to one of the wide players and you can use a link player between the midfield and the striker. We even used Cissé wide on the right to see whether that would solve our almost non-existent ability to turn the oppostion team's defenders.'

But the lack of a potent strike force remained all season: only thirteen goals came from the forwards throughout 2004–05. Fernando Morientes' arrival in mid-season, purchased from Real Madrid, did little to improve the situation. He seemed unable to play in a team without wingers and wasn't helped by the fact that he'd scarcely kicked a ball for six months. The staff knew the only way to paper over the cracks was to impose very strict tactical discipline and hope that individuals could produce the odd moment of magic to win a game here and there. But that was not enough in a competition that rewards consistency and a balanced squad. The Premiership statistics began to underline Liverpool's deficiencies as the number of defeats (expecially against poor opposition) mounted. The home defeat to Birmingham (a 0–1 which ended a good run of seven undefeated home fixures) was an accident waiting to happen after recent injuries to both Cissé and Baroš. Worse still, the defeat against Everton at Goodison Park in December (1–0) put the Toffees second in the table and confirmed them as genuine rivals for fourth place. It was also their first derby victory of the twenty-first century. One Evertonian contacted a radio phone-in show and labelled Liverpool's new manager 'Rafael Beneath-us'.

There was no obvious solution. 'The defeat against Everton was a repeat of our failings away from home. We lost the individual battles and the fifty–fifty balls; we didn't win the second ball. So, obviously, we ended up losing the match,' admits Benítez. Paco Herrera remembers the air of gloom after the game: 'We all sat back and thought, "OK, why is this happening? How do we solve it?" It happens week after week, so you cast an eye over the squad and you start to acknowledge that it is an imbalanced group, that it is struggling to cope with injuries, that it is not physical enough.'

One conclusion was that the team needed more Carraghers, more Gerrards, especially away from home. The players were not aggressive enough, so both Carragher and Hyypia, who were rarely booked, were told their football had to be more menacing. 'Without fighting hard for the ball, we cannot cope with the direct football that most English teams adopt,' Pako Ayestarán admits. Then, of course, there was the simple fact that Liverpool did not have the depth of Manchester United or Chelsea so couldn't cope when certain players picked up injuries.

All the analysis kept arriving at the same conclusion: the squad was not big enough and not good enough. 'It just seems that we have a team which was designed without a decent understanding of the requirements of the English Premiership,' is the honest assessment of Ayestarán. What made Benítez furious was that he recognised the key moments, identified the problems and applied some tactical solutions . . . but nothing changed. He hoped the last third of the season might provide momentum that would boost his side and see them overhaul Everton. But that push never occurred because the squad still was not good enough.

The match against Birmingham in February typified the situation. David Moyes' Everton had lost to Chelsea earlier in the day. Liverpool were still five points behind their city rivals but three successive wins (against Watford, Charlton and Fulham) had led Benítez to believe things were finally starting to fall into place. There were still eleven matches left until the end of the league season. It was the perfect time to put on that late surge. Instead, the team responded with one of their poorest performances of the season and lost 2–0.

Benítez was livid, and lost his patience at the post-match press conference. Up to that point he had always loyally defended his players in public, but by now he had decided that a large section of his squad was either treading water or simply not good enough, and he told the press all about them. Now he says, 'Gradually you build an impression of what kind of team you have and what kind of players you have. Before the Birmingham match we told the team that Everton had already lost and that we could close the gap, but they didn't react. Sometimes the problem you face is not tactical, nor is it the coach, or the team selection. Sometimes it just comes down to how much a particular result or performance matters to the pride of each player. In the Premiership, we never made progress in that area.'

Rick Parry agrees: 'There are not enough players screaming and shouting. I remember Alex Ferguson, who has built and broken several United teams over the years, saying, when it was time for

Paul Ince to go, that his squad was like a tinder box in the dressing room. They had strong characters – Schmeichel, Bruce, Cantona . . . fighters! And to keep control of them was almost impossible; things were always ready to explode. We haven't got enough of that.' Benítez could have done with another couple of Carraghers in the team.

The Carling Cup final presented another opportunity to boost the players' pride . . . or maybe strip away what little was left. But, sandwiched at the end of February between the two legs of the Bayer Leverkusen fixture in the Champions League, it left everybody floating in the same ocean of doubt. Chelsea, the runaway leaders of the Premiership, had not thrashed Liverpool. But, then again, Liverpool *had* still lost, 3–2. They came away neither buoyed by victory nor chastened by a crushing defeat. Psychologically, the team finished the day in pretty much the same state as they'd started it. However, the match seemed to confirm that Liverpool were *mediocre*, and that was the straw that broke the camel's back for Benítez. His last vestiges of tolerance for many of his players evaporated. The coach, coldly and clincially, admitted privately at the end of the game that half the team would have to go on this evidence. 'I was angry for losing to Chelsea because we had that final under control,' he says now. 'Chelsea came at us in wave after wave, but I didn't see them creating much danger. In my view it was simply our lack of experience which lost us the match. We should have played much more shrewdly in the last ten or eleven minutes.'

But the team had still to hit rock bottom. The league game against Crystal Palace was, without question, the worst moment of the entire season. There were only three league games left, and Everton, just four points ahead at this stage, had only drawn at home to Birmingham earlier in the day. But Andy Johnson's single goal sank Liverpool. Rafa gave his most revealing post-match interview to Sky Sports just after the fixture. He did not say much, but you could read volumes in his face and his broken voice. 'Let's think of the next match' was his answer to every one of the reporter's questions.

'Yes, the Crystal Palace result really did annoy me because that was the moment to get stuck in and put ourselves firmly in the top four', he says, still irked by it. 'But we were not up to it. I have not yet seen that interview, but it's true that when I was put in front of the microphone I was pretty pissed off. But I tried to control myself and not say what I really thought. I was actually quite composed. You cannot imagine what was inside my head at that moment.'

Composed? 'I have spoken to a few poeple about that interview,' says Jamie Carragher, 'and everybody thinks that that is the angriest they have ever seen him. Normally he is very controlled, but at times this season it has been difficult for him. We have been a very inconsistent team, whereas Valencia were probably the opposite when he was in charge. I think he said just before the Carling Cup final that even if we did win it there were going to be big changes. And I think that's right.'

Usually only his coaching staff see the side Benítez hides when the cameras or even his own players are around. On the Monday after a bad weekend result, they are often met by the despondent face of a man who views every game as an examination of his personal ability. This type of frustration is very hard to combat, and only the support of those closest to him can raise Benítez's spirits. Three-quarters of the way into the season, a member of staff at Melwood, intoxicated by what had become an exceptional European campaign, bounded into Rafa's office to offer his heartfelt congratulations on the team's achievements. Sadly, he choose the wrong day – the Monday after the Manchester City defeat. He departed bemused by the Spaniard's abrupt dismissal. For the manager, the Champions League could not compensate for the woeful domestic form.

The bad results left him sleepless, and matches were replayed in his head into the small hours of the morning. 'If I have something on my mind, I often get up at three or four in the morning and do an hour's work. You can think clearly and concentrate at that time and when I return to bed, I sleep. It's much better than tossing and turning in bed because that just keeps my wife awake as well.'

Sometimes he'd be tempted to phone his friends to discuss some tactical point or other, but generally he'd restrict himself to sending text messages instead, for which they must have been grateful.

'Frustration is the word,' says Paco Herrera. 'It's like you are an artist and you know what the picture is you want to paint, but you try to paint it and it doesn't come out well on the canvas. You cannot find the correct colour and then you end up wanting to start all over again. Rafa is one of the most demanding people I know: you win and he still finds mistakes. He is a perfectionist.'

'We must not sustain eleven away defeats,' admits Rafa. 'That is not normal for a leading team. We have to be able to turn more situations which appear as potential defeats into draws.'

Xabi Alonso sums up the players' feelings: 'You lose games where you might have taken a point and what stays with you is the feeling that we are really poor away from home, that we are not tough enough. We talk about this problem among ourselves but it still keeps happening. The boss has discovered what the causes are and with the help of new players we are going to solve it.'

The 1–0 defeat to Burnley in the FA Cup on 18 January is not viewed by Benítez in the same light as the tame league defeats. But it still taught him some tough lessons – and he will not be making the same mistake in the future. Around that time, Liverpool had to play seven matches in twenty-five days, so Benítez and Ayestarán decided that they simply had to rotate the squad to give some of the regular first-teamers a break. Given that seven days earlier a similar-strength Liverpool side had beaten Watford in the Carling Cup semi-final, they had high hopes that the gamble would pay off. But the gulf in quality between a Steven Gerrard and a John Welsh (to choose one example from the Burnley defeat) proved too great to be bridged. According to Ayestarán, 'No coach goes out wanting to lose a game, but one of our firmest beliefs is that in order to achieve your objectives you must have priorities. Napoleon sent troops to die after analysing the risks and benefits. The idea is very similar for us. We have a set squad and you can only squeeze a set amount out of it.

Therefore, you have to be ruthlessly clear about what your key objectives are and in which games you can or cannot afford to take chances.

'If any team, whether it's Valencia, Liverpool or Barcelona, changes four or five players in the first team and is then unable to beat a side from a lower division, that means either the squad is not competitive enough or a certain number of players are not good enough. Every footballer in your squad must be there because he deserves it. If you do not use this player, then someone has made a mistake signing him in the first place.'

The *Mirror* newspaper felt Benítez had got his priorities all wrong: 'Radio shows got inundated with calls suggesting the team Liverpool put out at Turf Moor was the worst in the club's history. The players were pelted with missiles from their own supporters as they left the field. Some fans even tried to jump the hoardings to get at the team. Even the Burnley players questioned manager Rafael Benítez's judgement in selecting such a weakened side.' The Burnley game was sandwiched between two other defeats (0–1 at home to Manchester United and 2–0 away at Southampton). After the loss at St Mary's, the *Daily Mail* was equally scathing: 'the worst Liverpool of the last 40 years', it jeered.

The Liverpool *Echo*, generally much more balanced than the London tabloids, pointed the finger elsewhere: 'the fans are not looking towards Benítez, but towards the board', it claimed. The feeling on the terraces was that the manager hadn't been given enough cash to build a decent squad. Nevertheless, the paper's Chris Bascombe says of Benítez: 'Rafa could have protected himself by playing a stronger team. "Oh, we played a strong team and we lost," people would have said. Whereas it was more like he didn't play a strong team, they lost and it was like he didn't care.'

Benítez defended himself by reminding everybody that Liverpool had already reached a final (the Carling Cup) and were still very much in the Champions League, but once the criticism really started to flow he began to realise exactly how much the FA Cup means to English football fans.

'You cannot succeed on every front, particularly with a squad like ours,' Rick Parry explains with hindsight. 'Is it a coincidence that Arsenal and Manchester United met in the FA Cup final but were knocked out earlier in the Champions League? It was a huge overreaction to say that we undermined the image of the Cup. I guess that because it was Rafa's first season, because he was foreign, it was just his turn to incur a media rant. You have to experience it to understand that there is still a magic to the FA Cup. Maybe he didn't understand that. Rafa wasn't disappointed; he was angry because those players should have done better.'

'The critics can't have it both ways,' argues Carragher. 'We got a lot of credit for playing youngsters like Darren Potter, Zach Whitbread, Stephen Warnock, David Raven and John Welsh in the Carling Cup, but then [we were] hammered for playing some of them in the FA Cup.'

'The FA Cup game was postponed,' recalls Benítez. 'When it was rescheduled, we didn't take the same group of players and we chose a line-up which lacked aggression. Traore scored an own goal and the control of the match slipped away from us. The decision we took in the FA Cup was pretty similar to that we took in the Carling Cup – let's play young footballers. But I realise that, without their usual cornerstone players, the team can become more tense and nervous, and it can lack confidence.'

The list of predicaments was growing longer than a Lime Street taxi queue on a Saturday night: an unsatisfactory squad, misunderstandings about the relative merits of competitions, away defeats, press criticism, a lack of money. And on top of all that, injuries. 'I did not use it as an excuse at all during the season,' claims the manager. 'If we do not have a player available, we'll just find another one to substitute him. But we had ten players who needed surgery of one kind or another. Could any team really get through the season in its best form with difficulties like that?'

It had started to get serious way back in September when Gerrard broke a bone in his foot. He came back two months later, but then a groin strain prevented him participating in the Champions League game against Juventus. Djibril Cissé broke his left leg in the match with Blackburn in October. The injury was so bad that his return against Juventus in Turin the following April was little short of miraculous. Luis García had hamstring problems in November; Baroš suffered a similar injury in December; and Xabi Alonso broke his ankle on 5 January and was out for three months.

Surprisingly, Harry Kewell started both the Carling Cup and Champions League finals for Liverpool but limped off each time. He spent the whole season telling the manager he did not feel fit, but Benítez never completely believed him. The conflict with the winger – spiced up by run-ins with his agent Bernie Mandic and the Australia coach Frank Farina – was just one of several player–manager battles that soured the year for the new boss.

(7)

STEVEN GERRARD: LIVERPOOL'S SPECIAL CASE

It Was All a Misunderstanding

In the twenty-third minute of the Champions League final, Vladimir Smicer replaced Harry Kewell. The gamble of putting the Australian in the line-up had failed. Benítez knew he needed a different type of player to attack Milan, one who could steal in between their defenders and midfielders, hold up the ball and make good use of possession. He had few options.

Kewell, limping badly, had to be persuaded to stay long enough for Smicer to boot up because the Czech international was on the bench just wearing his socks. Smicer had already been told by Benítez that he had no future at the club, and was warned that he had only a slim chance of playing any part in the final. He had spent the majority of the previous week looking for a new club, packing his suitcase and, understandably, not getting too many early nights. The result was that he wasn't in prime fighting shape, which explains the dramatic cramps which afflicted him in the first half of extra time.

In fact, Smicer almost didn't play at all. After Kewell broke down, a frantic debate took place on the bench about who should replace him. The fans would have preferred Didi Hamann, and he probably would also have been a welcome sight for the two Liverpool central midfielders, who were in a state of disarray trying to cope with the free running of Milan's mercurial Brazilian Kaká. But Hamann was not even in the frame at this point.

Instead, the debate was about whether the selection should be the Czech or a Spaniard who had arrived as a makeweight. 'We were unsure whether the choice was Smicer or Nuñez,' reveals Ayestarán. 'The clincher for us was Smicer's footballing quality. Even by that stage we knew that our battle was going to be getting possession, and then doing something clever with the ball, moving it quickly. We decided to persevere with the system originally planned, so Smicer was moved to the right, with Luis García between the midfield and Milan Baroš.'

For probably the first time ever in one of Liverpool's European finals, the fans booed their own player when Kewell came off. 'I stepped for the ball and my groin just went,' he remembers bitterly. 'My tendon detached in the seventeenth minute and no human being, no matter how brave, would have been capable of kicking a football after that. That night was the highlight of my career and became the worst nightmare. The British newspapers have tried to ruin my celebrations by deliberately lying about my injury. But that has been going on for over six months, so it doesn't surprise me. What is important is that the best manager in the world had the faith in me to start me when no one else thought I had a chance.'

After the final, the Australian finally had an operation – something his agent and his national coach had long been publicly demanding. Rafa, who doesn't like to be pushed around, had replied to some of Frank Farina's suggestions in the Australian media earlier in the year. 'I am not happy with people around Harry talking all the time and not doing the right thing for the player,' he had pointed out. 'His agent, Farina, too many people have been saying things. Well, we pay him, we know him, we control him and train him.'

Kewell, who had not played from December until the end of February, also believed he needed an operation, and figured that this was why he couldn't perform at his best. Benítez, however, decided Kewell had to wait. 'The boss knew right from the start of the season that I had an injury and that every time I played, he was taking a chance with me and that I was putting my body on the line because, at any given time, it could snap,' Kewell told *The Times*. 'That's what happened in the final. I knew after the problems I'd had that everyone would be thinking, Oh, yes, look at this. But what was I supposed to do? Play on? I know Liverpool's fans haven't seen the best of me.'

On the edge of the conflict, the supporters had long since taken the side of the coach. 'OK, so it transpired that in Istanbul he did have a genuine injury,' Chris McLoughlin wrote in *The Kop* magazine. 'His groin had snapped and he's had an operation to put it right. But the fact that so many of the 40,000-plus travelling Koppites in the stadium that night thought he was looking for a way out – and we all remember him limping off in Cardiff – said a hell of a lot about how he's perceived.'

So, given their tense relationship and the fact that a series of problems (groin, calf and ankle) had hindered the Australian all season, should Rafa have picked him? During the season, the Melwood staff had realised that he was a quality player but that he had too many physical complaints and lacked concentration in training and matches. And Benítez was having little joy in turning any of that around. Shouldn't all of that have been enough for the manager to look for an alternative?

One reason why he kept faith with Kewell was tactical. 'Benítez tried to field the most offensive team he had,' explains Paco Herrera. 'We saw Kewell really wanting to be part of things and it is better for a player like that to start, because if we needed him at the end and he'd broken down then it would have been a bigger problem.' Benítez justifies his risk too: 'It's true that Kewell spent a lot of time injured but he had been working to get better. He got to the final ready to compete.'

The conflict with Kewell was not the only one Benítez had to endure with one of the key members of his squad in his first year in charge at Anfield. On arrival, Benítez had made it plain that he preferred to talk about 'the team' rather than individuals. He was also against doling out excessive praise, even to Gerrard after the midfielder had decided to stay and ignore Chelsea's first big effort to sign him in 2004. But the coach soon became aware that the majority of his players only 'turned up' on the big nights and disappeared on their travels to less glamorous Premiership grounds. So he decided to change tactics and initiated a subtle public alignment with players like Carragher, who had the full-time commitment he appreciated, or Riise and Traore, whom he felt had lifted their performances through hard work in training and their willingness to learn.

Others like Milan Baroš, Sami Hyypia and Didi Hamann, soon started to experience the Benítez cold shoulder. The coach bluntly told Baroš to stop moaning to the press about his future and his spells on the bench – and to start scoring some goals! The Czech was heard singing, 'I'm going to Valencia!', in the small hours of the morning after the final in Istanbul because Benítez had told him that Liverpool were about to sell him. However, the Spanish club, who had recently appointed Javier Subirats as their new football director, had changed their mind only the previous night. Then Gérard Houllier, now at Lyon, surprised everyone by showing his interest in the player ('But they *hate* each other!' said a mutual friend). The Czech striker finally ended up at Aston Villa.

Benítez needed money to rebuild the side and could not afford to have strikers of comparable mould. The Cissé-Baroš partnership had never worked because the two strikers are so similar (they both want the ball at their feet and lack the generosity of a Peter Crouch, who is willing to assist and hold the ball for others), and they both seem unwilling or unable to help out in defence. Baroš was Liverpool's highest goalscorer of the season, but he stubbornly stuck to his own style of play even after a year of suggestions from the Anfield boss. He was simply not the striker Benítez needed in his system.

Sami Hyypia showed his anger in private when, without any explanation from the coach, he was dropped to the bench for three consecutive Premiership matches at the end of March. His place had been handed to Mauricio Pellegrino, an Argentinian central defender signed from Valencia in the winter transfer window. Benítez was testing the Finn. 'Players who react like that interest me,' he says. 'If they cannot accept this change of fortune, they are not right to play at this level. Some footballers need a bit of pastoral care, others don't need even a word. The truth is that if I tried to concoct some kind of explanation which even I didn't believe, then it would be better to say nothing at all to a player. What are you going to say to a guy you make a sub? It's usually better to say nothing.'

The Melwood staff reckoned that Pellegrino wouldn't play much but would have a very positive effect in the dressing room, which needed bigger personalities. 'His arrival forced improvement from Hyypia, the same way Josemi had improved Finnan's level,' reckons Benítez. The former Barcelona and Valencia centre-back is that rare beast: a footballer who thinks. A couple of years back he turned down a lucrative transfer to Celtic because his pregnant wife wanted to stay in Spain. Like Rafa, though, he is obsessed with football (he waits for his wife to go to bed before he watches tapes of matches). 'Obsession is bad for life, but good for football,' he says. Unfortunately, he doesn't speak much English, so his new team-mates have caught only glimpses of what he provided at Rafa's Valencia: suggestions, analysis of what the squad needs, motivation and even a paternal shoulder to cry on. 'He is such a nice guy that we felt sorry for him when his performances were below par. We would blame anybody but him for mistakes,' one member of the squad admits.

There was never any chemistry between Rafa and Didi Hamann, but Rafa understood his importance in a team lacking defensive midfielders and offered him a new contract half way through the season. But after he suffered knee damage against Everton in March, two different opinions on the treatment surged – the one from the club and the one from the doctor of his national side. Hamann followed the instructions of the latter and travelled to Munich to recuperate. As a consequence, Benítez felt it appropriate temporarily to withdraw the offer and it was all left to the end of the season. After the midfielder came back from Germany, he had face to face talks with the coach who asked him to come back to fitness as soon as possible as Xabi Alonso was suspended in the return leg of the Champions League semi-final against Chelsea. It was not designed as a test, but his performance that day plus his immense contribution in the final made Benítez conclude his experience was necessary. Although at some point Hamann thought his future was going to be at Bolton, he stayed after a new offer arrived at the beginning of his holidays. 'Three or four times I met Hamann for one minute. That is the sort of relationship I have with everybody, not just Didi. It's a matter of respect but maintaining a sensible distance,' the manager admits.

Carragher confirms that this is how it is for all the players, even himself, widely viewed as one of Benítez's favourites, but also says: 'The manager doesn't mind players having an opinion or saying what they feel. A number of times he has had team meetings and if something is going wrong or if there is something we need to do better, he'll ask the players as a group what their feelings are. I've gone in to speak to him perhaps three or four times and we'll have a chat at a personal level, maybe about my own game, and then maybe about the team, about where we need to improve. Maybe he sees me and a few of the other players as more experienced, and as he is new to the Premiership, he is trying to learn as much as possible.'

The biggest challenge of the season was, of course, the case of Steven Gerrard. Liverpool's captain received an unusual amount of personal attention from the coach to convince him that he was important and appreciated. However, he was also never allowed to forget that he still has a great deal to learn. Nevertheless, in both of Benítez's summer misunderstandings and a lack of communication between him and his captain were some of the reasons that almost led to Gerrard leaving the club he adores.

The Spaniard's strategy was similar each time: he set out his reasons for wanting the club to retain Gerrard and then left it in the hands of Rick Parry and the player. Benítez was aware from the very beginning that Gerrard had itchy feet. 'The first thing I had to tell Rafa, before he had even signed his contract, was that Steven Gerrard wanted to go,' recalls Parry. 'That was the first time I saw Benítez facing a problem – in fact, a real blow, which made his challenge a little bit harder than he'd imagined. I thought he might say, 'Well, that's it, I am going back to Valencia', but it was OK with him.' Rafa, typically, was not prepared to worry about something over which he had little control.

'We knew of Gerrard's frustrations in the summer of 2004,' insists Parry. 'He was passionate for success but above all passionate for success with Liverpool. We had numerous discussions that summer and I was disappointed when he said, "Yes, I know you are bringing in this new coach and I think it's good, but I still want to go." All those conversations happened while he was in Portugal [with the England team], never face to face. Strangely I still felt calm. I was thinking, "I am not rushing into anything, I want to hear Steve say those things to my face because it doesn't sound like him talking." And, of course, as soon as he came home, and was back with his family, he reached the conclusion he *couldn't* leave. It is "his" club. "I can't leave, I just can't do it," he said to me. It was as simple as that.'

It is obvious from Parry's account that Benítez's role in this first Gerrard u-turn was relatively minor. As we know, he'd met Gerrard in a Lisbon hotel during Euro 2004, and explained his plans for strengthening the squad, starting with buying Xabi Alonso and Luis García. He'd also told Gerrard that he wanted to rediscover the playing style which had once made Liverpool great, and incorporate elements of the Valencia side that had so impressed the Liverpool players and staff during the previous three years. But none of that changed Gerrard's mind. The return to his home environment and tension-filled conversations with his family, as well as with David

Moores and Rick Parry, did. On Monday 28 June, he gave an emotional press conference and announced that he would stay with Liverpool. The medical tests for Chelsea, which had been pencilled in for that very day, were cancelled.

Gerrard had decided to give Benítez a chance. But despite that, the man who had almost single-handedly saved the season for Liverpool in the final few matches of Houllier's reign soon realised life was going to be very different under his new boss. The previous regime had made a point of looking after him to the extreme. Gerrard knew, and was constantly told, that he was a key part of the project they were constructing. Benítez, by contrast, seemed almost indifferent towards his captain. The player, like other key members of the squad, could freely discuss tactics with the French coach. However, as we have seen, when he began to offer comments to Benítez at half time, the manager brusquely acknowledged him, not completely sure of what he had just heard, and then carried on regardless. All of a sudden, Gerrard was 'only' the captain again.

Then there was the fact that his friends Michael Owen and Danny Murphy had left. The Owen decision troubled Gerrard more because he didn't understand the tactical logic behind the transfer. And the way Benítez had treated Owen before and during the move to Real Madrid made the captain suspect that the new coach was nothing like either Houllier or Sven-Goran Eriksson. That summer, Houllier would have been round at Gerrard's house on his knees, begging him to stay. Rafa, more pragmatic, quietly followed the negotiations from a distance. For the first time in his career, the player didn't know whether his manager thought he was any good or not. And he certainly did not feel appreciated.

Chris Bascombe, of the *Echo*, cleverly pinpoints the contrasts in the attitudes of the recent Anfield managers: 'with Roy Evans, there was the sense that he was a nice chap but not a cold-blooded manager. Houllier was over-indulgent with Gerrard and others to the point of smarm. Eriksson is the same. Maybe he has never worked with a ruthless but democratic manager who doesn't want to divide the squad between good and bad players, but wants everybody to be seen in the same way. But that needs to be part of a good player's adaptation process.'

'Whether I go or not, Benítez is going to lead this team to great things,' Gerrard said publicly during the Spaniard's first season in charge. 'Rafa is really fussy about details. I think he realises that I can get better, so he is trying to improve all parts of my game, my movement, my work rate,' the captain added. 'He wants me to be clever with my movement. We have watched tapes together and I speak to him daily about what he wants me to do, what he wants me to improve.' However, there were so many corrections in the long training sessions that sometimes Gerrard assumed that Benítez did not rate him at all. The boss wanted him to be more disciplined on the pitch, to tackle in the right areas, to make more calculated runs, to score more. So what, exactly, was he doing *right*?

The quality of the squad was another worry for the midfielder. When he underperformed, it sometimes seemed to be borne out of frustration at the paucity of talent and commitment around him. Too many things were on his mind and his form was inconsistent, as he had admitted himself. 'The manager is right, I didn't play well enough this season,' Gerrard has said. 'There was a time when everyone was asking me about the future. I decided to wait until the end of it and get my head right. Then I started to play well.' He certainly excelled in Champions League matches, but many league fixtures which he should have grabbed by the scruff of the neck passed him by. 'The problem is that people expect too much of him now. All he has to do is have an average game to get slaughtered,' claimed the ever-loyal *Kop* magazine, but it later conceded, 'he hasn't been as individually outstanding as he was last season'.

That was certainly true, and the Liverpool staff was of course well aware of it. 'The pressure from the media, being a coveted player, rumours of huge wages. All that created a state of doubt,' explains Pako Ayestarán. 'That and the worrying sense that the clock was ticking caused the player to struggle in retaining his concentration, not only in games but when training at Melwood. He has been a key player in many matches, but he has not achieved the level of consistency which a footballer of his quality must produce.'

Rick Parry insisted halfway through the season that the player was 'above money. He is the future of Liverpool. It doesn't matter if it's thirty, forty or fifty million, we will not accept offers. Any idea we are going to accept offers for him and then tell him, "By the way, we've decided to sell you," is not on the agenda. But we are also realistic enough to know we can't keep Steven against his will. His decision will be crucial.' At that stage, the media speculated about the enormous salary Gerrard could expect at Chelsea (although it now appears he would never have been paid more than Frank Lampard).

In the meantime, his relationship with the coach was improving, although slowly, but Benítez suspected it would require hard work to convince his player to stay. 'We will speak at the end of the season,' Benítez was told on three occasions and that is how it stayed. The coach thought results and expected improvements in the performances would be good enough to clear the doubts Gerrard may have had.

Real Madrid, aware of the doubts in the skipper's mind, wanted to include Gerrard in all of the transfer negotiations they had with Liverpool. In the deal that brought Fernando Morientes to Anfield, they had demanded a 'preferential option' over the player. Benítez had refused. As he had promised in Portugal, Rafa kept Gerrard informed of all his potential signings. It was his way of making the player feel important. On the day that Morientes arrived at Melwood, Benítez sought out Gerrard and asked him: 'So, what do you think? Didn't I promise you this? This is the kind of signing you wanted the club to make, isn't it?'

Towards the end of the season, aware that the player was still unsure and confused about his future, Benítez met him to ask his opinion on where the team needed to improve. Gerrard's suggestions matched those of the coach and can be seen in the signings that were made in the summer of 2005. Rafa also, uniquely, asked his staff to look after the skipper, to show the affection he had come to realise Gerrard needed.

In March, Benítez had heard that José Mourinho had decided not to sign the midfielder, yet in the London media at this time Gerrard's move to Chelsea was being discussed as a 'done deal'. Rafa therefore prepared himself mentally and tactically for the possibility of Gerrard's departure and decided he would not sell him for less than £35 million. He had Mikael Essien or Valencia's Momo Sissoko pencilled in as Gerrard's successors.

Immediately after winning the Champions League, Rick Parry knew that an intense period of negotiations with the victorious captain and his Scottish agent, Struan Marshall, lay ahead. But Parry was in no hurry. After all, hadn't the player made his feelings clear to millions on TV by saying, 'How could I leave after that?' amid the post-match celebrations? However, while on holiday, Gerrard started to grow impatient. Not only he but everyone else seemed to have jetted off for the summer. No one seemed too bothered about renegotiating his contract. In fact, Gerrard was mistaken here. Benítez who hadn't gone on holiday, was desperate for Gerrard and Parry to get around the table and thrash out a four-year deal.

Stories started appearing in the press suggesting Gerrard thought the club wanted to sell him. Then an article was published in the Spanish newspaper *AS* on 30 June which claimed that the first round of talks had gone badly. Gerrard was convinced Benítez had contacted the newspaper and, furthermore, that he was clearly happy to sell him. Benítez, who was celebrating his wedding anniversary, had his mobile phone switched off and had no idea how the meeting between Parry and Marshall had gone. All parties involved forgot the newspaper was being consistent with the suggestion they had made earlier on in the season – that Gerrard was a Real Madrid target.

To cut a long story short, the twenty-five-year-old midfielder (who had been with Liverpool since he was nine) genuinely thought that he was no longer wanted, and was suspicious that the manager would prefer to build a team around Xabi Alonso rather than him. Add to this his annoyance at the board's tardiness and a craving to pursue the one club trophy to elude him – the English Premiership title – and you have an explosive cocktail in the mind of one of the most coveted and talented midfielders in the world.

'It was all a misunderstanding with Gerrard,' says Benítez. 'He was actually the first player who still had two years of his contract left whom we invited to sit down and renegotiate. But someone had told him that I wanted to sell him. I spoke to him five or six times face to face but somewhere along the line he started to doubt what I really wanted. I remember that on one occasion I bumped into Stevie coming out of a meeting with Rick Parry, and the player angrily asked me if it was true that I wanted to sell him. Three minutes previously I had been talking to Parry about a contract renewal for the player! I told him to go back to Parry's office and ask him what he and I had just been discussing. Again, he had been told false stories that were confusing him.'

It's doubtful we'll ever know the full details of the second Gerrard transfer saga. But certain things seem definite – Rafa did not want to sell Gerrard, Rick Parry's hurry to sign a new contract for the skipper was inferior to Gerrard's, and the player himself did not want to abandon his club whole-heartedly. The episode needed everybody to step back and look at everything with some sort of perspective and distance.

Stevie's agent had met the club to open negotiations on 29 June, but Liverpool, who were not shy of unequivocal declarations of loyalty towards the player, did not put forward any details of a new contract. That drove Gerrard crazy. The situation became critical on 2 July. Gerrard was planning to do a solo session, as he had been to Carragher's wedding, but before getting down to work he spoke to Benítez in the coach's office. 'Don't go to Real Madrid. Just listen to what Michael Owen is saying about his experience there,' Benítez kept telling his captain. 'Who's talking about Madrid?' was Gerrard's answer. 'Think about it, Steven. They are misleading you. I want you to stay.' Benítez thought he was talking to the player for the last time.

After Gerrard had left his office, Benítez, uptight about Gerrard's state of mind, asked Ayestarán to keep an eye on him and give him encouragement and support. But he was pessimistic and started to think again about Sissoko and Essien as possible replacements. No one, Benítez included, could have imagined the twists and turns which remained. The press, and not just the tabloids, was full of stories of a bust-up between the two men that weekend. The recurring theme was that Benítez wanted to sell Gerrard. 'The day people said we had a fight on the training pitch, I spent the whole day in the office, where we met. We did talk to each other very honestly,' Rafa remembers.

Immediately after that emotional weekend, Rafa introduced new signing Bolo Zenden to the press, and at the end of the presentation insisted he wanted Gerrard to stay: 'If I decide to go after eight years or so, I would like to see him as assistant manager, chief scout, if he wants, or maybe as manager.' He had suggested the same thing to the player minutes before.

Gerrard has recently acknowledged that the coach's surprisingly passionate declaration of support in private and in public were important factors in his late change of heart. But another factor was crucial too. On Monday, Gerrard issued a statement that he was leaving Liverpool. That evening, he sat down with his agent and his girlfriend and looked back on the turmoil of the previous few weeks. His mind raced back to the night in Istanbul, and he thought again of what he would be leaving behind. Preying on his mind was the fact that there is only one major medal he has not won with Liverpool, and it's the one he covets most. He wondered if he'd get as big a buzz parading the Premiership trophy down the Fulham Road as he would if he were aboard an open-top bus on Queen's Drive, with guys he'd been to school with lining the route.

Something else popped into his mind. Chelsea had faxed a bid of

£32 million, which was rejected immediately, but it had been received only ten minutes after Gerrard's agent had confirmed to Rick Parry the intended departure of his client. 'The speed with which they did it was too coincidental,' reckons journalist Chris Bascombe. 'If Chelsea had waited for him to put in an official transfer request, they probably would have got him. They forced the issue because they thought he was ready. But he was still not ready.' In Gerrard's mind, it suddenly became clear that Liverpool had not been manoeuvring behind the scenes to offload him. Chelsea had been the ones pulling strings, probably with their friends in the media, to try to sign him.

Rafa had said his piece very clearly and left the ball in Gerrard's court. 'I didn't follow the subject exhaustively on the Monday night in the hours leading up to Gerrard's change of heart' says the manager. 'I said what needed to be said, and, believing that he was on his way, I went to Melwood early on Tuesday morning. I contacted Rick and he told me that Stevie was staying after all. We had already started to talk about alternatives and were even then closing the deal for Sissoko.' A little later that morning, Rick Parry was able to tell on camera that Gerrard was going nowhere.

'Steve's agent told me that he had not manipulated the press,' Benítez remembers. 'And I said to him, "Look, in order to make progress we need to start from scratch." I did not want this confusion to create bad feeling. We also had to renegotiate with Carra, who was also represented by Marshall. After I told Steve I was delighted he was staying, I also said, "I don't have a problem with all this. If you are staying then let's just start from here and get on with it. I'm not the kind of guy who will remember what was said or what was published and then harp on about it. It's water under the bridge!"'

The similarities with what had taken place twelve months previously are patent. On both occasions, the doubts were not created by the money which was offered for and to Gerrard, but by principles and ambition. However, in contrast to the first revolving-door saga, Gerrard signed a new four-year contract in 2005, and promised that he was going to stay at the club for life. 'I never said I wanted to go,' he emphasised in his statement. 'I felt I was being backed into a corner and had to push things on. When I thought more about it, I wanted to stay.'

A photo snapped just after his dramatic turnaround confirms this: here was a man happy with his destiny. Gerrard is the personification of countless Merseyside dreams, and not even the burning of his No. 8 shirt by bitter fans when he seemed certain to sign for Chelsea can alter the fact that Liverpool is and always will be his club. Just look at his face on pictures of him holding aloft the European Cup. Would it have been the same if he'd been wearing a blue shirt?

After everything had been resolved, Gerrard apologised to his team-mates and even offered to give up the captain's armband. Benítez rejected the offer. Parry also apologised for misunderstanding the player's feelings and for not having pushed the proceedings through more speedily in the aftermath of Istanbul. And Benítez apologised . . . albeit in his own way. He told an incredulous press corps, 'Maybe my relationship with Stevie is down here and the one I have with my wife is much higher up. So perhaps I need to bring the relationship with Stevie up closer to the one with my wife!' In its own fashion, it was as sincere an apology as anyone else's after this whole sorry affair.

Throughout it all, though, one thing had remained unaltered: Benítez's opinion of the footballer. He thinks of his captain not only as a man of natural power and ability upon whom the future of the club might turn and who can slot into numerous different positions on the field, but also as someone who still has much to learn. 'Gerrard has quality, he uses the ball well, he's courageous and his physical powers are immense. On the pitch, he transmits and generates an extraordinary array of emotions for his team-mates and fans, and that makes him so important. One of the reasons he forced us to make such a big effort to keep him is the transcendence he has in the club and the team, things difficult to quantify. You can put in numbers his goals or shirts he sells, but not what he projects, the passion that generates and his importance for the fans. We are going to witness here his growing and maturing as a footballer,' says Rafa.

That process took a blow in Istanbul. In the first half, Gerrard looked out of his depth defensively and could not make his central-midfield partnership with Xabi Alonso work. As a result, for forty-five minutes Kaká ran the show. But from then on, Gerrard revealed just why Benítez is prepared to break so many of his self-imposed rules to keep his skipper happy. He showed why his is a special case.

(8)

HALF TIME

We Owed Something Important to all the Liverpool 'People'

It's the thirty-eighth minute. Milan launch a counter-attack with Liverpool distracted by an appeal for hand-ball in the Milan area. Kaká sweeps forward for the umpteenth time, feeds Shevchenko on the right, and his cross is turned in by Crespo at the far post. Five minutes later, Kaká evades Gerrard on the halfway line and plays a wonderful ball forward to Crespo, who chips it over Dudek. Milan 3, Liverpool 0. Game over. Surely?

JAMIE CARRAGHER: 'Nesta definitively hit the ball with his hand. It was a penalty! Some of us were protesting and were caught in the counter for Milan's second goal.'

RAFA BENÍTEZ: 'Hernán Crespo scored on the counter-attack while we were still shouting for a hand-ball by Nesta in their penalty area. I immediately started to note down in my handbook what we were going to do in order to overturn a 2–0 deficit. My thoughts at that time were that we were still alive in the game. I reckoned that at only 2–0 just one goal in your favour can grab you the momentum. But, of course, while I was busily writing down my notes, Milan went and scored their third.'

JERZY DUDEK: 'We went from shock to anger, 3–0. We are fucking losing 3–0! How is it possible?!'

GENNARO GATTUSO: 'Kaká played a magnificent first half. With the football we had produced it crossed my mind the final could become another "Athens", like the 4–0 that Milan produced against Barcelona in 1994. We really thought this could become a big goal-scoring match because we don't have the usual Italian mentality. The match would have died if we closed the doors, if we decided to defend, but that is not what Milan is about.'

XABI ALONSO: 'We had said before the match that Kaká *had* to be watched at every single moment. But Seedorf, Gattuso and Pirlo were playing together in a tight formation and we were losing the battle in midfield. When Crespo scored his two goals, I thought the vital thing was to get to half time at all costs without conceding yet another goal. I was also thinking that the break couldn't come soon enough.'

PACO HERRERA: 'In football everything is just a repeat of something which has happened before. The key thing is to understand what you've done wrong and learn not to repeat errors. So when they score a second goal against you ... and then a third with similar mistakes, you reckon that it's all going to end in tears. That we are not learning. Truthfully, at a time like that, it takes a moment or two to start assimilating what has happened and what to do about it because you are just so pissed off.'

PHIL THOMPSON (watching it in the Sky Sports studio at the Atatürk): 'Every time we went forward we took too many touches on the ball in the middle of the pitch before passing it. When we did pass it, we lost it too early, and they immediately shuttled the ball to Kaká, who would be lurking between our midfielders and our defence. In situations like that we had most of the team cut out of the game and we were getting murdered. It was just in that little chain of events all the time. Look at the movement for the third goal. It is played in to Kaká, but in one touch he softens the ball and then he gives it to Crespo, all in one movement.'

LEE MARTEN (fan, sitting in the Liverpool end): 'When Crespo put number three away, Turkish lira notes of various denominations began to cascade down on us from a supporter in the upper section of the stand. This guy had obviously seen enough and must have just thrown away all his money in disgust at the poor showing from the Reds. Quite a few people around us went away richer than when they arrived. A friend of mine reckons he managed to salvage the equivalent of about fifty quid in lira. I came away with a ten-lira note, which was on the floor between my feet.'

PAKO AYESTARÁN: 'If the other team has taken up good positions in midfield and then uses its movement cleverly it can put you at a tremendous disadvantage. That night, we didn't dominate in the important areas and gave away too much space in the centre of the pitch. That was exacerbated by the fact that our central defenders were far too occupied with the movement of Shevchenko and Crespo to push up and help the midfielders cope with Kaká. The Brazilian did us so much damage. We have to face the truth that in the first half Milan's game plan and the way they carried it out were absolutely fantastic.'

GENNARO GATTUSO: 'I went to the changing rooms mad with rage because I had seen Pirlo doing a nutmeg just before the break. I let everybody know that was definitely *not* the way, that we couldn't forget there were forty-five minutes still to play.'

DJIMI TRAORE: 'Leaving the pitch, I thought, "It's dead, it's finished"'.

JAMIE CARRAGHER: 'Walking to the dressing room, I was thinking about the supporters, my family and the great name of Liverpool. It was embarrassing really. In a cup final, normally, no matter if you're the worst or the best team, it's always a tight, tense game 1–0 or whatever, no matter who's playing. To be 3–0 down at half time in a cup final was embarrassing for us and for the name of the club. I didn't want it to go to 5 or 6–0. At this point some of my mates were getting text messages from Evertonians!'

RAFA BENÍTEZ: 'I walked into the dressing room rehearsing what I was going to say to them ... but also *how* I was going to say it. It's really difficult to come up with all the things you want to say in a foreign language. I was walking down the tunnel trying to find the right English words.'

PAKO AYESTARÁN: 'Rafa was calm. He's always that way, no matter what the situation. At 3–0 it is hard to be calm, but I've never seen him frightened or too nervous.'

DJIMI TRAORE: 'It is not in the English mentality to gloat if you are 3–0 up during the game. In England you learn that you stay focused until it's over. But that night the Italians "enjoyed" themselves too much at half time. I saw different things – clapping, hugging – as if they had already won the game. I have never said they were actually celebrating, but I saw signs.'

CHRIS BASCOMBE (Liverpool *Echo* correspondent, sitting in the press box): 'I have Traore saying on tape that he saw "celebrations".'

PIERLUIGI PARDO (Sky Italia television reporter): 'I was there, in the tunnel to the dressing rooms. Alan Kennedy was there. Marco Foroni of Sky Italia was also there. We did not hear any celebrations. Lots of rumours started flying around after the match and Traore may have heard them and made a big deal out of it. Some have said they were wearing "Champions" T-shirts underneath their Milan shirts. It would not be too surprising, as in every final all the teams ask their kit people to print them out. But they are normally left in a bag until the end, and I am sure that is what Milan did.'

XABI ALONSO: 'Celebrations? I didn't hear any.'

RICK PARRY (sitting in the directors' box): 'It's a good story, but it doesn't sound like Milan at all. You can see some clubs doing that, but Milan are a proper club, professional and respectful.'

PAOLO MALDINI: 'We are experienced players and there were no celebrations in the dressing room during the interval. We are a side that accepts the result on the pitch. But we do not accept what Traore was reported to have said.'

CARLO ANCELOTTI: 'To see that story published hurt more than the defeat. Our captain has denied it and deserves to be listened to because he's an example of loyalty all over the world. Our dressing room was completely separate from Liverpool's.'

GENNARO GATTUSO: 'It's an insult to hear someone say that people like Maldini and Costacurta were celebrating at half time. In fact, Ancelotti in the half-time team talk said he was worried and talked about continuing to play together, with the same intensity, just as it happened in the first half, because if an English team scores a goal, with their support, that leaves the game open again. I love English fans: they can help you change the most impossible situations.'

GIANCARLO GALAVOTTI (UK correspondent of *La Gazzetta dello Sport*, sitting in the press box): 'Traore was extensively quoted in an interview to the Press Association. After checking that the interview was actually recorded on tape, I sent my report to *La Gazzetta*. My paper decided to put the story on the front page with a full headline: "MILAN WERE ALREADY CELEBRATING AT HALF TIME!" To this day, Adriano Galliani and Carlo Ancelotti bear a grudge against *La Gazzetta* for it, and insist that the story related by Traore in completely false.

PACO HERRERA: 'I was in the changing room and I didn't hear anything. And Milan is a team with lots of experience and professionalism. However, it's certainly not true, as has been rumoured, that Ayestarán invented the whole story to get the players going.'

PAKO AYESTARÁN: 'No, I didn't invent this.'

RAFA BENÍTEZ: 'People told me that the Italians did make some comments among themselves. But I didn't hear the gloating that some have mentioned.'

JAMIE CARRAGHER: 'I never heard anything. I think the media jump on things and make a big deal out of them. I don't know if Djimi heard something, but I certainly didn't. We're talking about a top, professional team – people like Maldini, who I've got a lot of respect for. I can't see them doing that. Although I heard Gattuso was meant to have done something when he came back out, gesturing to their fans or something? Anyway, who could blame them? I would have been doing cartwheels myself with 3–0 at half time!'

STEVEN GERRARD: 'When we got to the dressing room, my mind went walkabout. I was sitting head-in-hands. All sorts of things were going through my head. It was weird.'

JOSÉ MANUEL OCHOTORENA: 'You could see that some of the guys were in a bit of a state.'

RAFA BENÍTEZ: 'We had talked with Pako on the way to the changing rooms about what we were going to change and how to cheer the players on. The problem is it is already tough enough motivating a team losing 3–0 when I'm speaking in my native Spanish. In English, it is much, much tougher. But we had already talked so much about what to expect in this match and how to deal with either a positive or a negative turn in the game that the words came more easily than I could ever have hoped. You cannot plan for the extreme, though, so the most important aspect was to lift their spirits in such a situation. I started with a motivational speech to get them fired up. I demanded that they start working again and try to solve some of our problems. I emphasised that there were still forty-five minutes left and, above all, we had to come off the pitch proud of ourselves at the final whistle because we had done literally everything within our power. I reminded them that it had been a hard, hard battle to reach such a massive game and that we owed something important to all the Liverpool "people" around the world, but most particularly in the stadium, who were expecting much more from us than we'd shown so far. I told them that if we scored a goal, then we would totally change the course of the game. They had to understand that the key to turning everything back in our favour was to score that first goal … and quickly. I emphasised that this was the most important challenge they faced as they walked back out at 3–0 down against Milan. I've seen posters that have been printed and pinned up on pub walls in Liverpool which claim to have my speech set down word for word. Well, even I can't remember it exactly, but they've got it pretty close.'

Don't let your heads drop.
All the players who go on the pitch after half-time have to keep their heads held high.
We are Liverpool, you are playing for Liverpool.
Do not *forget that.*
You have to hold your heads high for the supporters.
You have to do it for them.
You cannot call yourselves Liverpool players if you have your heads down.
If we create a few chances we have the possibility of getting back into this.
Believe you can do it and we will.
Give yourselves the chance to be heroes.

(Rafa Benítez half-time speech, as it is quoted on a poster in a Liverpool pub)

XABI ALONSO: 'It's true that some of the guys were in pieces, but I knew the importance of still having forty-five minutes left. I reckoned, "why not?" There was still hope and the entire second half was there for us to fight back.'

RICK PARRY: 'I don't think his speech was Churchillian or anything massively inspirational. That's not Rafa's style. He is still a leader for sure, but he's not generally one to shout or speechify. He is more tactical. He focuses on people's jobs and things that have to be done, rather than on grand emotional exhortations. He shows the way in calmly. He'll say: "Hang on. You are good players. Let's change things." He gives people confidence. You don't have to shout to do that.'

XABI ALONSO: 'Rafa didn't raise his voice at all. All he said was that we had forty-five minutes left, and he was looking for tactical solutions which would help us in the second half. Nobody got blamed; nobody got a bollocking.'

RAFA BENÍTEZ: 'After giving them this motivational talk, I started to write the new team formation on the whiteboard on the dressing-room wall. I told Traore that he had to get changed and that Hamann was coming on for him.'

DJIMI TRAORE: 'I took my boots off after I was told I was not going back on.'

PAKO AYESTARÁN: 'We had to achieve two things. First, we had to change the pattern in the middle of midfield where Milan were doing the most damage. So we had to put on a player who could hold a good line and control the flow of the ball. If that was successful then we could start to do damage from that area, too. Since we hadn't had enough power and movement in that area it was obvious to go for Didi Hamann. The second thing was more basic: the players had to believe in themselves again. If Rafa has to give somebody a bollocking he'll do it, and when he has to bawl and shout he'll do that, too. But it's rare. Above all he is an analytical man. These types of situations, losing 3–0, for example, call for more than just hammering the players until your aggression and your attack on them gets their character and spirit going again. You can tell them, "You are all playing shit and I'm ashamed of you", but such tactics alone are not going to win the day when the game is running so badly against you. We had to convince the players that the situation was merely a result of our errors and the fact that Milan had taken advantage of them so well. We needed to examine the problem, come up with an answer and then make the players both understand it and believe in it. That was the only way we could stem the flow of errors which Milan had taken advantage of so ruthlessly. If we could achieve all that then we knew we could go back out there and control the match. From then on it would be vital to score a goal within the first ten or fifteen minutes after the break.'

JAMIE CARRAGHER: 'The next big commotion was that the boss had brought Djimi Traore off. Djimi had his boots off and was just about to get in the shower when the physio announced that Stevie Finnan was injured.'

PACO HERRERA: 'The physio told us that Finnan shouldn't go back out, but the player thought otherwise and demanded to carry on. He was very upset and screamed he wanted to stay on. Being the boss, Rafa needed to make a speedy decision.'

JAMIE CARRAGHER: 'Finnan could have carried on because he'd had that injury before the game, but out of the blue the manager said, "No, we're changing. I'd have to take him [Finnan] off in twenty minutes anyway." So he took him off, and Traore stayed on. The physio probably played a bigger role in the changes than the manager!'

RAFA BENÍTEZ: 'Finnan was unhappy – not because of the tactical decision to sub him but because he told us that he believed he could keep going. His point of view was: "I've been training for a couple of days, coping with the pain and getting treatment, and I've managed to play the first half fine. I can play on, boss!" But I reckoned if he told me midway through the second half that he couldn't go on then I'd have to make a change which was beyond my control. So I preferred to do it then and took into account that I would still have one substitution left up my sleeve in case anything dramatic happened during the second half which needed a quick reaction.'

PACO HERRERA: 'All of this happened in the first six or seven minutes of the break. There were loads of changes and lots of commotion.'

XABI ALONSO: 'There was a disconcerting period. Finally the boss told us we were changing from a back four to a back three.'

VLADIMIR SMICER: 'It was pretty chaotic for a few moments in there. I was asking, "What do I have to do, boss? Where will I be playing? Am I going to be playing wide? Will I be the right-back or the wing-back?" Then we realised that the boss had written his second–half scheme with twelve players in the team!'

RAFA BENÍTEZ: 'Yeah, it was a total mess for a while. After I gave the speech, I first wrote on the board that Traore was coming off and Hamann on. I took Didi up to the whiteboard so he understood what I wanted from him and then, after telling Didi to go and warm up with Pako outside, I explained the tactical changes to the rest of the side. During my explanations, and with Hamann outside warming up, I was told that Finnan was injured. We were about to leave the dressing room and everybody else was getting up and walking around. "Come on boys!" someone screamed. Then I was reckoning on Cissé on the right-hand side of midfield, which I had put on the whiteboard. But someone told me, "No, boss. If Hamann is coming on and Kewell has already been replaced, then bringing someone else on would leave you with no more substitutions." "Ah, OK," I agreed. I never make three replacements at half time as it mortgages your future. So I took Cissé out of the line-up but I also deleted Luis García from the board because I wanted to move him to another position in the formation. Now I had ten players in the team! The system was changed on the board several times and that was what created the havoc.'

PACO HERRERA: 'I was occupied with Finnan, trying to calm him down, because he was pretty upset at being subbed.'

RAFA BENÍTEZ: 'With Finnan on the pitch, the idea was to play 3–4–2–1, with Riise tucked in a bit deeper. But then, with the realisation that Finnan was not fit to stay on, the logical thing was to tell Traore that he wasn't being taken off. We had to tell him he was back in the final! He had his boots off and was literally on his way to the shower. One of our major offensive problems in the first half had been the fact that we weren't threatening in and around their penalty box. So our idea was to change that pattern by using two players in the hole between midfield and Baroš, who was in the centre-forward role on his own. The vital task for these two support strikers was to produce terrific movement, which would help us creatively, but would also put massive pressure on Milan building the play out of defence, through Pirlo in particular. If we could do that then we guessed it would slam the brakes on the damaging work which Gatusso and Seedorf, but most of all Kaká, were doing further up the pitch. The next point was that using three centre-halves would make us much more secure at the back by staying tight on the runs of their twin strikers. Meanwhile, Hamann also had the role of making Kaká's life much tougher for him. You can try anything in a match tactically so long as you've worked hard on such ideas in training, and we had.'

PACO HERRERA: 'The tactical change was explained, and we told the players not to storm out there and lose their heads in the first few moments. Then one of us pointed out that we needed some sort of extra rallying point: something to lift the spirits and help the team believe that winning was still possible. There were too many players who were as groggy as a boxer after being flattened by a sucker punch. The team desperately needed some kind of rallying call. Then it came: "Hey, come on, remember the night we were losing 1–0 to Olympiakos at half time and then we stormed out and scored three goals in the second half? So why not tonight? Why not do it again?" As soon as that was said, one of the players picked up on it and started to urge everyone on in the right way, and little by little you could see and hear everyone's spirits rising until you could hear them all giving it: "Come on! He's right, we can do it. Let's go!" Maybe not everyone was totally convinced, but I can tell you for sure that the mood was changing.'

RAFA BENÍTEZ: 'Normally it's Xabi or Carra or Gerrard who'll be shouting, "Come on boys!" as an encouragement when it's needed. But in those first few minutes at half time there wasn't really any of that from them. Only in the last couple of moments before going out did the animation and the noise hit a more normal level.'

XABI ALONSO: 'You could see people were down in the dumps. But one or two of us pushed for something to rally around and words of encouragement about going back out and starting the comeback.'

DJIMI TRAORE: 'Later, when it was all over, we discussed the fact that we were all surprised that the manager had convinced us that we could come back. "If we score one goal, we can come back," he was saying.'

PAKO AYESTARÁN: 'I missed all that because after eight minutes or so, having said to Rafa the things I felt needed to be said, I went outside to help Didi with his warm up. When we came out, the fans applauded and we heard the sound of "You'll Never Walk Alone" echoing around. These fans have a deep belief: they have faith in the team and bring a tremendous boost of energy. A famous Catalan expression is: "Barcelona is more than a club". Well, to me, Liverpool fans are "more than just fans".'

CHRIS BASCOMBE: 'In the distance, you could just about hear the murmuring about suicidal tactics, a referee who didn't spot a handball and Harry Kewell's habit of getting injured in cup finals.'

DIDI HAMANN: 'While I was warming up, fans were still singing, but there was no belief in their voices. They were frustrated, of course.'

DAVID MOORES (sitting in the director's box): 'I was distraught at half time and my main concern was for the fans. They had come all this way and I thought, "Christ, I hope we put on a better performance in the second half." '

JOHN ALDRIDGE (on his way out of the press canteen at the stadium): 'At that stage I wished I could have gone home. It was such an anticlimax. I was thinking, "I can't watch." I felt sick in my stomach. All that way, just to be humiliated.'

KENNY DALGLISH (at that stage, on his way home): 'If I am honest, we all thought that was that. No one thought we had a prayer. I was so glum I left the pub where I was watching the match in Formby to see the second half at home.'

RICK PARRY: 'I was thinking of Basle [Liverpool had been losing 3–0 at half time in 2002 and came back for a draw] and of Olympiakos. But the fans were very low. They kind of rallied to sing some songs, although they didn't even do that at first. We heard all the comments, and some fans left. But there came a moment when they started rallying and saying, "No, we can still do something." We talked about it: "Let's score a goal, let's make it respectable, let's go out with our tails up, let's at least win the second half." '

PHIL THOMPSON: 'At half time I was going berserk in the TV compound. Nesta had handled the ball and instead of getting the penalty we conceded another goal. Richard Keys [Sky's anchor man] was looking at me and I was swearing: "The ref *had* to send him off. He *had* to give a penalty." My language was awful. I was so upset.'

SAMMY LEE (having a drink in a Chicago hotel room): 'Three–nil in the first half was quite comprehensive. I thought, "Ugh!", but I did say to the rest of the England staff that I thought Liverpool would win the second half. By that I meant that Rafa would go in and say, "Well, listen, it's now a case of restoring our pride. You go out, and whatever you do, you win the second half. And do *not* concede a goal." '

TONY BARRETT (correspondent of the Liverpool *Echo*, sitting in the press box): 'I saw people crying at half time. Someone said, "I will stay to see Maldini lift the cup. That will be the memory I will take with me." All of the guys from the same pub, the Holt in Kensington, left the stadium. They are die-hard fans, go everywhere, but they just couldn't stand it any more. Others, I'd say about forty more, went, too, but, after the start of the second half, they tried to get back in. Amazingly, they were allowed to re-enter the stadium. Before the players came out, people were singing "You'll Never Walk Alone", and that slightly changed the mood. There was a roar when Gerrard came out.'

SIR MICHAEL BIBBY (fan sitting in the Liverpool end): 'I decided to teach the words of "You'll Never Walk Alone" to a Turkish friend of mine who was seated with us. That is why I was singing it. We all thought it was a good joke when, before the start of the second half, people chanted, "We're going to win 4–3, we're going to win 4–3 . . ." '

JOSÉ MANUEL OCHOTORENA: 'Subconsciously, I think we thought that the final was already lost at half time. And my wife, just for something to say to Montse [Benítez] in the stands, said that we were going to win. I think she had to be the only person in the whole stadium who thought that we could get it back. When we started coming out on to the pitch, "You'll Never Walk Alone" was being sung.'

XABI ALONSO: 'From the dressing room we simply couldn't hear anything that was going on with the fans. Everyone has told me about how the support was getting behind us during the break, but I have to say I didn't hear a thing.'

RAFA BENÍTEZ: 'I didn't hear "You'll Never Walk Alone" from the dressing room. On the way out to the pitch I did hear it, but I was lost in my own thoughts.'

CHRIS BASCOMBE: 'When "YNWA" began it was the closest you'd get to Liverpool's followers uniting in collective prayer. But really, although the sheer volume had stunned the AC Milan fans, the line about "hope in your heart" sounded hollow. It was not a rip-roaring rally cry. It was the fans' way of telling their players: "We know we're going to get battered, but thanks for the trip anyway." '

XABI ALONSO: 'As soon as we got out on the pitch we could feel that the fans were up for getting right behind us and pushing us back into the game. You could feel their enthusiasm and that carried us right into the start of the second half. When we went out there we knew that these forty-five minutes were our last chance. Everyone wanted to turn it around.'

JOSÉ MANUEL OCHOTORENA: 'On our way out to the pitch I heard one of their subs, I'm not certain who it was, but Tomasson springs to mind, saying: "Let's see if we can play a bit of football now and enjoy the final." I was walking out behind Gattuso and Nesta. Gattuso was saying that the match was "already won" and that all they needed to do was "knock the ball about" and keep possession. Nesta told him to "calm down" but Gattuso just kept repeating that they have to keep possession.'

CHRIS BASCOMBE: 'I saw Gattuso lifting his arms in a victory sign to the fans when he came out.'

GENNARO GATTUSO: 'When I came back on to the pitch, I felt the atmosphere had changed completely. Italian fans are so different to English: they have a different mentality. And I made a gesture to my fans to wake them up. It was *not* a victory sign. They weren't singing! We were winning 3–0 and all you could hear was "You'll Never Walk Alone".'

CHRIS BASCOMBE: 'Then Steven Gerrard reappeared to a roar which would have made anyone arriving late believe it was still 0–0! Seconds later, as a means of clarification, the Kop-on-tour sang, "We're gonna win 4–3." "These Scousers haven't lost their sense of humour, have they?" observed a neutral in the press box. Didi Hamann was finally on.'

CARLO ANCELOTTI: 'At the interval all we said to ourselves was: "We must keep it simple and we must be careful because an English side never gives up." '

JOSÉ MANUEL OCHOTORENA: 'On the way out to the bench Paco Herrera told me, "If we get one goal then we are right back in this." I remember replying, "I'm not sure that scoring one will be enough to do that. We'll be on the scoreboard but ..." Looking back, of course, I can see he was right. What stays with me from that moment, even at 3–0, is the real optimism he had.'

PACO HERRERA: 'The poor kit man, Graham, missed the beginning of the action in the second half as he had to stay behind with Finnan. He is obliged to be the last one in the room and Finnan was getting changed. At least Finnan himself arrived on time to see the match start to turn around and then be transformed.'

(9)

THE ROAD TO ISTANBUL

Why Can't It Be Us This Time?

On the streets of Valencia, not long after the 'Miracle of Istanbul', a local daily sports paper launched a poster campaign based on Rafa Benítez's already mythical half-time talk during the Champions League final. The first of two images shows a group of tired and glum commuters waiting on the platform for the next train to arrive. One guy has stepped forward from the group to address the others and proclaims: 'We've got to get out of here and take on the world!' In the next image the group is leaving the station in team formation, with their faces set determinedly and their heads held high.

The world has largely assumed that Liverpool's astonishing fight-back was mostly attributable to the inspirational words of a leader who convinced his troops that the impossible was achievable. But Benítez's working regime and his degree of influence are much more complex and certainly less romantic than the posters would have you believe. He isn't the kind of leader who often raises his voice. At half time in Istanbul, he coolly managed to illuminate a way out of what appeared to be a hopeless situation through logic and tactics. A new strategy, the demand of an early goal, and a short motivational speech that reminded the players of the debt they owed to the fans buoyed the team and injected a much-needed sense of urgency. Rafa did what all great leaders are able to do: he showed others how to get themselves out of trouble.

In his book *Leadership*, Jorge Valdano, a former Argentinian international and now an extraordinary football writer, imagined an extreme situation in a match. (Incidentally, the book was published in 1999, six years before the events in the Atatürk Stadium.)

> The first half is finished and your team is losing three–nil. It is half time and these are the only moments when a coach can directly influence the unpleasant reality his team is facing. The players arrive in the changing room as beaten men. Is there a formula you can use in order to give all of your players a kick in the pants ... in psychological terms? As a player I was subjected to insults, understanding, threats, calm analysis, affectionate care and also total silence! What, if anything, is the perfect solution in such a situation? There is no textbook answer. However, we have learned that possessing the correct information and having a clinical eye, by which I mean the ability to analyse that information, as well as a certain speed of assimilation from the players, all help to find the correct responses to such a situation.

The 'information' Valdano mentions is the kind Benítez accumulates via his rigorous working methods. Although his team was inconsistent thoughout the 2004–05 season, Benítez was beginning to see glimpses of the kind of side he wanted to produce: defensively organised, able to move speedily into counter-attack, effective and mentally strong. 'Sometimes I recognise it as my team ... but not always,' he confessed halfway through the season. The 2–0 win over Monaco in September and, to an extent, the come-from-behind victory at Fulham constituted a couple of leaps forward in quality and organisation under the new manager. The 0–1 victory away to Deportivo La Coruña in November signalled another.

Deportivo had been semi-finalists in the previous Champions League, and although they were undoubtedly a team in decline, they were still considered a force in European football. But that night in Galicia, despite the quality of their rival, Liverpool played fearlessly and with an appetite for the game. 'That match was one of our most "serious" performances,' says Benítez. 'The team was very compact and well positioned throughout the match. We knew what each of us had to do at all times and when we won the ball back from Deportivo we did damage. It gave us renewed confidence and helped develop players like Igor Biscan.'

By picking Biscan, Benítez had shown his faith in the Croat (his inclusion kept Alonso, on the bench). And Biscan rewarded his manager's confidence with a terrific display. In the fourteenth minute, he was instrumental in the only goal of the game. He skipped past three challenges before picking out John Arne Riise on the left with an astute pass. Riise's cross was arrowing towards Milan Baroš in the box, but he was not required as Jorge Andrade bundled the ball into his own net while attempting to clear.

At the end of the same month, Benítez's team produced another performance which would become a benchmark for the rest of the season. The match against Arsenal gave the footballing world the chance to see how Benítez's work-in-progress would fare against Arsène Wenger's finished article. Henry, Vieira, Pires, Ljungberg and Reyes were all there, but Liverpool pulled off a tactical coup. Their formation put Xabi Alonso and Hamann in the centre of midfield, and, for the first time, gave Gerrard a freer role in front of them, which, as the season developed, increasingly seemed to suit his offensive instincts. The match proved that Benítez can get the better of any team ... even the best team around. Certainly this was the impression around Anfield that day. A late strike from young Neil Mellor, a magnificent shot that flew into the Arsenal net in front of the Kop, darkened the mood of the champions.

'We played really well in the first half, with great intensity,' recalls Benítez. 'We won all the fifty–fifty balls. Xabi Alonso scored first, but in the second half Arsenal began to use the ball better. That got them the equaliser. However, the game as a whole showed us that we *were* able to play football at the level of a team like Arsenal. Obviously, Neil Mellor's goal, to give us all three points as well, was the icing on the cake.'

Ten days later, in the Champions League, it looked for a while as if not only the icing but the whole cake had gone off. In their final group game against Olympiakos, Liverpool were obliged to win either 1–0 or by two clear goals to qualify for the knockout stages. Ultimately, the match against the Greeks gave more satisfaction to the players than to Rafa Benítez, as the final victory (3–1) had as much to do with the coach's tactics than with the confidence of a team spurred on by the Kop in full cry. After being behind at half time, following Rivaldo's free kick, the Liverpool players threw themselves into the match in the second half. 'It was a key moment in the season,' Xabi Alonso remembers with pleasure. 'We were in a difficult situation but we showed everyone, including ourselves, that we knew how to resolve it.'

The manager is more ambivalent. 'We had spoken throughout the week about not conceding a goal, yet we gave one away right at the end of the first half,' complains Benítez. 'And to do it in the way we did, with a cock-up in the wall facing the free kick, was a really tough blow. At half time I tried, as always, to use a mixture of psychology and information. I tried to motivate and lift the team, but a talk isn't enough. The key was to try not to panic and to stop the Greek counter-attacks. It was about playing the remainder of the game at *our* high pace without becoming obsessed about how quickly we scored.' Rivaldo, who was nominally playing wide on the left, had been floating into the middle of the pitch, and Benítez demanded that his players exploit the free space that the Brazilian was leaving on his touchline.

Rafa's leadership was rewarded with the correct response from his team, and his substitutions had an almost magical effect. Florent Sinama-Pongolle, who had come on at the break for Traore, scored the equaliser within a minute. Then Mellor sprinted on and he, too, scored to set up a frantic finale. With the clock ticking down, Gerrard unleashed a ferocious volley from twenty-two yards to sweep Liverpool into the last sixteen and send Anfield wild with celebration.

Pako Ayestarán says: 'Whenever they talk about that third goal, everyone always comments about how Gerrard put his heart, body and soul into the strike. Stevie put all the energy in the world into it, and luckily aimed it perfectly, too! But there was more to the move than that: the ball almost went out of play but Xabi Alonso fought to keep it in and from that point onwards we built the move down the left. Mellor improvised a head-flick and then Gerrard produced his brilliant shot. It is the kind of move which makes you realise that this team *does* know how to fight and make something out of nothing.'

Benítez, as usual, remained focused on the task in hand even after Gerrard's screamer. Rick Parry was 'fascinated, but not surprised' by the manager's response when the ball hit the back of the net. 'As everyone was going mad with excitement, the manager was thinking about the tactics. It just highlights his professionalism. I spoke to Rafa about it all later. He was keen to talk more about the things we did wrong in the game and what the team might learn from it. That has always been the Liverpool way. I think back to the great days of Shanks, Bob and Joe, and the stories about when the players reported back to pre-season training. Ronnie Moran, a loyal member of Shankly's staff, would be there to meet them in the Melwood dressing room. He would take their League Championship medals out of a bag and chuck them to each player without any comment or ceremony. Then he would launch into what was needed in the coming season. The lads quickly realised that you get nothing for yesterday. It's all about the next game. Ronnie was at the Olympiakos match, and seeing him there reminded me of that old story.'

In the crucial Olympiakos game, the usual two players lifted the level of the team when it was most needed – Gerrard and Carragher. They were decisive and demanding in everything they did – forcing opposition errors by waging war all over the pitch, dragging Liverpool into the match and overwhelming the visitors. In Spain, they would be called 'street-footballers'. 'They perform as if they are kids playing on their local streets, and nowadays most people don't do that any more,' points out Paco Herrera. 'When you played in the street you just threw everything you had into it – you didn't think about tactics or details. You just played for the love of it and for the joy of winning, of course. This is the main value of those two.'

Paul Flanagan, a diehard fan and personal friend of Carragher, passionately believes the defender is the *real* soul of the team, and is happy to reignite one of the Kop's favourite debates: 'Jamie is the ideal captain, the one that people will go on to write books about, but I suppose the club cannot give the armband to him. There are some other obligations with Gerrard.' Flanagan, of course, is hinting that Gerrard, unlike Carragher, needs constant reassurance of his value to the club. However, it should be pointed out that the *unanimous* reaction of the squad when he offered to relinquish the captaincy in the summer of 2005 suggests that Gerrard is also the players's preferred choice.

The skipper picked up a yellow card against Olympiakos which meant he would miss the first leg of the knockout stage. Liverpool had drawn one of the weakest teams left in the competition, which gave them a good chance of reaching the quarter-finals. But that's what Bayer Leverkusen thought, too. And adding to the Germans' confidence was the fact that, along with Gerrard, Xabi Alonso, Djibril Cissé and Florent Sinama-Pongolle were all sidelined too, in their cases through injury. However, Igor Biscan proved to be a more than able deputy for the skipper, and Liverpool swept aside the Germans with one of their most impressive, authoritative wins of the season. Goals from Luis García, slipping the ball past Jorg Butt after a perfect pass by Biscan, Riise, with a powerful free-kick, and Hamann, with another dead ball despatched into the net at the Kop end, had sent Anfield into raptures. But Rafa was still troubled after the match. An error by Jerzy Dudek deep into injury time, when he spilled the ball to allow França to score, gave Bayer a vital away goal. What had been almost an unassailable 3–0 lead was transformed into a shaky 3–1.

Benítez, though, kept his distress to himself. He had become concerned that there was too much negativity surrounding his team, too much talk about being the worst club left in the competition, which had resulted in a lack of confidence in some of his own players. He decided to do everything in his power to banish the inferiority complex. So, in the press conference before the second leg in Germany, employing a somewhat risky strategy, Benítez publicly contradicted Gerrard's widely reported belief that Liverpool were not good enough to reach the final. 'I prefer the players to say, "Why is it not possible for us to get there?" If Porto won the Champions League last year then why can't it be us this time? I don't want to hear any member of the squad saying that it can't happen. If we beat Leverkusen we will only be two rounds away from the final, and any team we draw will have to come to Anfield and face our fans as well as our players.' He was on a roll! Then he mentioned the name that makes every Liverpool player sit up and take notice: 'It was Shankly who made this club hungry for success. His work was the basis of the club going on to win four European Cups even once he'd left. That is what we are looking for now.'

Benítez did not forget to repeat all this to his skipper face to face as well. The coach also mentioned that Gerrard had to try to hide the glumness that too often soured his features. Sometimes his body language after a painful defeat screamed pessimism, and his constant efforts to do everything by himself indicated to the coaching staff that he did not completely trust his colleagues on the pitch.

Shankly, in his era, had been convinced that Liverpool could win any game of football under any circumstances. And his inspirational leadership transmitted that same belief to the players and the masses on the Kop. Benítez, similarly in total control of the club yet aware of its current limitations, was looking to instil the same sort all-pervasive self-assurance. To achieve this, throughout the season he returned time and again to the motivational DVDs prepared by his staff before key matches. Before the Carling Cup final in Cardiff, the DVD showed winning teams parading the cup around the stadium and celebrating with their fans. There were also clips of fans' reactions after the crucial victories against Olympiakos and

Arsenal. 'I used that strategy for the first time with one of the youth teams of Real Madrid and it evidently motivated the players,' Benítez remembers. 'In this way you can remind them of the joy you both experience and cause by winning a trophy.'

The press conference in Germany had the same objective of enhancing the team's confidence, and over the following weeks Benítez would continue to boost his players' morale with public displays of support. The team were still far from reaching their limit, they could go much further, play even better, reach the Champions League final if they set their minds to it. Slowly but surely, the message sunk in.

Rick Parry had been optimistic before the second leg against Leverkusen. After it, he was ecstatic. 'Away at Leverkusen, not only did we not let it slip; we were outstanding. Rafa's team gave a tremendous performance. That was probably the first time when you thought to yourself: "We really are a different team."'

That March evening in the BayArena, Liverpool took the game to their hosts. Gerrard had returned from his suspension and took the corner from which Luis García volleyed home his twenty-eighth-minute goal. The Spaniard would then score another before Baroš made it 6–2 on aggregate. (The consolation for Bayer came with a shot from Jacek Krzynowek.) Liverpool had performed well beyond the expectations of their technical staff: 'Some of us realised for the first time that an important achievement in Europe really was within our grasp that season,' recalls Pako Ayestarán.

Benítez, finally genuinely accepting that possibility himself, was gifted a new psychological weapon in the build-up to the next round. Juventus's Pavel Nedved had said he was very sorry for the magnificent Liverpool support, but the English club had 'no hope' of winning the quarter-final tie against his team. His sentiments filtered down to the Liverpool dressing room and were seized on as manna from heaven by the coaching staff. Nedved's words were debated at length and the press cutting was stuck up on the wall at Melwood. 'It was one of the few times that we employed that strategy,' says Ayestarán. 'We know that, if used cleverly in the right circumstances, the press-cutting tactic can generate a deep-rooted response from the players.' Benítez generally bows to Pako's opinion on matters like this. He trusts him to get the tone just right where motivation of the players is concerned. For instance, it was Ayestarán who rescued two framed posters which had been mouldering in Melwood's old gym and promptly hung them along the well-trodden route out to the main training pitches. The first says: 'Some people dream about success while others get up every day to achieve it.' The second cautions: 'Self-improvement is a neverending road.'

Ayestarán, a big fan of photography, was also determined that the training ground's historic 'aura' should not be lost. 'I asked for three photos of the Liverpool supporters to be hung up at Melwood,' he explains. 'One had to be with the fans celebrating something important like a goal. Another with them suffering, because they *do* suffer: they go home and they don't sleep and it is not the same getting up the next day having lost instead of having won. Finally, I wanted a photo just showing them supporting the team. Sometimes professional football is so busy and pressurised that we forget all about that. Now these shots are on the wall and looking down on us every morning.

'Recently I added one more picture. I had spotted an unusual image after the Istanbul final. It was of a father and his two sons, one aged about six, the other about thirteen. The expression on the man's face is sheer poetry. I think it must have been the moment when we went 3–0 down against Milan, and the guy just couldn't believe it. His mouth was gaping open and he looked so sad. The players need to remember and think about those types of situations. Liverpool players need to respect these people and never forget that, as footballers, they have a privileged and important role.'

These little details helped to make the Liverpool challenge in Europe a different prospect as the season progressed. Back in September, everyone at the club would have considered a quarter-final to be a good return. But the Olympiakos victory had suggested that something strange was happening, and the Bayer Leverkusen matches seemed to confirm it. But it was the quarter-final against Juventus which truly proved to the squad and others that their daily work was bearing fruit. 'Liverpool this season are less equipped for the marathon than the sprint. On the day, they could give it their all. They could raise their game. But you cannot say the league table lies,' said Arsenal coach Arsène Wenger at the time.

Nevertheless, Liverpool were slowly approaching the style Benítez wanted. According to the boss, 'In many matches, our players were not as strong or as good as the ones they faced, which is why our style ended up halfway between the normal physical football of an English team and the quality play you get at the high levels of the continental leagues. Our objective is to improve while playing good football, because being a strong physical team only serves you domestically. Until we achieve this perfect blend, we have tried to approach games with "new" tactics to surprise opponents and some of them have turned out quite well. Perhaps at the end of the away game against Juventus, the 0–0 draw which got us to the semi-final, the team realised that the long slog we'd put in at the training ground was finally giving us results. In Turin, we moved from four to five at the back. We worked hard on it and gave very specific instructions on the way to press Juventus until we felt we had it to perfection.'

In the previous round Juventus had knocked out Real Madrid, but in that tie the Italians had shown themselves to be the ideal rival for this Liverpool side. Benítez and his staff could see that Juventus were a well-regimented team, but they were sure Liverpool could concede possession of the ball (a problem for them all season) yet still be relatively safe. The Italians patently lacked creativity, that crispness that leads to the killer touch, and the right kind of players to do much damage. Benítez ordered a high tempo, pressure and flair to lift the crowd. There was total conviction at Melwood that success was possible.

So, twenty years on from that fateful evening at the Heysel

Stadium, Liverpool and Juventus met again in European competition for the first time. Before both matches the principal discussions surrounded the correct way to commemorate the Heysel disaster. Despite the reaction of a section of the Juventus support at Anfield, when they literally turned their backs on both the minute's silence and a mosaic created by the Kop, solid bridges of understanding were built between the two clubs. Liverpool asked for forgiveness for the tragedy which cost the lives of thirty-nine fans in a proper, respectful manner.

From the first kick, a Liverpool side fielding teenagers Scott Carson and Anthony Le Tallec due to injuries and suspensions that had sidelined seven regulars imposed a high rhythm and produced one of the best displays Anfield had seen for many years. The Kop lapped it up and themselves performed like it was the good old days. Sami Hyypia scored after ten minutes, volleying in a Luis García head-flick after a Gerrard corner. Then, in the twenty-fifth minute, Liverpool scored a second, a sublime twenty-five-yard strike from Luis García which sailed magnificently over Gigi Buffon. In fifteen minutes, Juve's keeper had collected the ball from his net as many times as he had during their previous eight games in the competition.

'People talk about the atmosphere against Chelsea in the semi-final, but my best memory of the season was the first half against Juve,' says Ayestarán. 'From the first goal we started to play at a very high pace, taking the ball away from the Italians. For the rest of the match I sat on the bench smiling because I saw that we had bags of confidence. Juve were surprised and the fans' songs were uplifting. I remember looking over at the stands and saying to myself: "We are going to win well here." Things got a bit complicated later but it was wonderful to feel so self-assured for most of that massive game.'

At key moments in most of their Champions League fixtures in 2004–05, Liverpool enjoyed the kind of good fortune which you need to win the competition. That night, Juve's Zlatan Ibrahimovic hit the post with a great shot, while Alessandro del Piero had a legitimate headed goal ruled out. During the second half, the Italians fought back strongly and an error from Carson, when he fumbled Fabio Cannavaro's soft header into the net, gave the Italians a seemingly crucial away goal. For the last fifteen minutes at Anfield and during the entire second leg in Turin, Liverpool focused on 'holding firm' to ensure qualification to the semi-finals for the first time since 1985.

With Gerrard absent and Xabi Alonso making his first start for more than three months, Jamie Carragher and Sami Hyypia were Liverpool's heroes in the match in Italy. Jamie did not put a foot wrong and Hyypia seemed the player of old – dominant in the air, assured on the ground. He even almost got his name on the scoresheet again when he was allowed a free header after Thuram had slipped, but it just went over the bar. Cannavaro provided the biggest scare of the night, hitting the post with a header, but mostly the Italians resorted to angling long balls into the Liverpool box. 'Easy, easy,' sang the Liverpool fans, and they were right, as Carragher and Hyypia headed away one speculative cross after another. Carragher, professionally ignoring the backdrop of bottle-throwing, a big banner that declared, 'Easy to Speak, Difficult to Pardon, Murderers!' and cries of 'We hate Liverpool' from the Juventus fans, concentrated on his task: blocking a fearsome drive from Emerson here, clearing a Zambrotta cross there, ensuring the offside trap worked efficiently, even lecturing Milan Baroš when the striker failed to mark properly at a corner. Juve's threat was reduced to the bare minimum and their coach, Fabio Capello, admitted publicly afterwards that he had been outmanoeuvred. It was the first time Italian journalists heard him say anything of the sort. 'We changed our system and Juventus were not able to react effectively,' assesses Ayestarán. 'I was expecting more from the Italians but I was never frightened of them. I always felt, from the initial moments at Anfield, that we had control of the tie.'

The hard work at Melwood had paid dividends again. 'I never

considered that match, or the one against Chelsea, a battle of the coaches,' insists Benítez. 'What happened was that we possessed one or two strong points and we tried to set things up so that we could take advantage of them. It all worked out pretty well. Juve resorted to hitting long balls but we were strong, orderly, together. I don't think it was a case of a victory by one coach over another, but rather a victory for one team which knew how to take advantage of its best qualities over another which couldn't do the same thing. Also, in Turin, we had the good fortune that Xabi Alonso was fit again and that gave us extra options both in winning and using the ball in midfield when we got it. In fact, the return of Xabi and Cissé for the last months of the season, with the energy they brought, gave us the push to win the Champions League.'

An added source of satisfaction in the Leverkusen and Juventus ties was that Luis García was finally finding the individual touches that rewarded the team's effort. As he showed off less, he scored more. It was a welcome turnaround. Frustrated by the lenient refereeing in the Premiership and by the intense physicality of a league which played non-stop football with no Christmas break, he had been toiling, shocked by the battering he was receiving week in, week out. 'I had literally no idea that they played such fierce physical football in England,' admits the Catalan. 'The day of my first game against Manchester United there wasn't even a booking for Rio Ferdinand after he clattered into me from behind when I received the ball at my feet. I remember the ref saying to me a few times during the match, "That's not a foul in England, son." I realised that I had to improve my physique, get stronger. Every loose ball is competed for as if your life depends on winning it . . . I need to be able to fight on equal terms. It's also true that the lightning-fast speed of the play makes totally different demands on you as a player in comparison with La Liga in Spain. Either you get right back up again after someone's booted you in the air or the coach will haul you off and get someone else on in your place in a matter of seconds. There's not one second of respite here.'

In contrast, the Champions League, at Anfield in particular, brought the best out of Luis García – most notably in the home leg against Juventus. His fizzing volley past Buffon turned out to be the decisive goal of the quarter-final. Anfield still features him in the 'Rafa Benítez Song' (two other imports – Josemi and Nuñez – who had been similarly lauded by the Kop, were dropped from the lyrics by the end of the season). His five goals in the Champions League and his skill, more visible when the team has greater possession of the ball, have suspended for now the fans' criticism. Most of them would agree with Kenny Dalglish's assessment: 'He has been superb but can be infuriating. He can also really strike a ball and Liverpool wouldn't have got to the final without his contribution.'

In the club's 112-year history, no Spaniard had ever coached or played for Liverpool before Benítez arrived, and, coming from a country which has not generally exported its finest playing talent, the process of adaptation for Luis García and his Spanish team-mates was bound to be difficult. 'It is not that there are aspects of the English way of life that I can *never* get used to,' he says. 'But it is certainly true that I found it difficult to adapt to the food and the rhythm of the day. If you have a siesta in the afternoon after training and get up about six then everything is already closed!' During their first winter together in England, Luis García used to invite the other Spaniards round to his house to play Monopoly or cards and watch La Liga on the TV. They had to study English, too, of course. Josemi, who landed in Britain without a word of English, remains the least fluent.

When Fernando Morientes arrived on a €9-million transfer from Real Madrid, he added a touch of star quality to the group. But it was a reputation he worked hard to shed, starting with his name. He'd never liked the Madrid 'star system' and wanted to establish a new identity for himself: so 'Moro' and 'Morientes' (his dominant names in La Liga) were out; instead, he wished to be known as 'Nando'. But identity change notwithstanding, Morientes fully understood that his arrival from Madrid added weight to Benítez's squad and, early on, he had something important to say. Privately, Stevie Gerrard had demanded that the manager and the board should sign top-quality footballers. Morientes immediately hit the ball back into Gerrard's court by saying: 'I want to learn English quickly in order to be able to tell Gerrard to stay with Liverpool!'

The striker made his debut along with ex-Valencia defender Mauricio Pellegrino against Manchester United on 15 January. It took only half an hour for Benítez to realise Morientes was short of both form and fitness. Adapting to the hectic pace of the English game was going to be much more difficult as a result. The manager soon decided that his new signing could not fulfil the strike role that he had envisaged for him. Instead, he would need another striker, and he told the board so. His revised role for Nando was the same one the player had performed during his year-long loan spell at Monaco: behind the striker, where he could use his ball skills, his movement and his intelligence to open up defences. Morientes himself recognises the challenge: 'I will have to change my style of play to suit the English game,' he admits.

In their second year at the club, the fans would be much more demanding of Luis García and Morientes than, for example, Xabi Alonso, whose process of assimilation in England was almost immediate. Xabi Alonso has never had Spanish television cabled into his Albert Dock apartment, and more than most he understands the philosophy of Liverpool FC: the humility, the hard work and the commitment required to be a player that the Anfield crowd will respect. 'One day I went to training and there was a funeral on the pitch,' he recalls. 'They told me that the ashes of a fan were about to be scattered. Liverpool had been his life. I was stunned. There is so much that has impressed me. At Anfield, even the silences are different; you can tell them apart. There is the one of respect for the memory of someone, the anxious one that shows the fans are completely caught up in the match and so on. Then there are some symbolic gestures: our dressing room is smaller than the visitors' dressing room because that's a sign of humility, but also a way of getting the players physically and mentally more united, closer. They remind you exactly where you are. I immediately appreciated that this was a club with a difference.'

Steve Gerrard's view of the Iberian incomers is that 'All the Spaniards are very good mentally; they train well, and work hard and we wouldn't have gone so far without them.' The midfielder had to make new friends after the sale of Danny Murphy and Michael Owen – a reason given by some for his unsettled season – but he found one in Xabi Alonso: 'Xabi is a fantastic passer; he's a nice guy on and off the pitch and doesn't play for himself. Liverpool is a better team with him in it.'

Nevertheless, fears remained that Benítez was buying too many Spaniards, and, while not agreeing with that assessment, Rafa knew that he had to retain an English nucleus in the team to provide an extra level of aggression. However, he couldn't see many viable alternatives outside the market he knew best. 'The English game has changed immensely since the Bosman ruling,' explains the Liverpool boss. 'Not only have fans become accustomed to the presence of foreigners; they have realised the crucial influence players like Cantona, Bergkamp and Van Nistelrooy have had in the success of Manchester United and Arsenal. What matters is that you have good footballers. If they happen to be English, then all the better.

'Although I'm interested in the Spanish players adding the missing elements for the team's development, I'm careful to maintain the best of English football at the same time. Liverpool's teams for many years were the least "English" in their composition and style, and now I'm talking about rediscovering the old style of play under Shankly. I don't want long, direct, high-tempo football to be the only thing we are about. Hunting the ball to win back possession and using that possession cleverly were absolutely fundamental under the Shankly regime and for many years thereafter.'

Chris Bascombe of the Liverpool *Echo* judges the foreign signings a qualified success: 'Nobody is going to doubt Morientes until he has had a long run in the side, and anyway, getting three good signings out of five from La Liga is not bad.' Others are not so sure. 'Without meaning to sound like a Little Englander, I think Benítez needs to beware of flooding his side with Spanish players, particularly as some of them still look lightweight,' writes the Liverpool *Daily Post*'s Len Capeling. 'The manager has clearly enquired about home-grown talent, else why should he reveal that the prices being asked are ridiculous?' Capeling hits the nail on the head: given the current market, Benítez can get more value for money in Spain than in England.

Two of the new acquisitions from La Liga, Luis García and Xabi Alonso, were in the line-up to face Chelsea in the Champions League semi-final first leg at Stamford Bridge. Knocking out the Premiership champions-elect would, of course, propel Rafa and his staff to new heights of adulation. On the other hand, being knocked out would raise many questions and increase the doubts among fans, and possibly even among the players. Amazingly, though, by this stage, nobody inside Melwood doubted that Liverpool were going to make it to Istanbul.

(10)

THE SEMI-FINAL

Anfield Gave the Team the Value Added Tax Factor – the Extra 17.5 Per Cent

The all-English encounter was a rerun of Liverpool's painful Carling Cup final defeat earlier in the season. But that loss was just one added ingredient in a tie laden with unsettled scores and emotions. With his rumoured move to Chelsea and his own-goal towards the end at Cardiff, Steven Gerrard was the focus of much of the attention.

'In Cardiff, to be fair, Chelsea dominated the second half and we were clinging on,' admits Rick Parry. 'However, they did not create much out of open play and we were not that uncomfortable sitting back. It took the freak equaliser, with Gerrard heading the ball into our net, and a few mistakes in extra time. For the wrong reasons, Stevie was again in the middle of it all. I said to him after the Carling Cup final, "We will draw them in the Champions League and we will beat them," to which he replied, "We are going to win the Champions League after knocking them out." Stevie truly wanted to make amends. Too many people were too quick to criticise him after Cardiff.'

More unfinished business was of a tactical nature. Liverpool's three defeats against Chelsea, the other two being in the Premiership, had been neither emphatic nor conclusive. 'We had never been outplayed by them,' argues Parry. 'We returned home frustrated after being defeated 1–0 in Stamford Bridge earlier in the season because they hadn't dominated us. Then Xabi got injured during their visit to Anfield in January but we still played well without him.

We should have got something out of that.' Frank Lampard, in a rash challenge in the centre of midfield, had left Liverpool without Xabi Alonso for over three months by breaking a bone in the Spaniard's foot.

It had been a huge blow. Xabi Alonso had been growing in stature and, around him, the team was starting to learn the passing game demanded by Benítez. Gerrard was clearly comfortable in his new, freer role behind the strikers with his back being covered by Didi Hamann. It was a midfield combination that worked better than the earlier Gerrard–Xabi Alonso central-midfield partnership which had left the Spaniard with too much defensive work (not the strongest aspect of his game) and the skipper too restricted. Three consecutive victories had generated a great deal of optimism in the club. Then Lampard dived. Suddenly, the pessimism returned. Though Lampard, to his credit, had rung Xabi Alonso the evening after the match to apologise and to assure him that there had been no malice in his challenge. Now they were about to come face to face again.

In the context of a European semi-final, Chelsea and Liverpool could not have come from more different backgrounds. Chelsea were the new boys, the nouveaux riches, and were just about to clinch their first league title for a half a century. Liverpool, by contrast, had more European tradition and history than any other English club. But it was the Merseysiders, not the Londoners, who were seen by everybody as the underdogs. 'Somehow, you couldn't quite connect the Chelsea fixture with Istanbul,' says Rick Parry. 'It was about beating Chelsea, full stop. You are not necessarily thinking about getting to the final. But the desire to beat them was enormous, and we were convinced we were going to do it.'

'Many elements came together in that match,' says Benítez. 'Chelsea were our domestic enemy as well as the last obstacle between us and another European final. Everybody's motivation was much higher so we stoked that up to the maximum. When we heard that a few of the Chelsea players already considered themselves to be in the final, we took advantage of it by emphasising the fact to our own players. We were playing on Chelsea's overconfidence by saying repeatedly in the media, "We are not the favourites, *They* are the favourites." I hoped that would relax our players in a useful way.'

Benítez's chess-player's mind went into overdrive as soon as he knew he would be facing Mourinho's men in the semi. While the team was psychologically convinced that it *could* win, the staff came up with the tactical game-plan needed to eliminate Chelsea. Paco Herrera recalls that, 'Before the first leg, I told one of Mourinho's friends, an agent, "Let him know from me that they are better than us. They've proved themselves in the league and if they played five matches they would win four. But also tell him they are going to win 1–0 in the first game but we'll win 2–0 at Anfield." Mourinho replied, through his friend, that this was not going to happen. He said that Liverpool would win 0–1 at Stamford Bridge and that Chelsea would win 0–2 at Anfield. It turned out better than I had predicted because we didn't lose in London, but all of us already had faith that, one way or another, we were going to beat them.' Mourinho's reply also hinted that he knew there was something missing from his side, Premiership champions or not. Or maybe it was just that, despite the thirty-three points that then separated Liverpool and Chelsea (thirty-seven by the end), the Portuguese coach had developed a good deal of respect for his opponents during their earlier encounters. That is just one reason why the semi-finals were never going to be the fiesta of goals seen in Cardiff, even though Chelsea had won 4–2 in each of their previous two Champions League home games, against Barcelona and Bayern Munich. Neither side was going to give anything away when they were just one careful step from the big night in Istanbul.

For Liverpool, the real challenge lay in the away game at Stamford Bridge. If they could hold out for a draw or, at the very worst, a 1–0 defeat, then the squad and its staff were convinced that they would turn it around in the second leg.

The atmosphere at Stamford Bridge was subdued. The travelling

Koppites' chant of 'You have no history' almost seemed to be glumly accepted on the Chelsea stands. The home fans offered the occasional 'Chelsea' or 'One man went to mow ...' in response, but without much conviction. Mourinho later admitted that it had been a mistake to allocate the travelling fans the area behind the dugouts. The infamous 'shhhhh' gesture, when he held a finger to his lips and turned to the Liverpool fans at Cardiff, was well remembered ... and repaid with interest every time he stood up at Stamford Bridge that night.

The mockery seemed to affect him. His communication with his players diminished as the match progressed, even as his frustration grew. 'Judging by the atmosphere inside the ground, you'd have thought they'd just been relegated ... It was Liverpool's players and the travelling Kop who were going to make their noisy mark on the first game,' wrote Chris McLoughlin in *The Kop*.

During the first half, when the London club dominated possession, they should have opened the scoring when Frank Lampard skied a shot from eight yards over the bar. But then Petr Cech first denied John Arne Riise from close range and, shortly afterwards, produced an even better save to paw away a header from Milan Baroš.

Little of note happened after the break, save for a last-ditch tackle on Mateja Kezman by an outstanding Jamie Carragher, and for a moment of controversy in the closing minutes that would heighten the rising sense of injustice and dislike of their rivals within the Liverpool fan base. Xabi Alonso was booked when referee Alain Sars wrongly judged he had fouled Eidur Gudjohnsen. It was published later in the English press that, after he'd writhed around on the ground for a while, the Icelander had said to Alonso: 'I knew you were a yellow card away from suspension.'

It was a disappointing match but a great result for Liverpool. In some quarters, though, the criticism of Steven Gerrard, quiet for the entire ninety minutes, continued. 'He tends to disappear too often in big matches ... especially against Chelsea,' went the refrain. Only later was it announced that he had an operation to remove an abscess from his mouth on the morning of the game after a sleepless night of pain.

'The key factor in gaining that result was that we'd got our analysis of Chelsea spot on and played with the correct understanding of their game,' claims Pako Ayestarán. 'It was all down to the work we had done the week before. We spent a great deal of time analysing Chelsea, using a lot of taped material – far beyond the normal extent. The team had the match planned and played it in their heads. Another fundamental point was that we convinced our players that it was *impossible* for Chelsea to beat us again. On this occasion, we knew that winning one match out of two would be sufficient. I loved this fixture in London. It wasn't a beautiful game, but it was one of those which you'll go back to watch again and again because it involved perfect planning and execution.' Paco Herrera adds: 'In case we needed a little push to confirm earlier confident feelings, after the result in London we thought we would definitely win at Anfield.'

Benítez also sounded positive after the match: 'We have played a good game. The team worked hard and controlled the game. They had some chances but at the end a draw is a good result. We had more counter-attacks and they started playing long balls.' Chelsea had seemed tired, which was reflected in their lack of offensive alternatives – as Rafa had predicted. 'We knew what to do against Chelsea. We know they have a lot of good players who can create opportunities. The most important thing is we need only to win at Anfield. It is a good situation.'

Mourinho must have sensed the confidence in the opposition camp because he continued to try to destabilise his rivals by saying that '99.9 per cent of Liverpool fans' believed that their team had already qualified for the final by drawing at Stamford Bridge, and that was a mistake. In the days before the return leg, to counteract Mourinho's psychological sniping, Benítez applied another idea taken from Shankly's book: he deliberately changed 'Why can't we win the Champions League?' to an emphatic 'We *will* win it!' and fearlessly announced his prediction to the world's press. Rafa, happy with the attitude of his players in training, felt it was time to be brave.

Anfield responded remarkably to the challenge of defeating the 'new enemy in the world of football', as the chairman of UEFA's refereeing committee Volker Roth had labelled Chelsea's Portuguese coach. Chelsea had claimed that Barcelona coach Frank Rijkaard had tried to influence referee Anders Frisk at the Camp Nou on the way to the locker rooms at half time. Rijkaard had come out of the scandal exonerated and with his reputation enhanced as a result of his dignity amid the allegations.

So, with anti-Chelsea sentiment more heightened than ever (there was also the small matter that they'd won the Premiership title in the period between the first and second legs), the stage was set for a classic European night at Anfield. It was to be this generation's Inter Milan or St Etienne.

Older fans could recall the night in 1965 when, with Inter Milan as their opponents, 25,000 passionate fans on the Kop had sung and swayed for two hours. That was a first-leg European Cup semi-final and Liverpool had won 3–1. Others remembered 1977, against St Etienne, when Anfield's gates were locked an hour before kick-off for the return leg of the European Cup quarter-final. That night a 1–0 deficit was famously overturned with only six minutes of the match remaining. 'The Chelsea game was the best atmosphere I have seen at Anfield,' says Rick Parry. 'The Inter match in '65 was special, but for sustained noise and passion, even before the match, this felt incredible.'

'We wanted the stadium to rock with noise. We wanted our style of play to whip the fans into an even greater fervour. Everything else was simply going to be down to what the players could produce,' recalls Benítez, who the night before the game had slept for only two hours after he'd played out in his head the match and all its possible details.

The hunger and the frustration that come from waiting for success for two decades were concentrated into one night that would surpass even the great occasions of the glory days. The Kop had started to build up the noise one hour before kick-off. The wall of sound grew louder and louder as the kick-off approached, and by the time both teams ran out it had become deafening. Everybody was singing the 'Rafa Benítez Song' with scarves, flags and banners above their heads. It was a truly inspirational sight that revived memories of the old, standing Spion Kop, a memorable moment of raw passion. Patrick Barclay of the *Sunday Telegraph* wrote: 'on such occasions it should be the players who have to pay for admission'. John Arne Riise admits, 'We could not have run as much as we did without such a raucous and sustained support.'

Jamie Carragher had predicted before the game that the atmosphere was going to be one of the best of all time. 'Prior to Heysel and Hillsborough, our fans expected to win things; perhaps they even took it for granted in those days. Now they have been waiting for so long and wanting it so badly, you can see that reflected on the terraces.' The local lad had suggested that 'this match is going to be my destiny'. He had dreamed of a night like this for so many years.

Another Red in the stadium saw the whole experience writ large on the face of Liverpool's captain, too. 'Gerrard is a Scouser,' explains the former Liverpool striker Michael Robinson, who was there commentating on the match for Spanish television. 'Every time he pulls on his boots and that red strip you can see the Liverpool lad, angry with the world, convinced that this club is great. And, dammit, he's going to be there when we once again *are* the greatest in the world. I'll never forget the look on his face as he came off the pitch at Anfield having knocked out Chelsea!'

Robinson vividly remembers how fifteen minutes into the game even his neutral co-commentator Carlos Martinez, with tears in his eyes, paid homage on air to Liverpool's stadium. 'He said that after fifteen years' covering Europe he had never seen anything like it.

For me, Anfield gave the team the Value Added Tax Factor – the extra 17.5 per cent!'

Chelsea simply could not compete. Just before the match started, Frank Lampard turned to the travelling fans a few times and gesticulated to them, trying to inspire some vocal support. It was no use. 'Had Chelsea gone one up it would have killed the atmosphere,' admits Carragher. 'But instead, never mind the start of the game, even in the warm-up the noise reminded everybody of all the times when you had to get in an hour before the match. They all wanted to get in and absorb that atmosphere by going as early as possible. And then to get the goal that early! Then the mood during the last twenty minutes was just pure tension, everything played on the edge of our box before those scenes at the end. Everything had come together to beat Chelsea.'

One of the banners that night read: 'Make Us Dream'. But the team didn't need to dream; they already believed. The wave of confidence and sound overwhelmed several Chelsea players, who were still trying to clear their heads when Luis García's fourth-minute strike sent the Kop into pandemonium. Their roar exceeded even the crescendo that had welcomed the teams into the stadium. Milan Baroš had raced on to Steven Gerrard's lofted pass only to be felled by Chelsea goalkeeper Petr Cech. The referee chose not to blow for a penalty, and Luis García prodded the loose ball over the line before William Gallas could clear it. Or did he? Rick Parry, for one, is convinced: 'I think a lot of the stuff in the media, those simulations, were rubbish. Gallas' foot was over the line and in the newspapers you had it a foot the other side of the line. Where did they get that? But at the end of the day it doesn't matter.'

After the goal, Liverpool produced a magnificent defensive performance, led as ever by Jamie Carragher, and by Didi Hamann, who was everywhere in midfield. Mourinho, giving tactical instructions from the touchline, tried and failed to find a way through the ring of steel which protected the Liverpool goal. Dudek had to make only one save in the entire two-leg tie.

Benítez, who spent more time on his feet than in his seat, knew his players could not hear most of his instructions. So, for once, his preference for understatement disappeared amid a flurry of passionate gesturing. This wasn't a man who had lost his cool. In fact, it was the complete opposite: he was focusing on his job and had to find a way to overcome the noise of the Kop. 'In the madness of it all, I knew that they couldn't hear me properly,' he says with a smile. 'In that situation you need to know the players can understand you. You can use different signals, or sometimes you talk with an individual player and pass on a message. I remember one moment towards the end of the match when I saw Nuñez wandering up his side of the pitch while, on the other wing, we were fighting to win the ball back. I wanted him to come in much tighter to offer support to the guys who were trying to keep the ball. I literally tried everything – shouting, screaming, waving my arms, yelling at other players to pass him the message – but to this day Nuñez doesn't know what I was trying to communicate to him against that tide of noise.'

The fans had changed their chant from 'We've only won it four times' to 'We're gonna win it five times', but the six minutes of injury time demanded by referee Lubos Michel were not well received. Anfield's edginess multiplied, and during that period there was one moment when the Kop held its collective breath: Eidur Gudjohnsen wasted a golden chance in the very last minute by shooting wide from only a couple of yards out. In the Kop, there was a sense of justice done that Gudjohnsen was Chelsea's villain that night after he'd got Xabi Alonso booked in the first leg. 'Ah, it went wide, I thought,' Rafa remembers, with the same calm with which you might say, 'Ah, the kettle's boiled.' 'I didn't have time to get nervous, it happened too fast. After that, Anfield went crazy.'

The noise was like Concorde taking off. The celebrations had an air of madness about them. There were cheers for the heroic performance and tears for those who hadn't been there to see it. Many, many fans on the Kop that night must have thought of the friends they'd lost at Hillsborough. Even Roman Abramovich was seen smiling and clapping in tandem with the ecstatic Liverpool fans. 'You'll Never Walk Alone' and 'The Fields of Anfield Road' were sung; 'We Shall Not Be Moved' was chanted; and, through the PA system, the police finally had to beg the fans to go home. Gradually people realised they had not just witnessed a victory against Chelsea: it dawned on them that, twenty years on from Heysel, they were in another European Cup final.

Michael Robinson could not control his feelings, either. 'People in Spain have talked a lot about the shout of "*Yes*" which I let out when the referee blew the final whistle, but I felt incredibly moved that they were going through to the final. When the transmission stopped, Carlos started to applaud and told me that I was crying!'

'I had twenty Spanish friends who came to the game, and they were amazed by the atmosphere,' says Rafa. 'I read the Spanish newspapers and saw the talk in the Spanish chat-rooms on the internet. People were writing about what a remarkable occasion it was, one they will never forget.'

The conviction at Melwood since the Juventus tie had been justified: the team knew how to behave in Europe and they deserved to be in the final. 'I'm convinced that ultimately we were European champions because of our own merit,' claims Benítez. 'If you do a proper review of the competition, you'll see that a terrific team beat some great clubs and did so deservedly. It's possible that we might have drawn the home game against Chelsea 1–1 and that would have prevented us getting to the final – but it would have been a miscarriage of justice. In those last twenty minutes it was a hell of a tough job to keep Chelsea away from our penalty area but you could see that we reduced them to doing something they hadn't done all season: hitting the ball long. That is a direct style of football that doesn't really suit Chelsea.'

The contest between Liverpool and Chelsea prompts an interesting conundrum. What would have happened if, as had been eminently possible during the summer of 2004, Rafa had gone to

Chelsea and Mourinho had gone to Liverpool? Chris Bascombe suggests an anwer: 'I'll tell you what would have happened. Liverpool would have been in the same position in the league and Chelsea would have won both the league and the European Cup. If Benítez had been in charge of Chelsea in that semi-final, they would have come up with something different in a hundred and eighty minutes to change the game.'

That tactical acumen would come to the fore again three weeks later in the Atatürk Stadium. In a strategic shuffle of his pack, Rafa Benítez would turn the game on its head.

(11)

SIX UNFORGETTABLE MINUTES

I've Never Seen Rafa Jumping Up and Down

Nothing's new in a game of football. All the moves, the passes and the tackles have been seen before. However, there is an infinite number of permutations of how those individual elements coalesce to make a match. And every now and again we are privileged to witness a succession of incidents that raises a great sport to the level of a sublime experience. On that night in Istanbul, Rafa Benítez was responsible for conjuring up just such an occasion for his team's supporters through his half-time intervention. Amazingly, it was the second time he'd managed it in his short managerial career.

Without Valencia's transformation in an exemplary second half against Espanyol in the Montjuic stadium in 2001, Benítez probably would have been sacked and could well have been forced out of coaching for ever. He would not have won two La Liga titles and one UEFA Cup with Valencia. Nor would he have been the Liverpool manager during that incredible 2004–05 season. The fixture took place in December, midway through his first season with the Spanish club. The league match against Espanyol was going terribly: the Catalans led 2–0 and the game was on course to become Benítez's sixth successive match without a win. Valencia had slipped to three points behind Alavés, the surprise league leaders after sixteen matches played, and in the VIP seats the travelling board of directors were talking of axing Benítez after 'six disappointing months in the job'.

'At half time that night I swapped Pablo Aimar for our striker, Salva Ballesta, and the system changed to 4-3-1-2,' explains Benítez. 'But the success of these types of changes depends on the type of players you have, and it does not always work out well. People have asked me a thousand times what I said at half time and the truth is that I did not say anything particularly special. Mostly I showed them the tactical way to turn things around.' Valencia won the match 2–3 with three goals in seven minutes. 'As is normally the case in such dramatic turnarounds, the goals came in a remarkably short space of time: before the other team can assimilate what's going on and before they can shake off the shock and react appropriately,' says Rafa.

José Manuel Ochotorena's wife and the unswervingly faithful fans clung to a faint hope of victory at half time in Istanbul, but the bookmakers, rather more pragmatically, were offering odds of 350–1 against Liverpool pulling off a win. For Benítez, the task was clear: move the ball quickly while avoiding more damage from Kaká, and score at least three goals. Understandably, not everyone watching the match thought that bringing on Hamann was the best way to achieve this; after all, he is a defensive midfielder and Liverpool needed goals. Putting three across the back, having Smicer as a right wing-back and Luis García behind Baroš were the other tactical changes. The substituted Finnan, for one, muttered about Benítez's decision and bemoaned his bad luck as he got changed.

As they usually do, the players donned fresh kits at half time, but on this occasion they seemed to have acquired a new mood, too. As they trotted out for the second half, the dominant sound – 'You'll Never Walk Alone', sung with increasing conviction – began to inspire them even more. When Gerrard appeared, three-quarters of the Atatürk Stadium welcomed its hero with a roar that paid no heed to the scoreline. The fans were shaking off their frustration in song, but truly in order to believe in the impossible comeback they needed the players to lend a hand. 'The team went back out with conviction, believing that the scoreline was not fair and that, above all, they owed something to the fans,' explains Benítez.

'We had started singing "You'll Never Walk Alone" through pure pride,' says Liverpool fan Matt Barragan. 'I went to Istanbul with my fifteen-year-old and nine-year-old kids, and they had spent the half time crying. The chant was half-hearted, we were tired, some had got up at three the previous morning, but during the last few choruses the sound became louder and louder.'

From the first moments of the second half, Benítez's players appeared much more decisive. They started to enjoy themselves, to pass the ball with vision and efficacy, and, most importantly, to deny Milan possession. Nobody was 'hiding', and an immediately obvious change of approach by Milan handed Liverpool a crucial advantage. That's how Xabi Alonso views it anyway: 'They made changes, too. Milan sat back and suddenly they weren't tight on us. In the first half they'd chased the game but after the break they stopped. That allowed us space and time on the ball so we immediately felt more comfortable. I had a chance – a shot from outside the box – which I think grazed the right-hand post. Suddenly we were doing and sensing things which had been denied us throughout the first half.'

Gennaro Gattuso's take on those first few minutes after the break suggests Xabi Alonso's opinion was shared in the Milan camp: 'You could see, with the change of Hamann, that Benítez had found the weakness of his side. Their system changed. All of a sudden we could not find Kaká with our passes and their team became more confident and compact. Their coach has to be congratulated for blunting our attack.'

Nevertheless, the final could still have been put permanently beyond Liverpool's grasp. Just before Alonso's shot, Dudek blundered as he failed to gather a bouncing Cafú cross at his left-hand post, and the loose ball narrowly evaded Crespo. Four minutes later, seven since the restart, Shevchenko came close to scoring from a free kick with a low, stinging effort. Dudek, though, made amends for his earlier error with a stunning full-stretch save to tip away the shot. 'The free-kick save from Shevchenko at the start of the second half was just as important as anything else I did in the match,' the keeper remembers. 'I saw it late and just had time to stick out a hand. Had there been a fourth goal at that stage, I don't think there would have been penalties.'

In the fifty-fourth minute, 'Stevie Gerrard's goal gave us breathing space,' says Xabi Alonso, sounding as phlegmatic as his manager. Relief surged through the men in red. At 3–1, the scoreline was psychologically less crushing; the game was suddenly on a more equal footing and it no longer seemed that luck had totally turned its back on Liverpool.

The move leading up to the goal didn't initially appear to pose too much danger: Riise's cross was headed goalwards by Gerrard, but from fully twelve yards out. The fans at the far end of the stadium needed a second or two to realise that it had beaten Dida. Joyful comprehension finally dawned at the sight of their captain, with the weight of 'humiliation' lifted from his shoulders, immediately rallying his troops in search of the miracle that now seemed possible. He appealed to the travelling Kop with a manic wave of both arms. Contrary to the legend that has already taken root, the first minutes of the second half, after the strains of 'You'll Never Walk Alone' had died down, were quiet at the Atatürk, so Gerrard's gesture was a demand to stoke up the atmosphere to white-hot intensity. He knew that Liverpool needed that to build their momentum; the fans understood and immediately responded. Suddenly the stadium was full of people with a wide-eyed, 'definitely maybe' optimism. Now they were producing a deafening noise.

Behind Dida's goal, there was utter silence. 'We never expected what was about to happen,' says Gattuso. 'The match was finished, the game had died already! It was inevitable that many of our players thought that. If you remember, there was a chance for Shevchenko early in the second half, saved by Dudek, so that told us that the match was going to continue the same way it had finished before the break. We certainly didn't think a disaster was on its way when

Gerrard scored the first goal. We didn't worry. It was still 3–1 then, no? We thought, "Any second now we can score again."'

The first Liverpool goal, though, was crucial. It signalled the start of a hectic period in which Liverpool looked unstoppable as they surged forward while Milan seemed inundated and apparently mystified. Just nine minutes had passed since the beginning of the second half and Liverpool were right back in the game.

It had all started with a long pass from Paolo Maldini looking for Andrea Pirlo deep in the Liverpool half which had been intercepted by Riise. The Norwegian played it back to Gerrard, who was on the edge of the Liverpool box. Xabi Alonso received the ball in the middle of the park, first looked to move possession to the right but then swivelled and pushed it out to Riise who was overlapping on the left. His first cross rebounded back to him off Cafú; the second landed square on the head of the Liverpool captain. Remarkably, this was Liverpool's only headed goal of that entire European campaign.

If anyone else (with the possible exception of Carragher) had scored the goal, the symbolism would not have been so great. The impact and momentum for players and fans would not have been so powerful. Gerrard's form had oscillated all season, affected by confusion over his future, his doubts over where 'his' club was going, the demands of the fans and his fierce allegiance to the city. But his unwillingness to accept the apparently inevitable had made him indispensable against Olympiakos, against Chelsea and now, on this turbulent Turkish night, against Milan. He had torn into the Italians from the first minute of the second half and now his determination was keeping his team alive, propelling them into the next few vital minutes. 'Steven Gerrard was everywhere. He was not going to be shoved off the stage. He first gave us the tempo of the game, the direction to go in and then he scored,' says Djimi Traore. 'After the first goal we started to believe. It was a lift to us and to the supporters, the key to what was to come.'

'Lets have it!' Lee Marten remembers thinking when he saw the captain's windmilling arms. But that belief which was also now coursing through the players, took a while to reach the directors' box, high up in the stand. Chairman David Moores was merely reflecting: 'Well, that's a bit of pride back.'

Two minutes later, Kaká was casually straightening his socks. Xabi Alonso, whom the Brazilian was meant to be marking, made himself available for the ball, which duly arrived from Riise. The Spaniard then slotted a pass precisely to Didi Hamann, even though Shevchenko had noticed that Kaká was otherwise occupied and tried to intercede. After one touch, Hamann fed Smicer, who had been screaming for the ball. The Czech controlled it deftly, then unleashed a low, perfectly placed shot from twenty-five yards. Dida was only able to palm it into the net close to his right-hand post. Smicer ran towards the Liverpool bench, apparently unable to comprehend the enormity of what he'd just done. His roar seemed to express two simultaneous thoughts: 'Is this *really* happening?'; and 'Is it really *me* who is helping to make it happen?' 'I am not a big shooter, but I felt I had to try something because there was no other option when I got the ball,' he says now. 'I hit it as hard as I could; my aim was to hit the target. When the ball went in, it was a great moment. I didn't know what to do.'

Smicer, a much better footballer than his time at Anfield suggests, and being used in a new position which required so much effort to adapt to that it caused his alarming cramp late in the game, had already been told by Benítez that his contract would not be renewed. He knew he was playing his last match for Liverpool, so this was his final opportunity to prove his worth to the club's fans. During his darkest days, Smicer had sunk to proclaiming privately, without a trace of irony, that he was not much use at football. The goal provided his redemption. The Czech already felt as if he had won, which is why he celebrated the goal like a winner, even though the scoreboard told a different story. If you still need a goal just to level the scores, you don't usually run off wildly, arms outstretched, fists clenched. But in Istanbul, Vladimir Smicer was playing two games that night.

Between the first and the second Liverpool goals there were two lasting images: Ancelotti, eyes wide as saucers, chewing his gum three times faster than when he'd come out of the dressing room after the break; and Kaká undoing the cord that had been holding up his sock while Liverpool built the move for Smicer's goal. The Milan coach was unable to respond to the changes in scoreline. And Kaká's nonchalance indicated that the Milan team had not yet grasped the significance of Gerrard scoring so early in the second half. By the way, Kaká's sock was never fixed.

In the massed Milan ranks behind Dida's goal, there was still silence and a lack of comprehension, disbelief. The smiles had gone; nobody was sending jubilant text messages as they had been for the previous half hour. In the rest of the stadium, bedlam and hope. David Moores explains succinctly: 'Vladi adds one more and you think, "Hang on ..."' Phil Thompson had started a bizarre goal celebration – tapping, not punching, the glass of the Sky Sports studio at the Atatürk as if he needed to break the barrier between himself and the fans. 'Second half starts, Gerrard goal, I'm up out of my chair and my arms are in the air,' he says. 'When Vladi scored the second goal, the look on his face, we are in this for good! Now I'm up banging on the window. No sound at all when it was broadcast at the end of the ninety minutes by Sky. We couldn't have any sound 'cause my language was so dreadful.'

Pako Ayestarán remembers, 'We scored our first goal and the guys started to believe. When the second went in, the faces of the Milan players were almost beyond description. They were totally out of the game at that point and didn't know how or why. They looked at each other as if to say, "what's going on?"'

'Rafa always says when you concede a goal, you are disorientated and groggy, like a boxer who's been hit by a sucker punch. If you concede a second, then you're down on the canvas, but you can still get up. But by the third, you can't get up again. We scored once, then twice, and while they were still reeling we thumped them again.'

'You could have made a short silent movie out of the faces of the

Italian players during those six minutes,' recalls referee Mejuto González in wonderment.

'The first goal gave us hope; the second, belief. There was still half an hour to go,' concludes Jamie Carragher.

In the fifty-ninth minute, Gerrard again surged into the box and Gennaro Gattuso clipped him. Cast-iron penalty. 'We had Gerrard raiding with aggression,' remembers Phil Thompson. 'If you see him coming at you, twelve stone of muscle, charging at you, you'd better move away. He was running and making headway in the forward position and that changed the course of the game.'

After Carragher had spotted Milan Baroš running across the edge of the box, he had given him the ball with a neat pass. Nesta had tracked the Czech but on his turn Baroš saw Gerrard, who was sprinting forward and had stolen a couple yards on his marker Gattuso. Baroš sent the ball with a first-time touch, almost a back heel, into the skipper's path. Gerrard collected the ball. Gattuso, trying to make up ground, tapped the Englishman's ankle when he was about to shoot and Gerrard crashed in the box. Mejuto González didn't book Gattuso but pointed to the spot. Carragher wanted more punitive action: 'I started to make gestures towards Nesta. Poor lad, I was trying to get the wrong man sent off! I only realised when I saw the video.'

Xabi Alonso stepped forward to take the penalty. 'I wasn't the only option. The boss has a list of penalty takers and my name was on it. He likes to have the most confident one from that list taking it. I just decided to grab the ball.'

But at that point Carragher had it: 'Luis García tried to take if off me, and I thought, "No, you're not taking it." I wanted Alonso to take it: he is a greater passer of the ball, a great striker of the ball.'

In spite of his instinctive desire to take the spot kick, Xabi Alonso was still shaky: 'I was tense, but being nervous is only natural. You can experience the tension in different ways: it can throw you completely or it can help you focus. It was the latter for me. Strangely, although I was nervous, I was also relaxed.' That came from confidence in how his team was now playing: 'I knew that we could score again, even if I missed it,' he admits.

Once the referee had waved away Milan's protests and Xabi Alonso had placed the ball on the spot, the clock had ticked on and we were in the sixtieth minute. Mejuto González blew his whistle, Xabi Alonso ran up and struck the ball sweetly and . . . Dida guessed right and saved it. Xabi Alonso had struck the ball well out and the keeper had dived full-length to produce a brilliant save. For all of half a second the Liverpool fans despaired. But then: 'After hitting the ball I didn't stop. I didn't put my hands on my head. I reacted quickly. I was ready for the rebound.' The ball went to Xabi Alonso's left, he got there before Dida or any defender and he blasted the ball high into the net. Xabi Alonso had hit the penalty with his right boot and the rebound with his left. The fact that he could do so gave him that crucial split second to finish the job. That was the day, as Jorge Valdano later wrote in a Spanish newspaper, that the 22-year-old 'became a man' – he will never face a 'first' penalty in a major final, nor have to 'miss' it for the first time. 'Football is a collection of moments and that was an important one, one that makes you grow, that tests you,' Xabi Alonso says. 'It was another step, another experience.' That penalty also taught him one of the few things that escaped the rigorous control of Benítez – that Dida is stronger to his right and tends to dive that way. José Manuel Ochotorena and a couple of the players noted that it might be an idea to place any future penalties to the Brazilian's left.

The world had just witnessed probably the most incredible six minutes in footballing history, about the time it would take you to shave, wash the dishes, read a newspaper article or send an email. To watch a Bugs Bunny cartoon. To cook and eat a fried egg or to boil two successively. From putting a pre-cooked meal in the microwave over to the second the bell rings and the dinner has to be taken out. It's how long people spend choosing from the menu at the restaurant. The longest anyone could endure a Chinese opera.

It's enough to make a cuppa, add and stir the sugar and then sit down to drink it. Put an advert break in and when you come back to the game everything's changed.

At the start of this chapter, Dudek saved with the palm of his hand a dangerous Shevchenko free kick and, by the time it takes to reach this paragraph, Liverpool had scored three goals. Have a look at your watch. It's true.

'I didn't celebrate the first two because we were still getting beat,' says Carragher. 'When the third went in, though ... I had seen Stevie running through and I just knew something was going to happen: he was either going to get clipped or he was going to score.' Didi Hamann could only shake his head in disbelief: 'This is not for real,' he heard himself saying. 'After the first goal, I knew we were going to score again,' he adds now. 'But when the third goal arrived I was shocked, surprised mostly. I looked at the clock and it wasn't fifteen minutes left, but a whole half an hour! We had to decide if we wanted to go for the fourth or be cautious. We went for the latter.'

Gattuso thought something similar. 'This is not happening, this is a dream,' I was muttering. 'We gifted the match to Liverpool. They obviously punished every mistake we made, but without those mistakes, the match was ours. None of us said a word. Or rather, nothing was said with words: the eyes were doing the talking. It's true you cannot change anything from the bench in six minutes; I completely agree with that. But maybe there were other things that could have been done to avoid that situation.'

In Chicago, it was around 2 p.m. and Sammy Lee was being hugged and congratulated by the England staff. John Aldridge screamed into his Radio City microphone like a man possessed. Michael Robinson threw his arms aloft and almost hit the roof of the television cabin. Phil Thompson was hammering on the window again.

As Xabi Alonso followed up to score, the entire Liverpool section of fans appeared to be impersonating demented trampolinists. Their adrenalin buzz was massive and spontaneous joy erupted throughout the stands. Spectacles flew uncontrollably from faces and disappeared, as kisses and hugs were exchanged between grown men. In the press seats, nobody was neutral any more: everyone had to line up with one side or the other. At the Milan end, fans put their heads in their hands and could not speak, let alone sing, for minutes.

Rick Parry admits, 'Yep, I hugged people I didn't even know.' David Moores, by then, was just another fan: 'When Xabi scored I was jumping around the Royal Box.' The Liverpool chairman was relishing the moment. Success always feels better when it comes after a long period of uncertainty; on this occasion, after eighteen months of constant pressure over the lack of fresh investment and Premiership underachievement when Moores himself had been forced to consider his position.

The cool reaction of Rafa Benítez to Xabi Alonso's goal (a quick hug with Ayestarán and some subdued back-slapping) was typical of the man. He also found time to rage at the fourth official because he felt that Gattuso deserved his marching orders. The boss's celebration, such as it was, came as no surprise to Pako Ayestarán, the man who knows him best. 'I remember when we went to Málaga with Valencia and a victory there confirmed us as league champions. Ayala scored with a header and Benítez came up to me to tell me the tactical situation on the pitch, while I marked down the circumstances of the goal in the notebook. People asked me afterwards, "How can you be almost champions of the league and, instead of jumping up and down, you are both talking about the move you've just seen as if it were any old game?" Well, I've never seen Rafa jumping up and down. The supporters can let themselves be carried away by emotion but a coach never should.'

The Liverpool comeback was kickstarted by the tactical corrections made by Benítez. Milan had been depending too much on Kaká, and Hamann had managed to snuff him out. As the minutes ticked by, Liverpool were transformed: Carragher led by example, Traore no longer seemed to be the player who had been so easy to beat in the first half, Hyypia felt more protected, Smicer ran like he'd never run before, Xabi Alonso passed the ball with conviction. The team moved like a sweetly played accordion – in synchronised waves.

'In the first half we ran a lot without putting them under too much pressure,' says Xabi Alonso. 'In the second half we still ran a lot, but the pressure was much more orderly and effective.'

The Italians had thought that the match was over at 3–0 and had looked forward to enjoying a comfortable second half, and that complacency had helped Liverpool, as Benítez recognises: 'We needed to attack and it happened that they let us do that. We scored a goal and started to look confident all over the pitch. When a team loses control of a match, it can take ten or fifteen minutes to get it back. But while they are recharging their batteries anything can happen ... or nothing. In this case we ended up scoring two more goals. There are no easy explanations, particularly when we are talking about an Italian team who are normally experts in the art of defending.'

The next day, Ancelotti was accused of having frozen, of not having reacted. But can you really change the direction of a match in just six minutes? Fabio Capello and Cesare Prandelli, the Fiorentino coach, have both publicly defended Ancelotti. A poll taken of Italian coaches reveals that not one of them would have done anything differently. Why change things when you are winning? And both before and after those six minutes, Milan held the initiative and were creating more than enough chances to win the match. If Ancelotti couldn't locate and eradicate the problem, perhaps that was because there wasn't one. Except for during those six minutes.

'Maybe we should never have gone 3–0 up. Maybe it was just too good to be true,' admits Hernán Crespo. 'Maybe it just wasn't to be. When things like this happen, you can usually go back and find where things went wrong, but I don't see what we did wrong. We still created chances after 3–3. What more could we have asked for? All I can think was that there was some inexplicable black-out for those six minutes.' Massimo Ambrosini can also offer no explanation, save for: 'We lost concentration, and we were unlucky. Three times we made mistakes and three times they scored.'

Would Benítez have done something if he had been on the Milan bench that night? 'Milan did the correct things,' he claims. 'Once the storm had passed they analysed our weak points and reacted accordingly. They put Serginho on because they realised we had a weak spot on that wing. They had to open up the game and take advantage of our tiredness, and they did it.'

'We had played, only minutes earlier, one of the best games of the season,' Ancelotti reflects now. 'The best first half of the season was the one we played against Liverpool. But when you concede some goals it means something has gone wrong. It means you have made big or small mistakes. We started the second half in the right way and then something went wrong. But we paid an exaggerated price for every single mistake we made. There is no proper explanation and if you concede three goals in six minutes you don't have time to make changes. It was impossible to do something immediately. This team was more experienced than the one that won the competition in 2003. They had been in similar situations. But there is a huge difference between this defeat and the 4–0 against Deportivo in 2004. Then, we started and ended the match badly. In Turkey, we started and ended very well indeed.'

But the verdict of the Italian sporting press has been very different. Once again the accusation has been levelled at Milan that they seem to be experts at snatching defeat from the jaws of victory. As Ancelotti well remembers, they were beaten by Deportivo La Coruña in the quarter-finals of the Champions League in spite of holding a 4–1 advantage after the first leg in Italy. Deportivo's sensational 4–0 thumping of Milan at the Riazor Stadium was the biggest shock of that year's competition, not just because the Italians were the defending champions, but because they had shown no defensive frailty all season. While Ancelotti is right to say that the Istanbul match and the night in La Coruña were very different, it is worth pointing out that there were some startling similarities, too. In both games, Milan's opponents punished every mistake and pounced on every opportunity. And in both, Milan perhaps contributed to their own downfall by refusing to play in the 'typical' Italian way and shutting up shop to defend a lead.

But you do not need to go that far back to find the same shortcomings in the Italian side. Admittedly, en route to Istanbul, they'd despatched some quality opposition, including Manchester United and their eternal rivals Internazionale (who were thrashed 5–0 on aggregate). But in the semis they'd met PSV Eindhoven and it was a different story. Milan won 2–0 in the San Siro, but in Holland for the second leg PSV led 3–0 and only an injury-time goal from Ambrosini saw Milan scrape into the final. On top of that disappointing performance, they had recently drawn in Serie A with lowly Lecce and lost at home to Juventus, which virtually guaranteed that the title would be heading back to Turin.

Some would say Ancelotti's Milan had found the formula for success. After all, they'd finished in the top three of Serie A in three consecutive seasons (winning it in 2004) and reached two European Cup finals (winning it in 2003). But some questions just wouldn't go away after Istanbul. How could Milan lose the Scudetto and the Champions League final, the season's two main targets, against technically inferior teams, and certainly against squads that were smaller and less talented? Why has Ancelotti's reign been characterised by the sublime *and* the ridiculous? Did they pay for overconfidence both domestically and in Europe? Is the pressure coming from owner Silvio Berlusconi, who wants the team to play offensive football and use two forwards no matter what the circumstances, affecting Ancelotti's decision-making? Was that why the coach didn't shut up shop in the second half in Istanbul?

Gattuso spoke like a wounded man shortly after the game: 'We have a winning mentality at Milan but it does cause us problems in Europe and may need changing. We need to attack by using our heads a little more than we have done. Milan need to find a way to go on the offensive without giving so much away defensively. We know that the political people at Milan like an attacking outfit, but our players need to know that it is not all about attack and that sometimes it is necessary to work hard defensively. With hindsight, I can see now we were affected by fear after Liverpool made it 3–1. That shouldn't have happened. Giovanni Trapattoni, when he was Italy coach, was labelled defensive, but trying to defend a result is sometimes the right thing to do.'

In the sixty-third minute, 'Riise had a shot which the keeper saved,' Carragher remembers. 'To be honest, when the third one went in and after that chance, I thought for a few minutes we would win it in normal time. But then I think they obviously realised the seriousness of the situation and came back stronger. In fact, all I was worried about for the last twenty minutes was that we did not do anything stupid again.'

Soon Liverpool were on the back foot again. A couple of minutes after the Riise chance, Dudek fluffed a Kaká cross. The ball fell to Shevchenko and his shot was cleared off the line by Traore. Hyypia wrapped an arm around Dudek's shoulder, but, to Carragher, that seemed overly sympathetic: 'Come *on*!' he shouted at the keeper.

The game had taken another turn, but it wasn't going to change again until 120 minutes had been played. Milan were winning the ball back and Liverpool's energy seemed spent. 'After scoring the three goals, we felt we could concede one ourselves, so we decided not to take too many risks and slowed things down,' admits Djimi Traore. It was time to defend. At the time, Traore thought he was probably playing his last match for Liverpool. If he'd been substituted at half time after his clumsy first-half performance, he may well have been proved right in that assumption. But out of the night's ultimate success came a new contract. And there was yet more courage to come from him in extra time.

Pako Ayestarán might have noted in his book that Dudek had committed another error; or possibly that Traore's improvement in the second half mirrored his season. The assistant manager's job, as ever, was to identify positive and negative features of both

Liverpool and their opponents, for analysis later when the dust had settled. At this stage of a match, he would usually have scribbled thirty or forty points. In the Atatürk, he'd come up with just three: 'In the first half, Milan's superiority was so clear and what we were doing badly was also so clear that there was not much to write down. And then I realised that it was the last match of the season, so we wouldn't get much from anything I did write down because there weren't any "next few matches" for a couple of months. As soon as the second half started I was aware that the game had become an emotional rollercoaster. I put my files down on the ground and prepared myself to experience some moments of incredible excitement.'

In the eighty-fifth minute, Benítez made his final substitution, with Djibril Cissé replacing Milan Baroš. For the opposition, Jon Dahl Tomasson and Serginho came on, too, with Crespo and Seedorf making way. That demanded a quick reaction from Rafa, who did not need to look too closely at his players to see which of them was physically able to move to right-back and counter the threat posed by the Brazilian winger. It had to be Gerrard, so the skipper was moved to his most defensive position yet. 'Stevie can play two matches in a row if he wants to,' claims his coach.

The whistle blew after ninety-two minutes, so the game became the thirteenth in European Cup final history to go into extra time. The message from Benítez was clear: 'Keep the ball, we're shattered.'

(12)

TIRED LEGS AT EXTRA TIME

I Suppose I Could Always Retire After That Save

'Before and during extra time I grabbed a few words with Xabi Alonso and Luis Garcia but very few others,' says Rafa Benítez. 'I wanted to see how they were and underline to them that the priority was to keep possession of the ball. I told them to stay patient so that we could try to take advantage of a dead-ball situation, if it came along, and, above all, to use the speed of Djibril Cissé.'

These simple instructions were being relayed from the coaching staff to the players as aching muscles were being massaged and cajoled back into life. They had to give another thirty minutes of effort. As his team-mates sat sprawled on the Atatürk turf, Steven Gerrard was waiting, champing at the bit in the centre circle, for the moment when everyone else got to their feet and battle recommenced. With the notable exception of the captain, Liverpool's players were running dangerously low on petrol.

Too often when the word 'experienced' is used about a footballer, it is simply a euphemism for 'old'. The Milan players' genuine greater experience of games at this level translated into something much more important at that moment: the intelligent rationing of their adrenalin and strength. Milan may have been an older team than Liverpool, but during extra time they played with greater freshness and vitality. After the shockingly dreadful impact of those momentous six minutes in the second half, the Italians had simply got back to work. They reasserted their control of the ball and almost totally dominated the game. Liverpool had already learned that it is more tiring to be on the back foot and defend constantly, and the lesson was about to become much tougher. It did not help that Rafa's team's efforts up to that point had been close to superhuman. That's the only way to explain the fact that, despite all fitness and medical checks that indicated the squad was in great physical shape, at least four players were hamstrung by their chronic fatigue in extra time.

In the fourth minute, Pirlo sent a direct free kick just over the bar. Liverpool were already starting to lose the ball quickly, and Milan were playing well again, moving the ball around and waiting patiently for openings. 'We thought they would tire as the game went on,' Rick Parry admits. 'In fact, it was the other way round. Those first twenty minutes of the second half made *our* legs go'.

A little later, in a short tragi-comic scene, Dudek first almost stepped back across his own goal line as he clutched a cross from Pirlo and then sprinted five quick steps forward with the idea of initiating a rapid counter-attack. Seven exhausted team-mates were left trailing in his wake. The keeper literally had nobody to pass to.

Xabi Alonso admits that the team was finding it impossible to do the basic things that normally come as second nature to them: 'Many guys could feel their hamstrings and calf muscles ready to give way. So those of us who were fresher knew we couldn't go upfield to support any attacks. We knew it was imperative to stay and defend; to help those who were really suffering.' Right from the start of extra time the Liverpool players knew that all of their efforts had to be devoted to closing up at the back, because no one was in a fit state to make a long forward run to support Cissé and then track all the way back again. Which left one option: long balls to the Frenchman and hope against hope that the Italians didn't score.

Eleven minutes into extra time, Tomasson was inches away from connecting with Serginho's long cross. Like most of Milan's attacks, this one came from their left-hand side. But Gerrard, in his new position as right-back, was at least making life difficult for the Brazilian wide man. 'Stevie is a force of nature and he understood very quickly what was required at that point,' says Rafa.

In the rare, sweet moments when Liverpool had possession of the ball, Dudek would generally send it long and high in Cissé's direction. Hamann, Luis García, Gerrard and Traore all did exactly the same. 'We understood that we had to cope with the situation as it was, and somehow get through to penalties without losing another goal,' explains Traore. Smicer, who had played twenty minutes less football than most of his team-mates, started to cramp badly.

In the last minute of the first period of extra time, Shevchenko got on the end of Cafú's deep cross to the far post but volleyed the ball straight into Dudek's arms. Then the referee's whistle sounded. Just fifteen minutes left to survive. At that point, Gerrard crossed paths with the Ukrainian striker and wrapped an arm around his shoulder. Shevchenko's face reflected the disappointment of his last effort, and Gerrard asked him if he was OK. Shevchenko felt there was still a ray of hope, still some time to take the match back to where it had been for the first hour, to make it Milan's again. He had enough power left in his legs, and trusted his midfield quartet to get the ball to him. But he knew as well as anyone that time was running out. Before moving away, Gerrard wished him good luck for the rest of the match.

As the teams were changing ends and the players were grabbing some valuable seconds of treatment, Pako Ayestarán shared his thoughts with Benítez. He recalls: 'We were all desperately hanging on for penalties. The team was at dropping point – four or five of the lads were running purely because of the size of their hearts but without any energy. It's an even more dangerous position to be in if you don't have the ball because you are just running around in search of possession. That is a draining and demoralising process. But that's pretty much how things were for us in extra time. We simply didn't have the physical resources to score another goal.'

Five minutes into the second period. It was obvious that Milan were back on top, and, with ten long minutes remaining, Liverpool somehow needed to recapture the epic spirit they'd displayed earlier in the game. Jamie Carragher resolved to lead by example. After another searching cross into the six-yard box from Serginho, the centre-back threw himself into the path of the ball. Cramp spread like hot oil through his legs, preventing him from rising. A stretcher was offered but refused: he insisted on getting up and hobbling off the field for treatment on his own two feet. Limping back on, he immediately had to make another diving block from yet another cross from Serginho.

'A broken leg is painful, but it eases off,' says Carragher with a laugh. 'Cramp is *really* bad, though. You just don't know what you can do to get rid of it. Every movement you make seems to aggravate it. It's hard to explain if you've never had it. I got it in my groin and I was thinking, "I'm getting married in a couple of weeks and I've got cramp in my groin!" '

Seven minutes to go. Rui Costa, who had replaced Gattuso just two minutes earlier took a corner. The ball evaded everyone but whistled harmlessly past the far post. By this time, the statisticians tell us that Milan had had 64 per cent of ball possession in extra time. Rick Parry knew what that sort of superiority meant: 'There was only going to be one winner during extra time, and it was not going to be us.' A couple of minutes later, Pirlo's free kick was deflected off Luis García for another corner. 'Yes, we could easily have lost the final in extra time,' admits Pako Ayestarán.

Three minutes to go. The defining moment. The travelling Kop had started to sing. 'Liverpool, Liverpool' when suddenly Dudek made a spectacular double save from Shevchenko: first pushing away a powerful header at knee height, then somehow blocking the follow-up shot at point-blank range. Shevchenko seemed stunned, and staggered away from the goalmouth as the ball went out for a corner. He seemed to be looking for anyone who could tell him how he hadn't scored. 'I was sure I would score from a yard out,' he says now. 'I hit it hard, but perhaps that helped Dudek as it bounced off his arm and up instead of going past him or coming back to me. I could have taken that shot ten thousand times and all but one or two would go in. I bet that if you asked Dudek, he couldn't tell you how he managed to keep it out. There is no logical explanation to what happened.'

While Shevchenko had his face in his hands and his mouth gaping in disbelief, Dudek was sporting half a smile, his tongue out, his eyebrows raised, seeming to be asking, 'How did that happen, then?' Later he attempted to answer his unspoken question: 'I managed to save his header, but it was obvious that he was going to get to the rebound – and get there first. I just jumped up as quickly as I could and tried to make myself as big as possible. Fortunately, the ball hit my hands. All of a sudden it was flying high above the goal and I just thought, "That's impossible! How is it possible?" Our goalkeeping coach, Ochoto, asked me after the match how I had done it. I said to him, "If I knew, I'd tell you!" '

'Dudek positioned himself even before Shevchenko made contact with that great header,' reveals José Manuel Ochotorena. 'He automatically put his body in the only area of the goal where he could maximise the potential chance of getting to the ball. And he had his arms positioned correctly. He got his judgement right and parried it. It was about technical ability as well as pure instinct. But what you have to do next in that situation is concentrate on the rebound. You have to get back in the game immediately and occupy precisely the right position to block a follow-up. The body instinctively tends to go to ground even more when the save is near the goal line, and, if your body position is hunched low when the ball is struck, then the likelihood is that the ball will continue on its trajectory towards the back of the net. But if the keeper gets up and stands tall then he's like a wall. We worked really, really hard on these concepts with Dudek in training.

'The credit for the save needs to include the technical knowledge which Dudek and the coaches brought to the situation, but also, crucially, our insistence on him practising it over and over and over again all season. I like to work a great deal on one-on-one situations – things like close-range shots. And we insisted on repeating these a great deal during the season. But, apart from repetition, intuition and reflexes are also important.

'Third, the degree to which the striker rushes his follow-up chance is crucial. On this occasion, Shevchenko suffered because of his anxiety at burying the opportunity. The chance to score was burning so clearly in his mind that he evidently thought it was best to get his shot off as quickly as possible. So he once again put the ball back in the area where Dudek was. In retrospect, you can see that he had many more options as to where to put it. In that precise moment, psychology was important because Dudek was more calculating than Shevchenko. There was, of course, a degree of luck, but it also became a one-on-one duel between the two players, and the stronger man won because of speed of thought, reaction and training.'

Up in the directors' box, Rick Parry, realising the magnitude of the saves, thought immediately of Ochoto ('the coach nobody knows', according to some Liverpool journalists). 'You look at the posture which Dudek adopted, not once but twice, and you can see that came after a lot of work with his coach,' confirms the chief executive. 'The reaction after the first save would have been so often to dive backwards, but Dudek made himself big. That was, for me, a classic moment in terms of Rafa's people and their methods. Maybe I'm biased because I was a goalkeeper, but that save wasn't an accident, you know.'

On the edge of the six-yard box, Jamie Carragher watched the double save as if it were in slow motion. 'It was a great ball in. Jerzy saved the first one but then I was just waiting for the ball to hit the net. If it had, we'd still have been given credit for what we'd done – getting to the final and coming back from three down – but at the end of the day, we would still have lost. It was one of those moments you literally cannot believe. Credit to Jerzy, but it was a bad miss from Shevchenko.'

Immediately after the save, the centre-back snapped to attention, turned round and demanded that his team-mates get into the box and focus on defending the corner. Traore, next to Dudek at that point, still had his arms outstretched in disbelief. 'Everybody was confident in Jerzy after the Shevchenko save. I realised that if we didn't concede before the end, we really could win on penalties,' he says.

Didi Hamann was on the edge of the box watching Dudek's antics: 'The header was a good chance but to save that and to save the rebound as well . . . it should have been a goal. Penalties were going to be a bonus, it was hardly believable that we were in still with a chance to make it into penalties.'

Gerrard had been in front of Serginho when the Brazilian crossed the ball into the box: 'I thought it was going in. "That's that," I thought.' The skipper, like everybody else (except Riise, who unashamedly kissed Dudek's cheek), forgot to congratulate the Polish goalie at the time. 'It was a corner. Everybody was so tired and we were on autopilot,' Ochotorena remembers. 'As well as the gesture from Riise, Carragher stretched out his hand to touch Dudek's, but I don't think they even made contact. At the end of extra time, they all went to congratulate him for the save.' Many in the squad now say that Dudek's save made them think they were destined to win.

Having been on the ropes for half an hour, psychologically at least Liverpool were now winning on points. The Milan players were finally buckling under the weight of so many squandered chances. 'Liverpool were clearly tired,' recalls Gattuso, who by now was observing the drama from the bench. 'But at that point I was already thinking, "Maybe it is not our fate to win this." Then, when I saw Dudek's double save, the "maybe" disappeared from that thought! Seriously, I *knew* we were going to lose in the penalties.' Crespo admitted after the match that Dudek's heroics had been the moment 'we said goodbye to the cup'.

Pako Ayestarán watched it all in amazement. 'Dudek saved the first chance and we all imagined that Shevchenko would side-foot it in. But he hit it hard instead.' Up in the stands, in the Liverpool end, the fans reacted, as they had done all match, half a second later than everybody else. Everything – all the goals, the double save, Carragher's tackling, even the penalty shoot-out later – happened at the Milan fans' end. From a distance, once they realised what had happened, they savoured another 'Gudjohnsen moment'. 'I suppose I could always retire after that save,' reflects Dudek with a grin. 'It was, by far, the most important one in my entire life. My brother called me the next morning and said I needed to see the match because the save was the "hand of God". When I don't feel pressure, I can be the best in the world.'

Benítez, who knows that the way in which players handle pressure is as important as their technical ability, had already decided to sign a new keeper. Whatever happened that night, Dudek would almost certainly be surplus to requirements next season, and he knew it. 'I have heard other goalies linked with the club, but that is the nature of the game,' the Polish goalie said resignedly after the final. But Jerzy, who up to that point had had a mixed match, now knew that this was his night. At that point, he felt ten feet tall.

The double save virtually heralded the end of the game, which, in fact, finished four minutes later. In playing out those last, agonising minutes, Liverpool managed to cross the halfway line just twice.

The final whistle went and it was time for the Midweek Lottery. The football version of Russian roulette. The penalty shoot-out.

(13)

PENALTIES

Penalty Shoot-outs Are as Much About Psychology as They Are About Technique

Rafa Benítez had told a white lie when he had announced before the game that his team had not prepared for penalties. 'We *had* practised, but not systematically. It was really just at the end of the last training session because the players like taking them,' he admits now. He already knew that the night before the 1984 European Cup final in Rome, which Liverpool won on penalties, the guys on the list to take the spot kicks had missed every single one in training. That fact supported his instinct not to prepare specially for the ultimate scenario. 'I didn't believe that it was going to be vital. You can knock them in with ease in the training session but when you are standing there in front of goal with everyone watching you in a full stadium you can still be affected by the fear factor.' He had his own way of choosing the penalty takers: it was based on the way individual players had performed during the season.

As far back as the pre-season tour of the USA, his staff had noted down all the statistics regarding the way their players took penalties: the power and quality of the strike, where a player liked to place the ball, their level of confidence and so on. It was all there. Although in Istanbul he was limited to the eleven men who remained on the field at the end of extra time, his list could still be composed with just a minute's thought once he had cleared up one minor detail: who actually wanted to take them? Once he had his volunteers, he would use his stats to pick the five.

During the season, Gerrard, Hamann and Baroš had taken the spot kicks. Baroš was off the pitch, so the other two were the first and second names on the list. The captain was not going to hide, even though his responsibility might have been especially onerous: 'I was on the fifth penalty. The gaffer asked me if I wanted to take one and I said, "Of course." So he said I could take the fifth. I thought, "Thanks a lot for that, gaffer."'

Some players then made it clear they didn't feel up to it. 'Rafa asked Didi Hamann first,' Djimi Traore remembers. 'Then he asked me and I said, "Oh, no, I prefer to let other players take them."' The German midfielder was not scared: 'I nodded when he asked me. Two minutes later he said I would take the first one. I was not too unhappy – I thought, at least I can get mine out of the way before anybody else!' Luis García, on the other hand, asked to take one. In fact, he pleaded his case to Benítez until the coach finally agreed, after a fashion. 'You will be the sixth player up,' he told his enthusiastic midfielder. He would take one only if the scores were still level after the first five.

Xabi Alonso, of course, had missed one during the match, and although he demanded to have another go, Benítez believed that the miss might have affected the midfielder's self-belief. 'The boss asked me if I wanted a shot at one and I said yes,' he says. 'Then, a few moments later, I asked him which one I'd take, and he told me none of them. He said that, because Dida had saved my earlier one, it was better for me not to take another. Then Rafa explained to Luis that he could see he was tired and put him sixth on the list.'

Benítez explains: 'The main thing you have to know when it comes to a penalty situation is who is going to take them, and in what order. I choose players who feel sure, or who give me that sense of security, that they'll score. Finally, I put them in order from one to five, and beyond in case the scores are level after five. Hamann was going to take the first one, although neither he nor I knew at that time that he had a broken toe.' Rumour has it that the German's injury actually occurred during the post-match celebrations in the hotel – another false myth of the Istanbul final, says Hamann. 'I felt the injury during the match but never told anyone, I did not pay attention to it. I must have done it seven or eight minutes before the end of the game after landing awkwardly. The Liverpool doctor saw it after the match, it was quite bruised. It was, in fact, a stress fracture.' The German midfielder took a penalty with a broken toe.

Smicer was to be number four, even though he was so tired that he could feel the cramp coming on again. He was at, or beyond, his physical limit. 'He didn't share information like that with me at the time. I suppose it's the kind of thing you tell your mates later,' says a grimacing Benítez. 'You see, when I asked him if he was OK to take one, he said yes and told me that if he got cramp again then, given that he only had to run four or five metres, he'd be able to cope without any problem. His cramps were caused by tension, but he's a beautiful striker of the ball. Anyway, at last I had a list of seven or eight penalty takers and I made my decisions about the order based on the characteristics of each guy. The first and the last had to be players whom I could be certain of, so I put Hamann first and Gerrard fifth.'

'In a final, the penalties depend on the state of mind of the player and his nerve. The most important thing is to have players who are totally committed to taking them. I knew that a few of those whom I left out would have loved to take one. This is a positive thing because it underlines that I had a group of fearless players.'

Specifically, Benítez is talking about Luis García, who was very disappointed, and Carragher, who had also asked his boss if he could take one. 'The manager said to me, "Do you want to take one?" and I went, "Yeah!" He was just going round asking people, so I thought I must be taking one as I was one of the first people to say yes, but then the boss just said, "This is the order we're going in," and I wasn't one of them. I don't think he's got much confidence in me! I'll have to show him the videos from the League Cup, where I took some.'

A few minutes before the shoot-out, Jerzy Dudek spoke to both

José Manuel Ochotorena and Carragher. The goalkeeping coach has no end of statistics at his fingertips. He has to watch every penalty that's taken in the Premiership and note down where the player aimed for. 'We try to get as much information as possible on all our opponents: how they take corners and free kicks, who takes them, how they hit their penalties, all that kind of stuff. We had also gathered a lot of info about the Italian league, but we understood that you always have to count on the surprise factor. We had basic information on all the penalty takers – this guy prefers to put it to the keeper's right or at mid-height rather than down low, etc. Those details we knew.'

This accumulation of information obviously increases the chance of the keeper choosing correctly where, when and how high to dive. But for Ochoto, that's not enough. 'On the morning of the match, we had gone over all the relevant information we possessed. But I tried to explain to Dudek that, during the match, he had to allow himself to be guided by his intuition to a degree. It is difficult to prepare for penalties because you never know what the keeper has in his head. It is a psychological thing. I told Jerzy, "You have got the information and now all you have to do is be Dudek. Allow your own instincts to guide you, and above all do everything with self-belief." I noticed he was really buzzing with confidence after preventing Shevchenko from scoring with that double save.'

After the shoot-out, when the dust had settled, Dudek remarked with a wry smile that Benítez was evidently not, after all, perfect. Despite all his meticulous preparations, Rafa's team had correctly predicted only two of the five Milan penalty takers – Serginho and Pirlo. His cheeky comment was not really a criticism, but showed Dudek's desire to claim the credit he felt he deserved. Justifiably, he insisted on being hailed as a hero after the match. And he was right: even the best-prepared managers and the most well-drilled teams sometimes make mistakes.

Two days before the final, Ochotorena had realised that he didn't have with him the DVD of the penalty shoot-out from the 2003 Old

Trafford Champions League final that featured Milan and Juventus. On that occasion, Milan had won on penalties after a 0–0 draw. Dida had saved three that night and Milan still had 80 per cent of 2003's squad. That DVD simply had to be watched.

Ochotorena made urgent arrangements to acquire the footage. José Paredes, another Spaniard, a friend of Paco Herrera, specialises in providing all sorts of information about players, even from the most obscure leagues, in the form of statistics and DVDs. The deal was done and the DVD duly arrived from Spain at Liverpool's Istanbul hotel the day before the game. It was then closely studied by Dudek.

But Jamie Carragher's intervention had almost as much influence on Dudek's eventual strategy and tactics, and helped to produce his glorious saves. 'I was worried that Jerzy is too nice,' says Carragher. 'He's a really nice fella, and I just thought he'd stand in the goal being dead polite and nice. He's a top man, dead professional and all that, but whatever you wanna call it, gamesmanship, cheating or whatever … fuck it … he's got a European Cup-winner's medal now. I told him to do *anything* to put them off. He hadn't been booked, so kick the ball away and get booked if you like, just do anything to gain an advantage.'

In the course of his inspirational rant, Carragher reminded the Pole about Bruce Grobbelaar. 'I told Jerzy what Brucie did to put the Italians off in 1984. Whether it worked or not, I don't know, but I saw the way he kept squeezing the ball every time one of their players walked up to the penalty box. Maybe it did have an impact or maybe Jerzy didn't have a clue what I was talking about. He says he was a Liverpool fan when he joined, but they all say that when they come here, don't they?'

Harry Kewell realised Carragher was screaming like a man possessed and decided to escort Dudek away from the Scouser's torrent of advice. But the goalie had already taken note. 'He was shouting at me,' he remembers. 'I was thinking, "Just let me focus on it will you?" I was quietly confident, relaxed. There were thousands in the stands but I only cared about the ball. But on my way to the box, I took his advice and did things to put off the takers. I started to dance as well.'

Milan won the toss, so the penalties were going to be taken at the end that had witnessed all the goals, right in front of the Italian supporters. 'At that point, I saw the size of their goalie compared to Jerzy . . . Fuckin 'ell . . . He was some size, him!' says Carragher. But if the defender was experiencing a moment of doubt, Rafa Benítez was not. 'We were all grouped together and I wasn't sure about what would happen,' says Paco Herrera. 'At 3–1, I was convinced that we were going to draw. But I didn't want to go to penalties because I felt we were the less experienced team. Rafa told me, "Don't worry, we are going to win. Now that we have got to penalties, we are definitely going to win!" '

Benítez had picked up on an almost imperceptible, but nevertheless significant, psychological shift. His confidence might be described as something like 'good vibes', and this innate self-assurance was of course a factor, too, and was picked up by the players. In addition to the burgeoning poise in the Liverpool camp, he could simultaneously sense the loss of self-belief among the Milan players. Their anxious faces were now reflecting their appointment with what some of them felt was their destiny to lose.

Benítez's job was over for the time being; his preparatory work had been done. As Serginho started walking towards the penalty spot, Rafa retreated into the background to watch events unfold from a distance. There was nothing more he could do. Now he was powerless. The players got together on the halfway line, and linked arms to form a huddle – each transmitting what strength and support he could muster into the bodies and psyches of the others.

Dudek, now possessing intoxicating, supreme self-confidence, greeted Dida outside the area and ran towards the goal smiling. He then held up Milan's first spot kick by engaging the referee in an unintelligible conversation . . .

Milan's first penalty – Serginho misses

Carlo Ancelotti agrees with Benítez about the importance of mental strength: 'Penalty shoot-outs are as much about psychology as they are about technique' is the Italian's assessment. In the stands, Milan's fans were shaking their heads, incredulous at the turn of events. The Milan players felt the same. A sense of defeat ran through the team like the Black Death. In just eight minutes, Milan's three specialist penalty takers, Serginho, Pirlo and Shevchenko, would all miss.

Their Brazilian keeper looked tense, serious, stiff – definitely displaying the wrong body language. Dudek, by contrast, was dancing on the line, flapping his hands around, jumping right and left. Ochotorena is convinced that if a keeper moves while the penalty is being taken, he puts off the taker: 'Those jumps were confirmation that he was feeling good about making the stops. In the Carling Cup against Spurs, he also stopped a penalty after making similar movements – although not quite so dramatic.' Dudek guessed correctly and dived to his right, but Serginho sliced his shot and blazed the ball high and wide.

Liverpool's first penalty – Hamann scores (0–1)

Ochotorena knew that Dida had impressive stats when it came to penalty saves, but he'd chosen not to share that information with the players so as not to dent their confidence. After Serginho's gaffe, it was Didi Hamann's turn: 'I was definitely helped by Serginho's mistake. I was more relaxed and thought, "I just hope it goes in."' He was the most experienced man in the Liverpool camp, which is why Benítez nominated him to take their first penalty. He avoided eye contact with Dida, fixing his gaze on the ground. As he ran up he shimmied and then slotted the ball neatly into the corner. Dida could not have behaved more differently from how he had at Old Trafford. Two years on, he was robotic, too stationary and even had his arms down by his side. While Dudek was trying to make himself look as big as possible, Dida seemed to be trying to shrink.

Milan's second penalty – Pirlo misses (0–1)

Dudek squeezed the ball in his hands, and, by handing it to the Milan players as they approached the penalty spot, consciously tried to make himself seem to be bigger than his goal. Pirlo stuttered during his run-up and his effort was saved by Dudek, again diving to his right. Before the kick, Dudek had added some of Bruce Grobbelaar's 'spaghetti legs' movements to his repertoire. Perhaps more significant was his forward movement from the goal line – he was a metre away from it when he touched the ball with his right hand. 'At the time of the second penalty, I was more subdued in case they were recording my reactions,' Phil Thompson recalls. 'I looked at Richard Keys and he said, "They are going to take that one again. There is no way they can allow that." I could not believe it myself when the ref let it go.'

As the saying goes, 'What goes around comes around.' At Old Trafford, Dida had moved off his line three times. His antics had sparked a public debate about a law that, since 1997, has allowed goalies to move as much as they like, provided they stay on the goal line. Referees were reminded after that final what was allowed and what was not, which had provoked stricter scrutiny of the goalkeeper's forward movement. Dida's Old Trafford performance had aroused great interest in the goalkeeping fraternity, and imitations had become increasingly fashionable.

José Manuel Ochotorena did not include suggestions about moving off the line in his technical chats, but all goalies know that moving forward closes down the angle. Another thing that both staff and players know and do not need to say is that in a penalty shoot-out, the officials rarely ask for the kicks to be retaken. Dida had successfully pushed the rules to the limit at Old Trafford; this time it was Dudek. Bolstered by his success against Pirlo, he resolved to throw himself forward again for the rest of the penalties.

Liverpool's second penalty – Cissé scores (0–2)

The French international had scored from the penalty spot against Aston Villa in Liverpool's last game of the Premiership just ten days before. His countryman Traore looked at the sky and prayed, while Cissé kept his cool and sent Dida the wrong way with a side-footed effort. That night, Dida would deal with all the Liverpool penalties in exactly the same way (including Xabi Alonso's effort in normal time): every time he dived to his right. It was obvious by then that he was more confident going to that side, and this information was reiterated in the Liverpool camp during the shoot-out.

With a two-goal lead in the shoot-out, Liverpool had a huge advantage. In the stands, Liverpudlian anxieties were finally receding. 'Milan missed their first two penalties and we decided this must be the least nerve-racking shoot-out in history: we were very relaxed,' remembers Reds fan Lee Marten.

Milan's third penalty – Tomasson scores (1–2)

He had to. Milan's situation was already desperate. He blasted his right-footed effort into the goalie's bottom-left corner, sending Dudek the wrong way. 'I did not disturb Jon at all with my moves,' the Polish goalie remembers. Again he had performed his routine of giving the ball to Tomasson, standing on the spot when the forward wanted to place the ball, delaying the taking of the kick with a slow walk back to goal, and then going into the 'Dudek dance'. But this time it failed. 'It had worked with the others, so I was not going to stop now' was Dudek's rationale at the time. 'After he scored, Tomasson made a point of telling the referee that my forward movement was illegal, but it seemed to make no impression on him.

People had forgotten that Dida did the same thing in Manchester. All anyone remembers is that Milan won.'

Liverpool's third penalty – Riise misses (1–2)

Someone must have mentioned to the Norwegian the progressively clear pattern in Dida's dives, but maybe it was asking too much to realise he would stick to the same plan until the bitter end. The Brazilian, still stiff and awkward, made a very tentative jumping movement on the goal line, but he had already decided where he was going to throw himself – to his right, of course – before Riise had finished his run-up. The midfielder struck the ball towards the bottom corner but the Brazilian denied him with a truly brilliant save, tipping the ball round the post. The ball was going so close to the post that it probably would have hit it. 'Riise was tired when he took the kick, but he still felt confident of scoring,' says Xabi Alonso.

Milan's fourth penalty – Kaká scores (2–2)

The Brazilian midfielder sent Dudek the wrong way with his firm right-footed effort into the keeper's right corner. This was the only penalty when Dudek went fully into Grobbelaar mode, even though most people would swear he shivered, shook and wobbled before each and every one of five. The so-called 'Dudek dance', rather than the Brucie-like wobbly legs, was actually his main tactic. So much so that clubbers 'did the Dudek' in nightclubs and beach resorts across Italy throughout the summer. The dance routine was even performed live on Italian television. The dancers were, needless to say, *not* Milan fans. A Scouse version has probably been seen on the streets of Liverpool every Friday and Saturday night since the final. Revellers at some of the coolest Merseyside nightspots have continued to perfect it, and have even had the chance to showcase it in the presence of Harry Kewell on one occasion.

Liverpool's fourth penalty – Smicer scores (2–3)

Benítez spent some of the build-up to the penalties with his head down, writing notes, as if the momentous events had nothing to do with him. But, although he was still confident, he knew that the fourth penalty could damage the Liverpool players psychologically. A miss would give Milan the chance to get back in front. But scoring would hand Dudek the opportunity to win the match with one more save. Smicer calmly side-footed the ball home and put Liverpool within touching distance of the trophy. His body, though, was giving up on him. 'I was hit by cramp just as I was taking it,' he confirms. As Rafa understood, it was tension more than anything else that caused the problem, because as soon as the ball was in the net the Czech was able to reprise his crazy goal celebrations of earlier that night. He ran off in search of the nearest Liverpool fans, while Gerrard and Carragher made it abundantly clear that he should get back to the centre circle and into the interlinked arms of his Liverpool team-mates before Shevchenko took what was to be the final penalty. Carragher had to break away from the Liverpool huddle himself to scream at Smicer before he finally got the message. He returned to the fold just in time to see Dudek save the next penalty.

Milan's fifth penalty – Shevchenko misses (2–3)

Liverpool are European champions.

(14)

THE VICTORY PARADE

One Year You Are the Best and the Next Year You Are the Worst!

'I saw him move to the right and tried to hit the ball in the middle, but Dudek's left leg was trailing behind him and he managed to lift it up and make the save. There is a thin line between success and failure.' That is the closest that Andriy Shevchenko, the 2004 European Player of the Year and the most consistent goalscorer on the continent, can come to explaining what happened to him in the very last second of the final. He could have won the match for Milan during extra time, and then he also missed the penalty which finally handed triumph to Liverpool. Two duels with Dudek; two defeats.

In addition, Shevchenko had been denied by other saves by the Polish goalkeeper as well as a goal-line clearance from Traore; not to mention a linesman's narrow decision. It had just not been Shevchenko's night. 'If even *one* of those chances had gone in ...' Shevchenko has admitted repeating to himself a good few times over the summer months which followed.

'I saw him coming up and thought, "Are you going to go for the usual place?"' Dudek remembers. 'Penalties are such a huge test of nerve for a goalkeeper.' In the radio cabin, John Aldridge predicted that the Ukrainian would score just as he had done from the penalty spot to win the 2003 final at Old Trafford.

Liverpool's players stayed in their huddle. Dudek went through the same ritual he'd devised for the earlier penalties. First he bounced the ball while waiting on the penalty spot for the striker to arrive; then he walked backwards to the goal line; and finally he attempted to distract Shevchenko by jumping up and down and throwing his arms around as the striker ran up to the ball.

'There wasn't really a "usual place" in the case of Shevchenko,' goalkeeping coach José Ochotorena says. 'There were many options – he has enough quality to put it anywhere – but obviously Dudek had decided he was going to go to the keeper's right. He threw himself there and it transpired that Shevchenko's effort was like a very weak, very low little lob. Dudek reacted well, kind of slowed his dive away from the ball and was able to get a decisive touch on it.'

'I was so focused that I didn't even realise my save from Shevchenko meant we had won,' Dudek confessed just after the game. But that ignorance lasted less than half a second. As soon as he was on his feet again he saw his celebrating team-mates charging towards him. Liverpool, once again, were European champions!

Carragher beat the rest by ten yards, patted the head of the goalkeeper and then just kept running. 'I've seen the pictures where we're all taking off from the halfway line and I've got a bit of a start on them!' laughs the defender. 'Some of the players had seen the save and were still stood watching!'

'The explosion of joy at a moment like that is so great that you just don't know what to do,' reckons Pako Ayestarán. 'I totally understand why Carragher started running towards Dudek but then started to run around as if he were being chased by the cops before sprinting off towards the stands! I can understand it because when I saw the penalty miss, I sort of ran around in a five-metre circle, twice, and then started to hug and kiss Rafa, then John the kit man, then one of the players, then Dudek. Then I pulled off my jersey and threw it towards the fans. As far as I remember, it was the only Liverpool jersey thrown into the crowd that night which was thrown back!'

'I don't know where I was running to,' says Carragher. After his zany zigzagging sprint, he fell to the floor, thereby giving the UK tabloids the opportunity to create yet another myth: that he'd suffered a blackout. 'That was bullshit. I fell on the floor, just overcome with emotion. It was a couple of seconds; that was it.'

Xabi Alonso went through a similar experience. 'After going 2–0 up on penalties we had to keep one or two of the guys calm because they were starting to choke in the belief that we'd already won. "Hold on, this is not over yet," we were saying. But once Shevchenko missed it was complete bedlam. I sprinted off, and we all huddled with Dudek. We kind of exploded with joy. We hugged, danced, shouted.'

After engulfing the goalie, team-mates started following Alonso and Carragher across the running track. 'I was celebrating with everybody on the pitch, but I couldn't believe we were actually celebrating victory in the Champions League,' admits Djimi Traore. 'It was the next day, in the parade, when I finally felt we had won it. From going out on to the pitch until the incredible end of the parade was one of the best days of my life.'

Stevie Gerrard was jumping around, humming 'Ring of Fire' and hugging team-mates, but his eyes were gazing up into the stands, which was probably where he wanted to be most of all. Liverpool had never forgotten that they were a winning club; they had not been allowed to. Now they were back where they belonged and the fans were celebrating the occasion with hugs, kisses, tears, shouting, shirts off and scarves around their heads, and their skipper felt like he was just another one of them. 'Credit to this man' were the first words Gerrard shouted to the ITV interviewer as he pointed to Benítez after kissing his cheek. 'He didn't let our heads go down. I am made up for these fans. They have saved for weeks and months to be here.'

After briefly shaking hands with Carlo Ancelotti, Rafa Benítez ran purposefully across to his players on the other side of the pitch. Just as he had done at the end of countless other games with countless other players, he felt the need to talk to one specifically. On this occasion it was Djibril Cissé. In some respects, for the manager, this was obviously just another game. Putting his arm around the player's shoulder and gesticulating with his free hand, he talked animatedly to the Frenchman. 'I speak to the players at that point because if I don't do it then, in the heat of the moment, the effect of my words could diminish,' he explains. So, amid the passion of celebrating the moment when he had won the Champions League for Liverpool and had broken a barren spell of twenty-one years, when he'd given the club their fifth such title, and when he, personally, had won his first trophy since arriving at Anfield, Benítez's first reaction was to try to instruct Cissé in some fine technical point he'd spotted, as if he'd been watching a five-a-side at Melwood. Now, even Benítez is a little embarrassed at being reminded of the incident, and he can't recall which tactical nicety he was trying to impart to the striker in that mad moment. 'Look, not only do I not remember what I said to him; I scarcely remember talking to him at all! I was probably telling him that he should have utilised his speed more at that late stage of the game when everyone else was tired.'

A little later, Benítez talked calmly about the substitutions, the injuries, Dudek's saves and everything else that had gone on that night. In fact, he seemed much more composed than the excited ITV reporter, Gabriel Clarke, who was conducting the interview. But the smile which kept invading his face told the viewers all they needed to know about the joy that was bubbling up inside.

Of course, the unexpected turnaround left the Milan players deflated. Only skipper Paolo Maldini, Gennaro Gattuso and Andriy Shevchenko stayed on the pitch for the duration of the Liverpool celebrations. The trio were visibly distressed but generously applauded their rivals. A few minutes later, the rest of the Milan squad, which had left the pitch straight after the last penalty, re-appeared, and they also clapped, hugged and shook hands with the Merseysiders. They had probably forgotten they had to receive their losers' medals – which would have been entirely understandable.

'It would have been better to lose 3–0 than the way we did,' says Gattuso. 'I had met Alex Miller in Scotland when I was at Rangers and he was at Aberdeen, so I went to him on the pitch to offer my congratulations. It was so painful. It had been difficult enough to do that at the end of the match, never mind during Liverpool's celebrations. It is not going to be easy to regain our normal mental strength. Something similar had already happened against Deportivo La Coruña the year before. I suppose we have to be brave and just have to accept that AC Milan are "different".'

And over the next few months they proved that they were not prepared to change, even after what they'd just been through. In the summer they signed two more world-class strikers, Alberto Gilardino and Christian Vieri, signalling their intention to continue to be the least Italian of Italian clubs. They were going to keep faith with their attractive, attacking football, no matter what.

'You'll Never Walk Alone' resounded from the Red Army and the players clustered together in a group to see Milan collect their losers' medals. Finally, with that always painful ceremony over, Liverpool stepped up to receive their winners' medals and the trophy. Fernando Morientes, who had been commentating on the match for Spanish radio, joined Rafa and his new team-mates on the pitch. 'I told Fernando, "Now you have another European Cup to show off," ' Benítez remembers.

Vladi Smicer was the first to kiss the trophy, while Djibril Cissé did a jig around the coveted prize until Carragher hauled the Frenchman back to where the other players were standing. It was the defender's last energetic act for a while: the vicious cramps were back in his legs, and later, when Gerrard was hoisting the trophy high in air, he was hobbling around at the back of the platform, wincing with pain.

'Are you happy?' Lennart Johansson asked Gerrard after handing him his medal. The skipper simply gestured towards the Liverpool fans. Then he kissed the medal and symbolically offered it to them. 'Champions League, you're 'avin' a laugh,' the travelling Koppites were singing. Soon after, Benítez collected his medal, but then Johansson ran out, so not all of the squad had received one when they left the pitch.

Now Gerrard was waiting to receive the trophy, and he leaned over to kiss it. Momentarily it looked as though Johansson was going to offer it to Carragher by mistake. 'Obviously all the players would love to have lifted the prize, but with me being close to Stevie, I know what it means to him, as a local lad, and it's great for him. I know, under Houllier, we had different captains and people lifting trophies together and all that, but I know he'd never get involved in that type of thing. I think it's right that only the captain lifts it,' declares Carragher.

Gerrard finally lifted 'Old Big Ears', the trophy that was going back to Anfield's trophy cabinet permanently – a right earned by the club for winning it for the fifth time. This was why the skipper was a Liverpool player. 'As he lifts it and everyone moves to the middle,' remembers Carragher, 'I got cramp again and was holding on to the barrier at the side. You can see it on the telly. It must have been that sprint to Jerzy that did it!' Josemi, wearing a Spanish flag as a skirt, managed to get to Gerrard first, so it was his image that was etched for ever in the pictures alongside the Liverpool captain and the European Cup.

In the next instant the players were all over the place. For the team picture, before the lap of honour, some were jumping, some were seated on the floor. Gerrard gave Xabi Alonso a kiss . . . on the lips. 'Ah, that "peck",' recalls an embarrassed Alonso. 'We were all in the team group and he took my face and planted a great big smacker on me. And the way things were, I just thought, "OK, I'll give him a kiss on the lips!" We were all just letting our joy, everything we had inside ourselves, flood out. Normally we are more laid back.' Gerrard's unbounded enthusiasm carried over into the dressing room, where, face to face with Paco Herrera, the skipper dished out more of the same treatment.

In the official team photo, taken just after Liverpool had received the cup, there is one unfamiliar face. Next to Sami Hyypia, with his arm draped around Didi Hamann and his fist punching the air, is nineteen-year-old former Tranmere Rovers trainee Lee Dames. He even managed to lay his hands on the precious silverware. It was only when he asked Gerrard to hand him the cup so he could have his picture taken with it that he was rumbled and ushered away. Lee's infiltration into this unique moment occurred because he had opportunistically grabbed a tracksuit from a steward and then a jacket from the deserted dug-out. His dad Paul, who watched the whole incident on television in a Liverpool city-centre pub, was flabbergasted.

Then came the lap of honour. 'While we were wandering round the track, I told Pako that we'd really pulled off one hell of a feat,' reveals Benítez. 'I wasn't showing that was how I felt but it was my overwhelming emotion at the time. I was very proud of our work – I like a job well done! This particular triumph seemed to me to carry extra merit because it meant my staff and I had won two European trophies in two seasons with two different clubs. Mourinho had done that in the preceding couple of years with Porto, but to achieve it with two different teams is much more difficult.'

But Benítez was not leaping up and down with joy. That had only happened once before, and probably will now never happen again. 'I did it on the balcony of the town hall after winning the second Spanish title with Valencia,' he says. 'The fans were going so mad with joy at what we had achieved for the city that I couldn't help but show my euphoria.'

Rick Parry was engulfed in wave after wave of kisses and hugs from family, fans and anyone else who could reach him. 'The abiding moment for me in Dortmund, in the Alaves UEFA Cup final, was when the players lined up and sung "You'll Never Walk Alone" in front of the crowd. It was a moment of triumph that worked as a great interaction between fans and players. It was different in Istanbul: there was a sheer release, especially when they ran with the cup to the left-hand end of the ground. That passion between the players and the fans, the stories that still come back from fans, the emotional outpourings and tears . . . all that was partly because we had won the European Cup again, but partly because of the nature of it, the surprise, the *relief*.'

As much as Jamie Carragher and some of the others tried to get close to the fans with the cup, the stadium security men created such an effective human barrier that not much physical contact was ever achieved. Parry concedes, 'It's understandable because they have a job to do, but sometimes a bit of common sense is required. Things can go wrong so you do have to try to be a little measured. But you also have to understand that that sort of feeling is unprecedented and probably will never, ever, happen again, so let's just let them enjoy the moment.'

After the triumphant procession of the cup, it was time to celebrate inside the privacy of the dressing room, where the rules are different. But the media got in the way of that. 'The disappointment for me was that I couldn't get to the dressing room straight away,' remembers Parry, who had come straight from his box in the stand. 'Some of us, players, directors, were grabbed in the flash interview area on the way to the changing rooms, so there was never a moment when everybody was together. The players were doing television, some were getting treatment, Rafa was in and out. There was never a moment when we could organise a great huddle with the door closed. People were in and out, non-stop. At that point, Gérard [Houllier] went round the players and they were respectful and shook hands with him.'

What was the former Liverpool manager doing there, you may ask? Was it just one of those things, as Parry implies? Houllier, had *he* been in charge of Liverpool that night, would have gone crazy at the idea of, say, Kenny Dalglish or Graeme Souness muscling in on the celebrations. But he had done this at Melwood in the early days of Benítez's reign, too. Back then, Rafa had not needed to intervene over what most would consider a lack of respect because the visits had soon stopped. (Somebody at the club had finally lost patience and explained to Houllier that it would be better to allow the new regime time and space to flourish.) The ex-manager, though, was still regularly seen at Anfield as he was the Liverpool commentator for the French television channel that covers the Premiership.

Looks were exchanged when the Frenchman strolled into the dressing room, but nobody challenged his right to be there. Houllier had been at the match with his brother Serge, who was chasing around trying to get a spare shirt from a kit man. This is how he explained the dressing-room situation to Patrick Barclay of the *Sunday Telegraph*:

> It was one of the best moments of my life when I saw the reaction of the players. I'd been outside with my brother Serge, who is also well known to the lads, but I was feeling a bit apprehensive because, after all, it was they and Rafael Benítez who had won the trophy. The only thing I had contributed was the fourth-place finish the previous season that got them into the competition. But, when Benítez saw me through the open door, he was really good. He called me in and it was great that the players wanted to share the moment with me – there were quite a few hugs – because you cannot live with people for four, five or six years without becoming attached to them and I was so proud of their performance that night. There were no mixed feelings at all – I'd always known that at some stage I'd have to leave the club. But I never fell out of love with Liverpool for a moment, never bore a grudge. I'm a fan for life.'

'I would not have gone down to the changing rooms,' says Houllier's old assistant Phil Thompson. 'It was Rafa's day, the players' day and there was no need to be there. I *was* jealous, though.'

Xabi Alonso's words echo those of most of the squad and staff: 'It was a bit strange to see him there. The dressing room was a private moment of ecstasy, embraces and expressions of joy shared among team-mates. We just wanted to celebrate together.'

Then came a momentary trough of depression. 'By the time everyone is draped around the dressing room, after so much running during and after the game, having embraced everyone there is to embrace, it can produce a little "low" in anyone,' says Pako Ayestarán. 'You are left utterly without energy. It's even a bit of an effort to go on celebrating. You find yourself thinking, "This can't be right. I was just happy a moment ago sitting here next to Ochoto and now I feel absolutely nothing." There is a little, personal Bermuda Triangle moment when all your natural emotions kind of disappear. You put a bit of effort into it, grab a bottle of beer and join the toasts, but your body is still saying to you, "Nope, I feel nothing that I should be feeling." Then, bit by bit, the contagiousness of the moment and of everyone else's growing happiness gets you back to enjoying the importance of the achievement and the happiness of success.'

During this subdued moment, when the players were coming in and out of the dressing room, defender Mauricio Pellegrino realised that the twenty-five medals UEFA had provided for the winners were not going to be enough for the entire squad and the technical staff. So he went to the empty Milan dressing room and collected a handful of discarded, unwanted losers' medals. They now hang on the walls of such young players as Zak Whitbread, Darren Potter and Florent Sinama Pongolle. It was that kind of thoughtful gesture which had made Pellegrino, whose six-month adventure in Liverpool was drawing to a close, so popular among the squad.

Despite Houllier's inappropriate appearance in his ex-team's dressing room, Benítez's demeanour never wavered. At one point he seized the opportunity to collar Rick Parry and explain what lay behind Liverpool's 'schizophrenic' display that night: 'I told Rick that the line-up we chose always ran a certain risk of Kaká and Pirlo running the central midfield. It had always depended on us getting a grip on them and we hadn't done that well. Kaká played brilliantly and with total freedom because Seedorf, Gattuso and Pirlo worked their socks off for him the entire time.' Then Rafa went on to explain the thinking behind the half-time substitutions. Whether Rick Parry cared about any of this is debatable. After all, Liverpool had just won the Champions League. Who was bothered *how* they'd done it? But he listened patiently nevertheless.

A few hours later, Benítez was still focusing on the technical minutiae of the game with Spanish journalists in his hotel room. By that time, he had dined with his players and the rest of the squad in the hotel restaurant and had felt obliged to say a few words after the chairman had spoken. Yet another inconvenience of public life and success. Before leaving the restaurant, the legend goes, Milan Baroš managed to drop the cup on to a grand piano and dented one of the handles. The curators at Anfield's museum have promised never to repair it as 'it adds to the character', but Baroš denies it was him.

Text messages were pouring in to the players', directors' and manager's mobiles (chairman David Moores even received one from Tony Blair!). 'It was great to have one from Ferguson; it was a nice gesture,' says Benítez. The boss took days to plough through them all and send replies. In Valencia, another text message went round the fans – 'Homage to Benítez on Sunday. Pass it on'. On that day at the Mestalla Stadium, numerous banners congratulated their former coach.

The fiesta continued all night in various parts of the team hotel. Some players, like Xabi Alonso, surrounded themselves with friends and bottles of champagne. Others happily joined a party that was in full flow upstairs, flitting between it and the downstairs bar, which stayed open for a few extra hours. Baroš and Smicer (who had an enormous cigar jutting out of the side of his mouth all night) headed out into the centre of Istanbul to taste the atmosphere. They finally got back to the hotel around 4.30 a.m. But even then 'I didn't go to bed at all,' remembers Smicer. 'There's no need for sleep after a night like this. The feelings were so strong, I was so happy. I just wanted to go out on a high and I am proud I showed I can play. There was lots to celebrate, although I'd been told two months previously that I wouldn't be getting a new contract.'

One man who didn't manage to join in all the fun was Jamie Carragher. He was simply too busy! 'We had a party upstairs but I couldn't enjoy it because I was getting so many people in. I must have got about forty people in there. My dad and all that were in the hotel, but my brothers and them were outside, so I was having to get them in. Every ten minutes I was going back down trying to get more people in, making up lies and saying they were my brothers or uncles. Some fella actually got in the party by saying he was my brother. Someone asked me, "Is he really your brother?" and when I said, "No," they threw him out.'

On his way to grab a little sleep before the bus left for the airport, Stevie Gerrard appeared clutching the cup in one hand and receiving congratulatory handshakes with the other from all and sundry as he processed down the corridor. It was five in the morning. Countless muezzins were singing out their early morning calls to the faithful from the minarets of Istanbul, and Liverpool fans were still arriving at Taksim Square on their weary way back from the stadium. Although the vast majority of the crowd had dispersed in decent order despite the difficulty of finding buses that would take them into town, some, of course, had been reluctant to leave the impromptu party that had started in the stands as soon as Shevchenko had missed the last penalty. It had been three hours before the exhausted stadium staff had finally evicted the last of the stragglers. Hordes of fans in red and white had stayed in the stands to sing the old songs over and over again. Then they had pocketed handfuls of the special confetti which had been scattered over the players while the cup was being handed over to its new owners. Much of this was later sold by the bag on eBay. The last photos were taken, the last text messages of congratulations sent, the last tears cried. 'I've never seen so many adults crying together in one place,' says John Aldridge, readily acknowledging that he was one of them.

Michael Owen's sister Karen sent him a text from the stadium: 'You should have been here'. He received it in Spain. 'I was in touch with Stevie throughout the week before the game,' the ex-Liverpool striker told the press. 'I left messages for several players after the match and Stevie was the first to reply. He's my best friend there, along with Carragher and Hamann. I sent them messages as well, but it took them longer to reply. They were probably having a bit of a drink! But I never regretted moving to Madrid. I would have regretted it all my life if I *hadn't* gone to experience playing in a different country, learning a different language and a different kind of football.'

Sammy Lee, in Chicago with the England team, felt as much a part of the Red family as ever. 'They were all thrilled with the victory. I came across some of the [England] players in the hall of our hotel and later in training, and they were all congratulating me. I am not there any more, but they were still congratulating me. I made sure I phoned my lad to see that he was OK. In fact, I phoned everybody – all my friends. They were all in Istanbul.'

In Liverpool one out of every five workers was beginning a night of celebration that would leave them too delicate to make it into work the next day. And in the streets of Badajoz, well after midnight, Josefina and Paco Herrera's neighbours streamed out on to the streets to dance, hug and cry. They were taken aback by the intensity of what they had seen and were delighted to see Liverpool's chief scout, such a decent man who had lived side by side with them and whom everyone adored, being a central part of the action. The final had been watched in Spain by a massive TV audience. Spaniards like to see their boys doing well.

After three hours' sleep, Rafa Benítez went down to Reception and got stuck into the 'morning after' press conference. He started with a bit of self-defence: 'I don't think I got it wrong to begin with. We conceded in the first minute. Then, soon after, we lost an important player to injury in Harry Kewell. Everything changed.' Rafa had the pressmen's undivided attention, and he clearly wasn't going to waste the opportunity that gave him. 'Never call me the "special one"!' he entreated. 'I am one step closer to what the other managers achieved here. That is all. I have to do a lot more before I could be considered on the same level. Now it is important to build on this success. What has happened in this final doesn't change things. I knew the players before the final, and after the final I still know them,' he said. That message that was directed at Milan Baroš, Jerzy Dudek, Vladi Smicer and Igor Biscan. Without making all the details public, Benítez was making plans straight after a great victory, just as Shankly had done during his time at the helm.

But despite the victory, the doubts remained. In the summer Liverpool's fans would continue to express concern over Benítez's judgement. For example, did Peter Crouch really possess the quality needed to wear a Liverpool shirt? However, Benítez has defended the acquisition of Crouch as a solution to the urgent need for height in Liverpool's attack. It's the type of signing he's made throughout his career: buying a player who fulfils a specific need in the team and appreciates the 'collective' philosophy on which the club operates. 'Sometimes it's not only about having the *best* footballers but the *right* guy for what you want to achieve,' claims the manager. 'We had to improve the quality of the squad. The best way to motivate players is to make them feel their place is threatened by somebody else. The greatest mistake Valencia made in my last year there was not to sign anybody to increase the competition.'

The case of Luis Figo, who came so close to signing for Liverpool, is similar. Lacking the money to sign one of the specialist inside-right players he really wanted, Benítez looked for someone with the characteristics the team required who came within the budget. Figo seemed to fit the bill. It was never a matter of looking for a big name (although Figo is obviously that) and then trying to find a spot for him in the team, as so often happens at Real Madrid.

'Those who have come have given good performances for their teams and some are already prestigious, like José Manuel Reina, the best goalkeeper in Spain,' says Rafa. 'Momo Sissoko is a personal gamble based on the knowledge we have of him as I coached him at Valencia. Bolo Zenden is versatile . . . *and* he was on a free. Crouch is a striker who in England is absolutely essential because he is very tall, impressive with aerial balls and can keep the ball. He will be good for us as one of our problems when we played away was that we hardly had possession and won too few aerial challenges.'

It's debatable whether Benítez should be forced to make these self-justifications. In just twelve months he's shouldered and then shaken off the burden of the Shankly years. The Spaniard's name will now forever be uniquely associated with a legendary moment in the club's history. 'He has aspects of many managers,' the Liverpool *Echo*'s Chris Bascombe says: 'the hands-on approach of Shankly, the calm of Paisley and Fagan, the meticulous streak that Houllier had when he arrived. But nobody calls him the "new Bill Shankly" and that is a good thing.'

What Rafa said in Istanbul at that early morning press conference could not have been clearer; and it probably would have pleased Shankly, who never rested on his laurels. 'We need a new mentality for the Premiership, especially away from home. We cannot change everything but there *will* be changes.' With that, Benítez boarded the bus that took him to the airport.

At both of Istanbul's airports, and especially at tiny Sabiha Gokçen, thousands of fans had to cope with hours of delays. Friends lost each other in the rush to find a plane. Fans were kept in a marquee and had to buy food vouchers at exorbitant prices. But despite the chaos and their inevitable exhaustion, their mood remained jubilant. Throughout that Turkish morning there was always someone, apparently wide awake, to put the loyalty of the hundreds dozing in the tent to the ultimate test. That self-appointed inquisitor only needed to intone the first line of 'You'll Never Walk Alone' to provoke an army of zombies into rising from among the semi-conscious mass of humanity to reprise a few verses of the blessed anthem before lapsing once more into catatonic slumber.

Virtually nobody, it seems, returned on their appointed flight, and passports were scarcely ever checked. Some fans, like Mark Challiner, 'mistakenly' boarded the squad's plane. He was meant to be flying to London, but ended up next to Sami Hyypia en route to Liverpool. 'All the players found it really funny,' he says.

'I was thinking, "Life cannot get any better than this",' said Stevie Gerrard. Back in Liverpool, he would be forced to reassess that opinion.

Those lucky enough to head back to England in the early hours of

Thursday morning tried to catch up on their sleep, just as the players were doing. A drowsy Brian Oliver, sports editor of the *Observer*, recalls hearing the voice of the captain describing the weather as his plane was reaching London: 'Look out of the window and you'll see it's a beautiful day. As far as I can see there is only one small cloud, just hovering over Stamford Bridge!' Applause broke out.

The vast majority of those who had been in Istanbul didn't get home in time to witness the biggest outpouring of public emotion the city of Liverpool had ever seen. That day, a street party with 750,000 guests took place. Some who had been at Shankly's funeral, fans who had travelled to all the previous European Cup victory parades, those who had danced and sung at the 2001 'treble' celebrations and many, many more all awaited the arrival of the team. That sunny day was already losing its heat when the team's plane touched down at John Lennon Airport just after 4.30 p.m. Then they headed into the city, escorted by twenty mounted police officers.

'Luis García's eyes were bulging when he got on to the double-decker bus,' remembers Jamie Carragher. ' "This is amazing," he was saying. Then Stevie told him, "You ain't seen nothing yet!" ' But the true extent of the scenes would soon surprise even the skipper, who admitted to the press, 'It was unbelievable. None of us imagined there would be so many people there, waiting to cheer us on. I can remember the celebrations following the cup treble in 2001, but this was something else. The lads were just buzzing. For some of the foreign players, it was a real eye-opener. But this is Liverpool Football Club and that is why we never gave in against Milan when it looked like a lost cause.'

Red and white flags and red shirts mixed with the white strips of Valencia CF. Pensioners dug out their old Liverpool flags and waved them on their front lawns. 'At moments like that you realise football truly is a religion here,' says Xabi Alonso. The crowd's collective hangover and their marathon wait for the team's return were remedied by imbibing just a little more beer. The fans made enormous efforts to catch a glimpse of their heroes: climbing lamp-posts, traffic lights, police surveillance vans, even the glass roof of Lime Street Station. Someone spent an hour atop the head of St George's statue. Kids were sitting on their dads' shoulders; babies were dressed in Liverpool kits. 'The coach just wouldn't move,' remembers Carragher. 'It totally surpassed the celebration for the treble. At least then there were times when we could pick up a bit of speed; but this time we were just crawling. That's why it took so long and ruined our night out!'

'Rafa and I had both enjoyed wonderful moments with Valencia,' remembers Pako Ayestarán. 'After thirty years without winning La Liga there were huge celebrations in Valencia. But here the difference is the total passion. The loyalty for the Liverpool team deserves much respect, and it also commands our perseverance and dedication. Without these supporters the club would be different. Those of us who arrived last summer were totally bowled over, from the first minute, when people stopped us in the street and said: "Thanks for coming!" The parade just cemented those sensations.'

The coach was tortuously snaking through the red and white sea that was Queen's Drive. At the back of the bus, Hamann, Gerrard, Carragher and Cissé took it in turns to put on their own show. They passed Anfield, with kids clambering on to the Paisley Gateway and two young girls in white lace dresses holding a banner proclaiming, 'Today was our communion party, but we'd rather party with you.' They continued towards the city centre and finally stopped at St George's Plateau. It was clear by then that the whole city had decided to shout together, dance together, chant together.

'Football is so changeable,' says Benítez. 'One year you are the best and the next year you are the worst! I'm actually pretty pragmatic about it. What you have to do is focus on the day-to-day work. You must do things better and better, and it is the result of this work which will stay with you at the end. If other people thank you and you get results then so much the better.'

For the moment, nobody on the bus wanted to face the fact that Liverpool hadn't actually qualified for the following season's

Champions League. But you could feel that there was a shared sense of optimism on the double decker. The communal spirit and the images of the parade shouted out the message to those who needed to be convinced: 'How could you not be swayed by such a massive, public display of strength? How could you even *think* of leaving all this out of next year's competition?'

'If things are not done properly you have to correct them and sort them out,' says Benítez. 'I think it's obligatory and fair that the champions defend their title, and most people agree with me. It was not logical that we had to start from the first round, but we accepted it and got on with it.'

Liverpool simply *had* to be allowed to defend their trophy, even if it meant having to qualify from the very beginning of the competition. Gabriele Marcotti of *The Times* acknowledges that (after all, the European champions have come back to defend their title every year since 1957), but he also points out a downside to Liverpool's inclusion:

> The sad thing is that all English clubs have no reason whatsoever to be happy. By deciding to scrap its rules and admit all five English clubs, UEFA has done serious harm, both to its own credibility and to its long-term independence. England's PR campaign and behind-the-scenes horse-trading will leave them beholden to other countries for years to come.

Forcing a change of rules, Marcotti believes, has created a dangerous precedent.

Near St George's Hall, a tribute read, 'Who needs Toffees when you can have Turkish delight?' but some Evertonians were certainly also in the street. In fact, a crowd twice the size of Liverpool's population was celebrating the victory, relishing that feeling of once more being at the centre of the footballing world.

'I watched the people who had come out to greet us really closely,' says Paco Herrera. 'We had won the European Cup, but the experience of winning had been different for the players and the staff compared to the fans. Parading around Liverpool like this allowed us to imagine what it had been like from their point of view. From all the faces I saw that day, three in particular stay with me. The first was a woman at her window looking out at us defiantly while her neighbours were shrieking like crazy people. Suddenly I realised that the woman had a sign in her hand saying: "I Support Everton". She was looking at the victory procession as if to say, "So what?" Then there were the animated faces of a couple of two-year-old kids, their mouths open and their foreheads scrunched up as they screamed, "Come on!" To me, that is Liverpool.'

When the bus entered the city centre, at around 9.30 p.m., it was getting dark and the monumental buildings around William Brown Street, which was packed with 300,000 people, were illuminated. The crowd erupted into cheering and singing as the team approached St George's Hall. As the procession drew to an end, a few of the players and directors looked at Rafael Benítez and wondered whether, as he hugged his two daughters, he was allowing himself to enjoy the moment. In twelve months, they'd got to know him well. Deep down, even in the middle of all the madness, the Liverpool manager knew that his work was just beginning.

(15)

THE NEW SEASON

Rafa Needs to Feel in Control and in the First Year there were Too Many Things that Escaped Our Control

As the opposing armies of fans gathered for the 2005–2006 FA Cup, the rain was hardly a consideration; so gently did it fall in the hours before kick-off that it didn't even get them wet. Cardiff had been divided into two zones, one blue and the other red, with the aim of keeping the opposing factions of Liverpool and West Ham apart.

The noise grew as fans made their way towards the Millennium Stadium. It towered over them, always seemingly just a few streets away.

A left turn brought them into a smaller road and then, suddenly, a corner of the Stadium revealed itself like some strange UFO that had just landed among the buildings. By the time the team that would eventually lift the cup with a dramatic flourish stepped on to the pitch, the weather had improved, but the tension was taking its toll.

A key member of the Liverpool backroom staff cast a worrying look over the players and confided to a colleague that some of the assembled squad were about to fail the team. He reeled off the names one by one: 'His mindset is not right; neither is his, or his, or his. They are scared. We are going to struggle.'

Rafa Benítez was having similar thoughts. The final was going to offer yet more proof that the club's development was far from complete. There was more work to be done and new players to bring in. It was true that Liverpool in this, his second season in charge, was a better side than twelve months before, but still it contained footballers not equipped for the highest level of competition. Maybe some of them were capable of holding down a place in an Aston Villa or a Celta Vigo, but they did not appear to be the kind of players Benítez felt he needed for a side which had entered a new era, one marked by regular appearances in finals.

This second season was to be Benítez's opportunity to learn who had, and who did not have, the necessary tools to compete at this level, and the final in Cardiff was a fitting way to end it: with a new title, but also with enduring mixed feelings regarding the club's forward progress. The Spanish boss may have had his doubts about the pace of changes at the club, but with the new contract that weeks later he was going to sign, the Anfield Board was rewarding to some extent his latest triumph and reacting to the renewed interest from Real Madrid for the Liverpool boss. But more importantly, they saw the new deal as a way of underscoring their commitment to Benítez and his ambitious plans, both in terms of new signings as well as more fundamental restructuring. So besides another trophy in the cabinet – two if you include the European Supercup – the real legacy of the 2005–2006 season was that Benítez had managed to place another building block in the club's renovation.

The squad, still in the process of redesign, had to reconvene early since UEFA had decreed that Liverpool would, after all, be allowed to defend their Champions League title, but only on condition that they compete in the earliest qualifying round. The success of Istanbul had finally sunk in, and players and staff returning from their break felt that they were coming back to a group that now had a clearly defined ideology and leadership. They could see, in hindsight, what a culture shock Rafa's first season had been. Without doubt, the Champions League victory had given the club a huge confidence boost, and rescued a season on the brink of disappointment. It was a matter of building from there.

'Everything is much easier when the foundations are laid,' says Paco Herrera. 'We felt at home when we walked into Melwood that second summer; it felt as if we needed a little break to realise it. We all spoke the language, had better vocabulary, we could express ourselves better, whether it was talking about our feelings or giving instructions to the players. And we were the Champions of Europe. Rafa needs to feel in control, and in the first year there were too many things that escaped our control,' adds Ochotorena.

Benítez too believes that things were different the second time around. 'Players were humble returning from holidays,' he recalls. 'The press, the staff, the fans, they were all happy and expecting more of the same. There was an instant mythology of many things from that final, and that makes sense because it is almost impossible to repeat something similar. In Spain, they gave recognition to a Spaniard succeeding abroad, although to win accolades in my country is not easy. In fact, I have received twelve awards of one kind or another in the UK, and only two in Spain in the last couple of years.'

The first Benítez season had helped players and staff get used to each other and, in the case of the new arrivals, to familiarise themselves with their new surroundings. The 'Big Idea' (team effort, defensive work, generosity, strategy in set pieces) was imposed and worked on incessantly in training until it had become almost second nature. From day one of the second season, work on the training ground centred around repetition of the same tactical strategies so that the players learned them by heart and, very importantly, so that they could see Benítez had not changed his mind about the basics, that he continued working with the same beliefs.

His good eye was brought to bear in the signing of players that also helped the team grow – Momo Sissoko, Pepe Reina, Peter Crouch . . . The Spanish boss had made some mistakes in the transfer market but he reacted and remedied some of them. Josemi and Antonio Nuñez, for instance, were not suitable for the Premiership though they have proved to be solid players, as they are now regulars at Villarreal and Celta, two of the most consistent teams in La Liga. 'For one reason or another, some have not settled; they never got used to the way things go here,' Carragher admits.

But in a way it was a case of 'new year, old problems'. That summer the board, who acted early on the three new names mentioned above, did not finish the job with the sharpness Benítez would have liked. There was the possibility of signing Nemanja Vidic, Luis Figo or Dirk Kuyt, but eventually two of the positions that clearly needed reinforcing (centre back and right wing) ended up being filled by players who were already in the squad. As Bascombe puts it, 'When Liverpool won the European Cup, that should have been the platform for "instant cashing-in", and it wasn't.' There was not time for either anxiety or complacency though, as the season started early.

That forced premature return is now remembered as a blur. Benítez can instantly recall every detail of matches played years ago or quite literally the height of the Real Madrid B team players he had under his wing in the old days, yet it took him much longer to summon up how he spent a couple of breaks in the summer of 2005 – they were so brief they hardly have a place in his memory. 'Where did I go? My wife would kill me if she knew I can't remember. Ah, yes, I only had a little break to Edinburgh and the Lake District, only a few days,' Benítez, almost embarrassed, finally remembers. 'The competitive matches started very early. I was pleased with the beginning of the season, an average of three goals per match in the first five fixtures of the qualifying rounds. We attacked. We were superior in possession. The only worry was we had to win those matches or we were out, but at the same time we had to pace ourselves because there were more than fifty matches in front of us. I was thinking, "How about it if I get it wrong with some rotations?" During the qualifiers, we didn't have time to react if things did actually go wrong. But after winning the first matches of the three rounds, everything was easier.'

So how did Liverpool manage to reach the end of the season fresh enough to win an FA Cup in May that went to extra time and penalties, when their first competitive game was played on 13 July the previous year (the 3–0 victory over the North Wales minnows of

TNS)? Much of the credit goes to Pako Ayestarán. He studies every season down to the last detail. He decides where and when the team needs to find its best physical condition, or where and when Liverpool can afford to drop back slightly from peak condition. When to push the players, when to slow down, which matches can be won without being in ideal shape, maybe with a single goal and without the need of the spark one finds when Liverpool are riding on top of the physical wave. The choices about which matches to prioritise imply a certain amount of guesswork but some, of course, pick themselves. 'It allows us to meet Chelsea or Manchester United in great condition. You see Chelsea sitting comfortably on top of the table but we arrived at the fixture in one of those top physical moments and you know then we have a very good chance to beat them,' Paco Herrera says.

The challenge of the 2005–2006 season was probably the biggest Ayestarán has ever faced. Under the supervision of Benítez, he had to manage a year that started with little pre-season work, with three qualifying ties before the group stage of the Champions League and a trip to Japan for the FIFA World Club Championship followed by the return flight to England to play three matches in six days. Being European Champions was clearly not entirely a bed of roses. When the team needed extra attention, tactical work or were coming up to a big match, Benítez spent more time with them. For Rafa, work now means going to the office as much as participating in training sessions, more and more being left in the capable hands of his assistant, whose influence has gone so far as to change Melwood itself. He built something called 'Pako Hill', a structure with a twenty-five-degree slope at the edge of the training compound. 'We haven't used it yet, we don't know what it's for, but we're a bit worried,' jokes Carragher.

Even as the season's preparations went on, the technical staff laid out its own expectations for the club. It was a kind of 'internal bet' among Rafa and his men: finishing second in the Premiership. Second place was considered as valuable as first place. While winning the title would have been nice, they understood that continuing to progress was a more important, and more realistic, target. Chelsea were seen as a cut above – a view shared by the bookmakers – but Liverpool wanted to win the battle for runners-up. The idea was that the 2005–2006 season would be the one where they sorted out their squad problems and laid the foundation for an assault on the Premiership crown the following year.

The European Supercup (held as usual in Monaco on 26 August and pitting Liverpool against UEFA Cup winners CSKA Moscow) was the dress rehearsal for the new season. The coaching staff watched the match with eyes as big as dinner plates. Benítez would be checking on his new signings (Reina, Sissoko and Barragan all played), monitoring the return of Gerrard (after he had turned down Chelsea's approach and renewed his commitment to the club) and verifying the mental state of Djibril Cissé who, by now, would be realising that the coaching staff had doubts about his ability to lead the front line. Rafa felt that the team had made a considerable jump in quality, confidence, technique, tactical acumen and psychological strength, which helped them battle back from being a goal down after 28 minutes. Two goals from Cissé (the first one coming eight minutes before the end of normal time to level the game) and the final victory in extra time helped create positive impressions in what was generally a pretty dull game. 'Rafa made it quite clear in the press conference that we could possibly lose. There was not much of an atmosphere, the Supercup is a glorified exhibition game,' says Chris Bascombe.

There was still work to do in the transfer market and reinforcing the attack remained the priority. Despite denials from sources within Anfield, efforts during the latter part of August were focused on acquiring Michael Owen. Thus, the new season was starting again with transfer negotiations that quickly developed into a soap opera centred around one of the most prominent players in the club's history. Owen's obvious desire was to play for the Reds, but he ended up at Newcastle. Why don't players end up where they really want to play? The return of Robbie Fowler, whose Anfield contract was inferior to the one he left behind at Manchester City, clearly showed that hardly anything can stop a footballer once his mind is made up.

'The issue was an easy one – the financial conditions of the transfer and the situation of the player worked against the move as Liverpool could not afford it,' Rafa Benítez says. 'Real Madrid put a lot of pressure on Michael to go to Newcastle after they offered £16 million. Real kept asking for us to match that evaluation because they wanted the money to sign Sergio Ramos and we didn't have that kind of figure in mind.' His move was not helped either by the price tag of £120,000 per week that his advisors were placing upon his services. Officially then, it was all about money; but, rightly or wrongly, the impression at Anfield remains that Owen did not come because he did not want it badly enough.

'Michael never said he *only* wanted to join Liverpool.' Bascombe adds. He came close when he admitted in public that he would only go on loan to Newcastle, but the player did not follow that up with total faith in what Liverpool had in mind. Benítez planned either to get him on loan, to pay Real £12 million for him [both very unlikely] or to try to sign him again in the Christmas transfer window, but Owen doubted that that last one was the best solution. The player was worried not only about his future in the England side in a World Cup year, but also he was not completely sure Benítez liked him enough. His mind was full of questions – will he keep his promise and come back for me in Christmas? Will I play enough at Liverpool under him? Is it really him who is pushing for this transfer deal? Maybe he took the Spaniard's reluctance to pamper him as meaning that he did not like him, but the Spanish coach is clear about his feelings: 'I told him, "I have no problem whatsover with you". Imagine, I have him next to Peter Crouch, it would be fantastic! It would be a partnership to kill opponents.'

'When faced with a similar situation, Milan Baroš publicly rebuffed any interest from Lyon and joined Aston Villa for a smaller fee,' Chris Bascombe wrote in the *Echo*. 'Fernando Morientes took the same stance last January when, in the wake of Liverpool interest, Newcastle offered more. For Owen, the risk was too great. Time was running out. He was told by Madrid that there was no prospect of a deal with Liverpool, and if he didn't go to Newcastle, he'd be on the sidelines until January. The shadow of the World Cup loomed large. It seems international ambition overrides a burning desire to return to Anfield and the next six months couldn't be sacrificed.'

But someone had lied to the player – he was never going to be on the sidelines at Real. 'Michael had spoken to Eriksson, and he knew the national coach was going to keep his place in the side even if he did not play regularly,' Benítez says. 'But through mutual friends I had heard from Vanderlei Luxemburgo, the Real coach, that Owen was going to play matches and if there were injuries, even more often than not. He was going to be playing regularly till December or January when we could come back for him.'

The player admitted he was uncertain that a Liverpool bid would be accepted in time and did not want to stay in Madrid till Christmas. 'I wanted to play for a club who really wanted me. I flew by private plane into Liverpool airport and went straight into a meeting with Rick Parry, the chief executive, and Rafael Benítez at a friend's house in Liverpool. Rafa and I sat together in the lounge while my adviser discussed my playing contract with Rick in the dining room. We were together for about two and a half hours, and I would say that it was a good meeting – the most positive I had heard out of Liverpool.'

'I wanted Michael in my team,' Benítez adds. 'I had spoken to him a few times on the phone but when we met in Liverpool I told him he could play with Peter Crouch. I also said to him, "I will bring you but I cannot pay what Newcastle are offering for you [£16 million]. If I asked Real to let you go on loan, they would probably say no. So if they do say no, you force your way out. It is the only way", I kept saying. I was very conscious of our time limitations as that conversation took place a day before the end of the transfer window. "But if, despite our efforts, Real say tomorrow you cannot go, don't worry about your near future", I told him. "We will come back for you". Then I chatted with his agent who kept saying money was not an issue, that it was easy to sort it out with Real Madrid. I told them, "If you want me to assume such a huge investment, and if it is really so easy to sort out, you sort it out with Madrid, bring the fee down or get them to accept a loan deal".'

On the journey up to Newcastle, a doubtful Michael Owen spoke again to Rafa and Rick Parry. 'But after some horrendous advice, he was pictured meeting Newcastle officials,' Bascombe remembers. 'Hardly the actions of a man trying to send a signal to Real Madrid he didn't fancy moving to St James' Park. As Owen strolled around a Northumberland estate on Monday night, he was inadvertently knifing his and Liverpool's ambitions through the heart. Having been set a morning deadline to make his decision, he returned to north Wales resigned to moving to Newcastle.'

'On the journey home from those talks [with Liverpool and Newcastle], my mind was still spinning,' Owen confesses. 'Would Liverpool's offer be in time, and be accepted? What would happen to me if I stayed at Madrid? How much would I miss European football if I signed for Newcastle? I arrived home at around 9.30 p.m. and sat in the kitchen with my mum, dad and wife Louise. With growing doubts about the Liverpool deal, my mind was made up.' Or was it?

'In case Michael needed it, the proof that I wanted him is that we even made phone calls after the famous Monday walk of Michael with some Newcastle officials, even early on the next day before he signed for them,' Rafa remembers. Owen prefers not to admit publicly that, after that family reunion on the Monday evening, as Bascombe wrote in the *Echo*, the player was still trying to move to Liverpool. 'On Tuesday morning he was having second thoughts and made a series of frantic phone calls to Anfield officials. With the St James' Park medical team due to arrive at his North Wales home to complete the formalities, Owen was still waiting for the call from the Anfield hierarchy. When it came at around 11 a.m. that morning, the conversation between Owen and Rick Parry confirmed his fears. Liverpool had neither the cash, nor the will, to spend more than £12 million to buy him back. Sending an SOS to Anfield was fine, but without a white flag, surrendering any intention to join Newcastle, it was hopeless. Sadly, this was a concession Owen felt he couldn't take without a definite assurance that his ambition to join Liverpool would be realised.'

'I am convinced Michael thinks in his heart that it could happen again and that he will be back at Liverpool,' Bascombe says now. For Benítez it will never again be a priority. In Liverpool people are stunned that the player chose the Newcastle option, given his reservations about the move. The impression is not only that Owen – who cried on the phone to friends when he realised his dream move to Liverpool was not going to take place – did not want to stay in Madrid under any circumstances or that he was not sure about how badly Benítez wanted him, but also that advisers around the player were crucially obsessed with the business of such a big move to Newcastle. In the end, there were too many people and too many doubts working against his transfer to Anfield.

So that left Liverpool with a strike force composed of one player unable to adapt to the Premiership (Morientes), another who did not work enough (Cissé) and a third who had recently arrived with a need to disprove the notion that the club was taking an outrageous gamble in signing him: Peter Crouch. Cissé was essentially forced to stay after the Owen transfer fell through, even though the club did have some loan deals lined up for him. The French striker felt he did not have Benítez' complete trust and, early in the season, told the manager that he needed to play. Just as Owen was preoccupied with his England team chances, so Cissé was similarly worried about his place in the French national squad. 'If I don't play, I won't be able to go to the World Cup,' he told Benítez. With France being blessed with a great generation of centre forwards – Henry, Trezeguet, Guvou, Saha, Anelka – his position was made even more desperate.

'Fans see a player on the bench and wonder, "Why isn't he playing?" But maybe he can have one good game but not the next four. You can use the players who can amuse the supporters, but if you want to win trophies you need workers, for ninety minutes, every week, every training session; workers with enough quality for winning.' Benítez was not talking specifically about the French striker but he might as well have been. A year later, when Cissé's leg broke again during a friendly between France and China prior to the World Cup, his move to Marseille, negotiated at the time, seemed to have found an almost irreversible obstacle, but the need to finance new signings and the misgivings of the Spanish coach towards his quality made it happen.

After the three qualifiers in the summer of 2005, Liverpool managed to get to the Champions League group stage, the real start to the competition. They were grouped with Chelsea, Real Betis and Anderlecht and it was important not to lose the first match against the London rivals and the final 0–0 was considered a good result. Before the game, Anfield had been awash with reminders of last season's European campaign; from the special photo section in the match-day programme to the chants from the Kop, to the supporters proudly displaying cardboard cutouts of the quintet of European Cups only yards from Mourinho's dugout. It was difficult for Chelsea to escape what ultimately transpired to be a consequence of their last appearance here. The atmosphere on that triumphant May evening in 2005 was one of the finest the arena has ever witnessed, and although September's volume didn't quite reach the same decibel level, there was nevertheless an impressive wall of sound.

Anfield continues to treat the Chelsea matches as the pinnacle of the season, but inside Melwood it was decided that there would be no special psychological preparation for that game. Such efforts may have been necessary in Rafa's first year as a way of building confidence, but continuous meetings create their own mental obligations, tensions and pending issues. And after all, Liverpool were already European Champions!

'In the Premiership, they were better, but in the knockout competitions we were better. We are more competitive in cup games,' Pako Ayestarán says. 'From the technical staff's point of view, they are important opponents, but no more than that. For the players it is different, of course. Playing in the semi-finals of the Champions League and the FA Cup is a powerful enough reason to give your best. But how appropriate that those fantastic performances of our players coincide with Chelsea being the rivals.'

The behaviour of Mourinho forced a little change to the original plan: Chelsea became another match and José another coach – unless he directly attacked the team. Rafa Benítez says: 'After losing against Chelsea at Anfield 4–1, I heard Mourinho say that we played basketball, that we were all about route one football. All of a sudden stats that we know are private and can only come from within the club appeared in the press. It surprised me and I took note. Then he mentioned in Portugal that we played defensively and that the only thing we know how to do is defend. I cannot accept disrespect from another coach. There was lots of respect before, but someone, and it was not me, crossed the line. To make his team look better, José has attacked another one. It is then that I don't feel so comfortable about it, and I may say things to balance it out.'

Rafa rarely uses the press to launch attacks and, even in the Mourinho battle of minds, his strategy is omission rather than insult. For example, in the preview to the FA Cup semi-final, asked about the value of Mourinho as a coach, Rafa replied, 'The real responsibility for Chelsea's success is Abramovich.' Of course, Benítez's English has improved since his arrival in Liverpool, but he is clever enough to hide behind its undeniable limitations as a means of defending his ground. 'I am not completely happy because I still can't express exactly what I want to say. In Spanish I could say ten thousand different things, but here I have to be very careful – words are taken out of context. I have no time to study new words, and finally when I talk under the pressure of a microphone I go for the safety net and probably use too many clichés'. And if he wants to make a particular point, the words are rehearsed beforehand with Liverpool's loyal press officer, Ian Cotton.

'My two daughters, Claudia and Agatha, speak English with a Liverpool accent,' Montse, Rafa Benítez's wife, says. 'One of them does not speak Spanish, but understands it. She is only three, actually, so we are not too concerned.' That is the kind of thing that could destroy a love affair between a coach and his ideal club – siblings that seem to have lost touch with their original country. In fact, both daughters speak to each other in English, but Montse dismisses that as a real worry. 'We do not really care about this. They will have time in the future to recapture their Spanish roots. We don't have a sell-by date for our stay in Liverpool.'

Not even in the toughest moments, not even when Rafa has to talk to his daughter in a language of which he does not have complete command, has Montse heard Rafa look for an excuse to give up. 'His life is football. When things are not totally right Rafa arrives back from a match and analyses it, thinks about things all night, talks about it, explains it to me three or four times. He talks and thinks loudly. My role is mostly to listen, and if he enquires after my opinion, to give a different point of view alien to football. But we don't talk about tactics or referees. The things we talk about are a player that has disappointed, a decision he took. Rafa lives football every single hour of the day, and I have always understood and respected that.'

During this second season in charge, there were a couple of those tough moments. One came as early as the end of October with two consecutive defeats: 2–0 against Fulham and 2–1 against Crystal Palace in the Carling Cup. 'But we reacted very well,' says Paco Herrera. 'We studied the situation, looked for the positives, reminded everybody of the basics, tactically and mentally. We quickly found solutions.'

'They were deceptive results anyway,' Benítez says. 'Against Crystal Palace we had lots of chances in the first half, and against Fulham we played the whole match in the opposition's half. We were so superior that I thought, "It is not possible this is happening".' Certainly the team was not too far from its best form. After the Carling Cup defeat, Liverpool had ten consecutive victories. In the middle of that extraordinary run came the FIFA World Club Championship with the chance to win another title, or perhaps more appropriately, the obligation to win another title. 'It is OK if people do not give the European Supercup enough value,' Benítez says. 'But the Intercontinental is another story. It is the only title Liverpool has never won, so again we took it very seriously. I have seen that final against São Paulo on video again and I think it is extraordinary we lost it [the Brazilians won 1–0]. It's full of inexplicable decisions. Lugano should have got a red card for a tackle on Gerrard, not just a yellow; three disallowed goals ... We were clearly superior, although we have to think that for South Americans this competition is the top of the world: to beat the rich Europeans is to them like winning the World Cup, they want to win it at all costs.'

Two days before the final of the World Club Championship Francisco Benítez, Rafa's father, died. The Spanish coach and Liverpool were already in Japan. Some might have expected Rafa to fly home but reluctantly he decided not to. Francisco had been suffering from heart disease for a long time, and his son had already said his goodbyes. The haste with which death is dealt with in Spain meant that the funeral would take place within a couple of days of his demise. 'I had been in Spain a couple of months before he died,' Rafa, always one who keeps the expression of strong emotions at bay, explains. 'His heart was working at a third of its capacity. He had been a very energetic man and he could not walk two metres in less than ten minutes. His legs were black for lack of blood circulation. There was nothing I could do. The flight connections to Madrid would have meant I would have missed the funeral anyway. I wanted my mother to be comfortable and my brother said she was. And in any case, if I can avoid a funeral I do, especially now that I am getting older and friends are dying; it is hard to take.'

Back in England, after the disappointment of Japan and the death of his dad, Benítez immersed himself in the game and the fortunes of Liverpool. Halfway through the season, a couple of results confirmed that the early positive impressions the coaching sessions were creating were producing a solidity and consistency essential for success, and the feeling that the spectre of away defeats was a thing of the past. 'In fact, it is at home that we have played worse in the second season. We didn't dominate or play with the flair of the first one,' Ayestarán says. The victory in the Liverpool derby (winning 3–1 at Goodison Park) and the spectacular 5–3 scoreline against Luton at Kenilworth Road in the FA Cup after being 3–1 down, and then scoring three goals to go 4–3 up in the space of twelve minutes, convinced them all that the hard graft on the training ground was paying dividends.

'The previous year we were not able to manage some away matches,' Benítez says. 'We had more quality than the opposition but kept losing. The second year the team was more solid at the back, in midfield, and in attack. We are more consistent. Even when we did not get the three points earlier on, against Spurs or Boro, we felt we could easily have won. Gerrard had seven goal chances against Boro!' These were two goalless draws, but Benítez felt the team was improving. When the positive scores started arriving, the confidence did the rest.

The away defeats, though, were not the only ghost carried through from the previous season. In February the victories against Arsenal and Manchester United – both 1–0 – seemed to give the impression that Liverpool were getting closer to the top teams in the Premiership. However at the end of Benítez's second season, the staff agreed statistics still proved that the team had to win points away against the likes of Arsenal, Manchester United and Chelsea. These fixtures have resulted in six away defeats in the two Benítez years, so they have become a sort of litmus test of the team's Premiership quality. As long as these key away victories, at Stamford Bridge, Old Trafford or Arsenal (whether that be at the old Highbury or the new Emirates) continue to elude them, Liverpool's technical staff will know that there still remains work to be done to improve and strengthen the team.

'The target in the second season was to improve, but specifically to beat teams that we can normally beat, especially away,' Benítez remembers. 'And we wanted to see what happened with the ones who were our equals. Luckily we have not done too badly: we lost against Chelsea, against Arsenal with a rare mistake from Gerrard, and lost in the last minute against Manchester United. We have the feeling that we can now beat them.'

The double defeat against Benfica in the last sixteen of the Champions League coincided with one of the predicted physical drops of a very long season. It was also a reality check. Coming close to winning the European cup for the second consecutive year would have been a small miracle. 'The one in Lisbon was a painful defeat,' Benítez says, as if for Rafa there is any defeat that isn't. 'If you lose against a team that is superior to you, we accept it. But we played with lots of problems: Gerrard was not well, the horrific Sissoko injury, and so on. Despite that, we did not feel we were in danger of going down. And then we conceded a goal from a set piece, one that was so predictable that we had analysed it together beforehand. That affected how the second match went. Again, we went 1–0 down after two or three consecutive mistakes that I cannot accept. It is very hard to lose like that. Possibly we weren't in our best physical shape, but what hurt me most, though, was the feeling that we always fail in the little details, the same ones that kill us when we play against top teams in England.'

Arsenal defeated Liverpool four days after the disappointing Benfica result. Peter Crouch couldn't hit a barn door (one goal in thirteen matches); the team had lost its spark. The physical dip was taking its toll but then came the complete turnaround in form, one which, arguably, was the consequence of the planning. Five goals were scored against Fulham, three against Newcastle, three against Everton. The squad had reacted well after the difficulties, had hit form again and Crouch scored four goals in three matches.

'I have always backed Peter Crouch. He was not signed to score twenty-five goals a season, but to help us in what we need up front. For the style of football in England, he has been essential. He wins balls, fights for them, defends, generates second moves close to the rival box by winning aerial battles and having an eye for a pass. He can keep the ball, he can play it; that is what we want from him. This is what has helped us grow in away matches – his work, that of Momo [Sissoko] and the security of Pepe Reina.' Carragher concurs with his coach: 'Those three are the spine down the middle. We now have a physical presence – we are stronger, more solid.'

'Would Rafa have signed Crouch for Valencia?' asks Chris Bascombe, making the point that Rafa had quickly identified how to progress in England. Along with that obvious improvement, one thing became clear as the season moved on: the coaching staff were now targeting the FA Cup as one of the potential titles to win. In Benítez's first season it had been decided that players could be rested for the domestic cup competitions. Although that helped the European campaign, Liverpool's early exit from the Cup against Burnley had created the biggest crisis in the Benítez era. Now that the new inhabitants of Melwood realised the importance of the FA Cup, those rests did not coincide again with FA Cup fixtures. Would that extra effort be too much of a gamble for such a long season? Would it pay off?

(16)

THE FA CUP TRIUMPH

As Soon as it Started I Realised it was going to be Difficult to Beat West Ham

Rafa Benítez lives on the Wirral, indeed, he is a close neighbour of one Robbie Fowler. Montse, unlike the partners of some foreigners who have come to Liverpool in recent years, has found many reasons to enjoy Merseyside and, because she is Rafa's co-pilot on his all-consuming English adventure, she actively sought them out. Remaining a prisoner in their house was never going to be an option. Montse, a former lecturer in law at the Open University, now uses her time to improve her conversational English (thus enabling her to correct her husband's in the evening). She also goes to drama classes and she paints. She does not see her life now as a stop-gap existence, dead time in a parenthesis. This is her life and the life of her family. 'It is a total immersion,' Montse says. They rarely go out together or venture away form the area, but when they do, they have a couple of favourite places in the Lake District, 'where there is a bad signal for mobiles', she laughingly admits. She is well aware of her husband's love affair with the telephone.

Montse's praise for Liverpool is fulsome. 'There is a respect for Rafa from the staff and fans we haven't seen before. And that respect embraces me. I can only appreciate that and thank everybody for it. If you need something, they quickly find it, send it to you. Liverpool is a genuine family.' The regard in which Benítez is held manifests itself in many different ways and Montse has seen all kind of demonstrations of the fans' adulation. When they are in the car people who recognise them will often sound their horns, others will go out of their way to touch Benítez on the arm or shoulder; some will ask for an autograph; some tell him how much he is loved. To prevent this adulation spilling over into their children's lives, the headmaster at their school, in a letter sent to all parents, wisely requested that they be treated as normal. 'To be honest, all that worship, at first it disconcerts you a lot,' Montse admits. Now it is part of their lives. Both Rafa and Montse are reading about Liverpool and especially about Shankly, to understand the club's history and to try to comprehend what is behind that devotion. 'Liverpool is full of people who have suffered, and football is a way of life, as well as a source of happiness. It is very easy to see that,' Montse concludes. It was she who told Rafa and their friends that they were now living their lives as if they were going to stay for fifteen years on Merseyside. 'Till somebody thinks differently, this is our home. You have to forget about going back to Spain. And about our kids speaking mostly English; it is really nothing to worry about.' As a child, Montse spent a couple of years in Portugal and ended up speaking different languages. She thinks that living abroad enhances life, not diminishes it – in fact, it even helps your public profile. 'It is a bit sad, but in Spain you have to go abroad for people to recognise your quality. It takes a while for people to admit it, but they finally do, and they have recently done this in Rafa's case.' So when there was the real possibility of leaving for Madrid around March 2006, Montse was asked her opinion and she was clear in her mind. 'All these people deserve all our respect back. We cannot leave them.'

That empathy with Liverpool, a feeling that runs through the Spanish staff, was clearly the key factor when Real Madrid contacted Rafa Benítez just after a new chairman, Fernando Martín, had taken charge of the Spanish club. At that time there was talk of a shortlist at the Bernabéu that included people as diverse as Fabio Capello, Sven-Goran Eriksson and Arsène Wenger, but Benítez was contacted first. It sent a tremor through the club. First, the Board found it hard to accept that an approach was being made by Madrid until Benítez confirmed that it was true. Second, Benítez himself quickly had to take a cold hard look at what he had achieved at Liverpool, not just in terms of trophies, but also in terms of how the longer-term strategy was developing. Finally, the people around Rafa also had to have their say.

Rafa conferred with his assistants and told them about the offer, and put on the table the two possibilities: we can stay or we can go. They all agreed that it was not the moment to go. For them there was no doubt that their future lay with Liverpool. Benítez understands clearly that he has to finish what he has started. As one of his friends puts it: 'He could be another Alex Ferguson; his adaptation and that of his family is total.' Despite that, it was necessary to arrange a meeting with Rick Parry to make sure the club was in tune with his thinking. He took the opportunity to reassure himself that his decision to stay was the correct one. 'It was mostly a case of sitting down with Rafa over a weekend, but he made his mind up quite quickly,' Rick Parry says. 'We talked things through, about future plans. You can understand why it is a temptation; every Spaniard wants to manage Real Madrid at some stage. But again he chose Liverpool.' Rafa got a new contract – with an extra year on top of the five already agreed, and improved financial conditions – that ensured he would remain on Merseyside until 2010. Almost without having to negotiate, he got the reassurance he was really looking for.

What did Rick Parry have to say that convinced Rafa so quickly? 'Nothing. We just confirmed that we think on similar lines, that we were happy with the way things were going. Nothing new, really. I think he appreciates the value and honesty of the club; the fact that we don't make false promises.' At the same time that Liverpool were announcing to the world, via their website, that Rafa Benítez was not only staying but that he was going to sign a new contract (which was finally signed on 2 June), Fernando Martín was being interviewed by a Sky Sports crew. He still had hopes of convincing Benítez, probably because he was not aware of what was really keeping him on Merseyside.

So in March 2006 Rafa decided to stay, but not before he had thought about it, albeit briefly. Some hardcore fans might be inclined to the view that Rafa should, by that date, have been in no doubt that Liverpool is one of those few clubs in the world where the respect and power that the manager gets is beyond anything he might dream of elsewhere, and that he should already have come to regard his post on Merseyside as the summit of his career. In fact, it is probably the first case in Liverpool history where the job at Anfield is not considered by its holder as a pinnacle. Benítez, as well as being a pragmatist, is also Spanish. His childhood had spawned different dreams to other Liverpool bosses, and probably coaching Real Madrid and being the Spanish national coach are two of them. It is unrealistic to imagine that he can totally deny or reject his long-held aspirations.

Robbie Fowler's return to Liverpool is a story made of similar childhood dreams. He came back to end his 'unfinished business' with the club he loves. It became one of the most memorable stories of the 2005–2006 season. He wrote in his autobiography: 'I honestly don't believe that I have ever been happier in my football life than the moment when I sat in my car outside Anfield, a minute after I had put pen to paper to bring me home.' It was the end of January 2006, twelve long months after Benítez had first mentioned the possibility of signing him. On that occasion he went, instead, for Morientes. The first serious contacts were established in the summer of 2005, but Fowler fractured one of the discs in his spine, an injury that took a long time to be discovered, and delayed any chance of him returning to Anfield. Robbie, by now already playing again, and Rafa met at a private party after the Champions League match against Chelsea, but it wasn't until later on that, with the permission of Manchester City, both of them met at Benítez's house, just a quarter of a mile away from Fowler's, to discuss their future together. They shared a drink of water and a long conversation.

'The team needed better stats in finishing,' Benítez says. The financial risk was minimal; the sporting one, much higher. When he signed Robbie, Benítez was understandably worried about his fitness because he was in very poor physical condition and needed a lot of work on his fragile body. Recuperation after his injury had not been overseen to the best standards. Cautiously, Benítez waited until the end of the season before increasing the original six-month contract. Many people were surprised as it seemed an easy decision to make; one where nobody was going to lose, but Benítez did need convincing. The Spanish coach wanted to see a clear enhancement in Fowler's fitness and to reduce the sporting risk to the minimum – he wanted to have a player on board that he could use, not just a talismanic has-been. Finally, the good statistics, his physical improvement, his clever movement, his attitude and, importantly, the needs of the team, persuaded Benítez. Liverpool requires that kind of player in the Premiership, while in Europe what he offers complements the team.

'It is very difficult to find a player who is not obsessed by money, by his contract; but that what he wants to do is to continue playing, to make an effort, to work hard to play for the club he loves,' Benítez says admiringly. 'There were expectations about his goals, and they arrived finally at key moments after having three disallowed. He has helped us to continue the good relationship with the fans, to strengthen the union with them.' Fowler, a returning god to add to the Pantheon, scored the winning goal against Bolton and then against Blackburn, and the first one against West Brom away. These were well-timed dividends for the gamble taken.

As he had played for Manchester City against Scunthorpe United in the FA Cup he could, of course, take no part in Liverpool's campaign. In the first round proper, Liverpool spectacularly came from behind to beat Luton. The core of the team was playing that day – Hyypia, Carragher, Xabi Alonso (whose second goal of the match, a sixty-yard strike, ended the contest), Kewell, Gerrard, Crouch. Then they delivered a workmanlike, professional performance to go 2–0 up at Portsmouth and to hold out comfortably in the last thirty-five minutes after Pompey had briefly threatened with a goal of their own. Next came Manchester United.

By admitting, before that fifth-round match, that it is very difficult to beat Liverpool if they score first, that Benítez's team only 'had to play for five minutes' to get the win, Sir Alex Ferguson was suggesting that they were impostors incapable of performing for the whole match. But on the day, the reality was that Liverpool bossed the midfield and dominated the game from the outset. Following Peter Crouch's headed goal after nineteen minutes, the afternoon became even worse for United as Alan Smith suffered a broken leg after blocking a John Arne Riise shot. In the sixth round, Birmingham, who until then had never lost against Benítez, suffered a humiliating defeat. An early goal from Hyypia started the rot. Steve Bruce's team conceded seven goals as Liverpool advanced to the semi-finals where they would meet Chelsea, yet again.

By that stage of the season it was clear that Steven Gerrard, voted PFA Player of the Year by his peers, had become Liverpool's best player. His new contract gave him the stability he was craving. He knows now it will be very difficult for him ever to move from Liverpool but he is convinced that, so long as the Board continues to support Benítez and his ambitions for Liverpool, then the Spanish coach will, in turn, make those giant strides that turn Liverpool back into a great club; one that he, long term, wants to be associated with. 'Steven Gerrard started scoring goals at the beginning of the season,' Benítez remembers. 'And as I saw his progression I decided to find him an extra individual challenge. I saw as a real possibility his scoring twenty-five goals [he ended up with twenty-three] and he would have got it if it wasn't for some games he missed because of little injuries. He was placed on the right of midfield, where we had seen him a few times the previous season. We found the balance with Sissoko, Xabi and, on some occasions, Hamann. He creates lots of problems to rivals from that right-hand side. When he makes his diagonal runs he is difficult to stop, and if he decides to put a cross in they come with menace too.'

To begin with, Gerrard did not like this new position and Benítez was aware of that. 'We knew it, but to benefit the team he accepted it,' Rafa says. 'If he had had a poor match, you would sense his unhappiness with the tactical position. But finally when the team started winning and he was playing well, he felt comfortable and happier. We have imposed the team mentality and the captain was a good example of it.' Occasionally, and at the end of the season, Gerrard returned to a holding midfield position along with Xabi Alonso. This is a combination that has not always worked but Benítez planned to use it more often in the future once they had rectified a long-term deficiency by signing a natural right-sided midfielder. In fact, Xabi and Steven may have to battle often for a place in the line-up as Sissoko also seems destined to be a regular in the side because he has such a high work rate. 'Gerrard is such a powerful player that when he goes forward it is almost impossible to defend against him. You, as a coach, cannot hold him back continually; he needs the freedom to roam around because those movements clearly make a difference. We have to find a balance between the times that he can be left free and those when he has to follow tactical obligations,' Benítez warns.

In the FA Cup semi-final, Gerrard ran Chelsea ragged along the right flank, and a revitalised Kewell did the same down the left. José Mourinho complained that John Arne Riise's opening goal shouldn't have been a free kick in the first place but, with thirty thousand jubilant Liverpool supporters celebrating inside Old Trafford, the Chelsea manager's moans were overwhelmed. Then Luis García, the usual hero against the London rivals, reappeared and scored his inevitable goal; a deceptively elegant shot, after a forty-yard sprint, that put the tie beyond the West London club.

Mourinho's tactics that day had played right into Liverpool's hands. Of Chelsea's decision to use right-back Paulo Ferreira in the midfield and to play with two strikers, Crespo and Drogba, Pako Ayestarán concedes, 'Any other choice would have done us much more harm.'

Liverpool had planned for the possibility of either two or three forwards being used against them so, when Chelsea's formation was known, Benítez reminded everybody of the things to do and of all that had been rehearsed in training. What Rafa did not know was that Mourinho had not even practised the new system during the week. When the Chelsea players heard about it on the morning of the game, they were, to put it mildly, somewhat surprised. 'I think he tried to find a one-on-one in our defence; a striker against a centre back, and try to hurt us through the centre,' was Paco Herrera's analysis of events. But what actually happened was that the Liverpool fullbacks did not suffer at all, and it was easy to combat the Chelsea attacks through the centre as the Reds now have a physical presence equal to most.

Didier Drogba pulled one back for the Blues to set up a frantic finish with another 'Gudjohnsen moment' when Joe Cole, deep into injury time, blasted over from eight yards out. Liverpool held on to make it through to their thirteenth FA Cup final. Backstage, along the corridors of Old Trafford just a few minutes after the final whistle, Mourinho crossed paths with Benítez, but did not look at him and did not even congratulate him on Liverpool's victory. His palpable rage was a recognition of his own mistakes that day. Also, here was proof that Benítez's team had moved to a higher level, had joined a new elite – the one inhabited by real contenders. Maybe you offer paternalistic respect to a rival not on your level but, as with Mourinho that day, you detest the one who comes and takes your crown.

When the Cardiff FA Cup final arrived, Rafa Benítez was again ready to wield that axe with a squad that was still not up to scratch. The previous months, his staff had prepared for a better season with the early signings of the Argentinian centre back Gabriel Paletta and Valencia left back Fabio Aurelio, only confirmed in the summer but agreed much earlier, and the deferred capture of Mark González (who returned to the club after his successful six-month loan spell at Real Sociedad, where he had to go as he could not get a work permit). He knew that with Cissé going, and once Craig Bellamy was signed from Blackburn, he had to spend the summer of 2006 waiting for the right moment to make a final approach for a striker, Dirk Kuyt being the chosen one, and for the right winger; Daniel Alvés of Sevilla was the preferred option but was too expensive and Jermaine Pennant became a more than decent second choice.

Benítez has always tried to avoid signing the so-called prima donnas but has changed his tune a bit, and now admits that there is nobody he definitely would not sign. He now concedes that acquiring someone with a controversial past like Bellamy has to be considered if it fulfils the needs of the team. 'If you ask any manager, they would tell you that we look for the ideal centre back, the ideal midfielder, and so on. But when you do not find that, you try to get something close to it; somebody that would guarantee loyalty to work and commitment. There is always something positive you can get from someone with a notorious past. But the final decisions depend as much on the market as on the wishes of the manager. Bellamy and Pennant, aware as I am of their quality and love for the club, are a risk I am willing to take.'

Looking forward to Benítez's third season, the enormous shadow of Abramovich's Chelsea dominates the scene. Their acquisitions of Michael Ballack, Andriy Shevchenko and Salomon Kalou make the idea of the Premiership title yet more difficult. When so much money is clearly the significant difference between teams, the legitimacy of the 'domestic' title is placed in doubt by football people. But nevertheless that is what the objective is. 'We are the team that shoots more on goal, that crosses and heads the ball in the box more often. The problem is that we are not effective enough – we have to finalise better and service the players better up front. We had more clean sheets than anybody; we are the second-best defence. We only need to give another little jump. Will that jump be enough to get to the top? I don't know, when you see what others are able to get,' Benítez admits.

Liverpool are poised at a critical moment. Fewer points in the coming season after the fantastic second harvest would create doubts in the minds of the fans and even in the mind of Rafa Benítez himself. What would be the consequences of that happening? 'There are echoes of Houllier really,' Bascombe says. 'The position we are in now is the one we were in in 2002. The only difference is that we have a better coach, better players, but it is still the same situation and the next signing is going to decide if we go back to 2002. There is only one place to go after last season. Rafa has done in one season what Houllier did in four, but now we have to challenge for the title.'

'Our philosophy has always been to try to improve,' Rick Parry says. 'Knowing that along the way we can pick up a cup is a bonus. Progress in the league has been tremendous; narrowing the gap on Chelsea from thirty-seven points to nine is fantastic; but for me an even bigger achievement is to get so many points over Arsenal – the first time we have been ahead of them since 1996. Eighty-six points is fifty per cent more than the previous season. You can analyse it so many ways. The next progression of course is the big one.'

Work always yields results. We are not about getting sporadic success. With the working method that Pako and Rafa use, followed up by the rest of the staff, the team grows progressively. If the signings settle in well, Liverpool can win the league,' Paco Herrera says. Alas, this loyal assistant to Benítez moved on from Liverpool during the summer to become the director of football at Espanyol, but not without having left his imprint – a reserve team with a different philosophy to the rest of the Premiership. 'We decided to have twenty-two players we rely on in the first team and, parallel to that, build a B team like there is in Spain, a project for the future, with players that can be part of the first team in three years maximum, acquired with hardly any money and then developed.'

The FA Cup Final against West Ham, though, had come too early for these new men. In the week of the final Luis García, Fernando Morientes, Pepe Reina and Xabi Alonso were called up by Spain, but only Luis García went as he was suspended for the final that Saturday. The rest had to stay put, a decision not welcomed by most of them. But Benítez wanted them to have their focus on one thing only – winning the Cup Final. Already at their hotel in Cardiff late on the Friday afternoon, the players were well rested for the match. Benítez and his staff, once they had all settled in, sat down together and started planning and organising the forthcoming pre-season . . . till eleven at night! Nothing is left to chance at Liverpool.

The next day, after breakfast and a stroll near the hotel, close to the Millennium Stadium, the players gathered to receive their final instructions before the 3 p.m. kick-off. 'We prefer things to happen quickly. It was good that we did not have to wait too long for the match to start,' Carragher says. The line-up had been chosen some days before the final and was comprised of the best eleven for a fixture that, they thought, would have the usual ingredients of a Premiership match: pace, physical aggression, long balls. So the ones were Reina, Finnan, Hyypia, Carragher, Riise, Gerrard, Xabi Alonso, Sissoko, Kewell, Cissé and Peter Crouch. On the bench, just five subs: Dudek, Krompkamp, Hamann, Morientes and Traore. The final they were about to compete in would prove to have the entertainment value of Russian roulette.

RAFA BENÍTEZ: 'We knew West Ham is an offensive team not scared of going forward. We knew they score goals, but also that they concede them. It was going to be an open final.'

PAKO AYESTARÁN: 'The plan was to play down the flanks and to have a fluid game, to move the ball around, to dominate that way. But not everybody had a good game. It was a surprise the way we played the first few minutes because the warm-up had been excellent, and normally I can pick up if a player is suffering an excess of tension in the exercises before a match. But as soon as the match started I realised it was going to be difficult to beat West Ham.'

PEPE REINA: 'The first goal was a very quick movement. Xabi lost the ball to Benayoun and he played it short to Ashton. He threaded it to Scaloni in on the right and his low cross ricocheted off Carragher. I think I read the pass well, but Carra couldn't hear me scream "my ball". It is not a mistake but bad luck. In the second, with half an hour gone, I spilt a shot off Etherington and Asthon tapped in the loose ball. It was my mistake, clearly. The ball goes away from me, but not too far. The striker was quick to react. I should have got hold of the ball; it didn't come with much power.'

RAFA BENÍTEZ: 'We weren't doing much in wide positions or through the centre. In fact, we weren't doing much, full stop. So we decided to change to a 4-5-1 and to try and create some danger by playing the ball through their midfield and defence. So Cissé moved wide left, and that way the full back had someone to worry about and open up spaces at the back. He could also use the huge space left between the full back and their winger. Kewell was moved to the middle of the attack behind Crouch.'

OCHOTORENA: 'We weren't imposing our game, and to add insult to injury we had to come back from behind. Players were not switched on to start with, maybe because of the pressure of coming out on the pitch as favourites. We were being dominated when the rest of the season we were learning to dominate. It was a match that nobody controlled, a match without an owner. It was very useful that Cissé scored, after a pass from Gerrard, before the interval.'

PAKO AYESTARÁN: 'We were upset on the way to the changing rooms. I talked with Rafa about what needed changing but it was pretty obvious – we had to play more down the wings and there was space to use in between their defence and midfield, but sadly the player who can use it cleverly was suspended. So, inside the locker room, Rafa started giving instructions.'

RAFA BENÍTEZ: 'It was important to go back to the locker room after getting one goal back. There was no telling-off at half time, although I was disappointed. I insisted to them that there were things that we spoke about before the match that were not being done. We had conceded two goals and, now we were playing 4-5-1, we needed to have the ball again to make the new system work. We needed to be more precise with our passing. One thing was clear – you cannot compare this match or even half-time to Istanbul. We had much more confidence in what we were able to do; we thought we could win it. I reminded my players that West Ham concede more goals in the second half, and that we score many more in the last 15 minutes of the game; so we were sure that if things went well, we could still come back and had options to win the Cup.'

PACO HERRERA: 'The second half started and Reina made a crucial double save from Harewood and then Benayoun. West Ham had started on the front foot and we needed to change procedures very quickly if we were to win it.'

RAFA BENÍTEZ: 'Pepe is not the kind of player who would think for twenty minutes about his mistakes. He was focused when the second half started, and kept us in the game with his double save.'

PAKO AYESTARÁN: 'After that save, we controlled the game, but had to improvise again after Kewell's injury. We felt Morientes could guarantee us a better control of the ball and he came on.'

PACO HERRERA: 'Then we scored our second goal after Xabi flew a ball into the box, Crouch nodded down and Gerrard smashed it into the top corner. We only needed to maintain the possession long enough to make sure we did not lose control of the game again.'

PEPE REINA: 'The third goal we conceded I would say was also my error. It is a difficult one to stop because Konchesky's cross-cum-shot is a confusing ball. But to be honest, if it goes in people rightly blame the goalkeeper. I could have reacted quicker or differently, I could have read the swerve of the ball better, to have been better placed, more in the centre. I will have time to analyse it because I will watch it a thousand times.'

OCHOTORENA: 'I don't think it was Reina's mistake as he was placed ideally to receive a cross, which is really what it was.'

RAFA BENÍTEZ: 'We had talked about the heat of that day and how it could affect Xabi, who had been injured. But he played because he felt well the day before. When he came off, I thought maybe it was better to play with Krompkamp on the right because he had fresh legs, and Paul Konchesky appeared to have cramps. We needed to get more control of the midfield as we were having to run back a lot when West Ham attacked with pace. A few minutes later, I put Didi on for Crouch. He has experience, so I explained to him that he needed to keep the ball and play more with the wingers because we had been playing a lot through the middle and losing the ball.'

STEVIE G: 'The pitch at Cardiff is really big and it was trying out there. It was really humid, and I'm the type of player who builds himself up for these big finals days before. So I just ran out of steam after seventy minutes and started cramping up.'

PAKO AYESTARÁN: 'We were out of the game, we had given up, players were hobbling; Riise, Finnan, Gerrard ... West Ham were going to win. Then Stevie G. scores. That is the difference between having or not having a player that at any moment can save your day. The quality of the strike in his second goal ... Well, you have to admit that there is not much you can do against that.'

PEPE REINA: 'In extra time I was thinking, "I hope they do not score". They didn't. I was not thinking about me becoming a hero; it was the best for the team because we were clearly in a poor state.'

RAFA BENÍTEZ: 'Pepe is famous in Spain for saving penalties and we had confidence in him. Before the shoot-out the goalkeeper coach was talking to him about what to do. We reminded him that we had information about their penalty takers, not all of them, but some. About who would take ours; we knew Cissé would be a problem as he was injured; Gerrard, Hamann were clear choices. In fact it was easy to decide as most of the players had some kind of muscular problem or other.'

OCHOTORENA: 'I was convinced Reina could become a hero that afternoon. I reminded him that it was his chance to be the protagonist. I told him to be focused, confident. He had made mistakes that could have cost us the match, and I felt we had to support him. During the year, without having exceptional matches, he performed consistently. He had to adapt to a new football he loved, but that he only knew from the TV. In England there are more crosses to the box, more contact; more risks have to be taken. He has suffered those difficulties, and it was time to finish the season on a high.'

PEPE REINA: 'I felt I could give something back to the fans that had been patient with me. I remember in a match against Birmingham, a Spanish fan spent the whole ninety minutes shouting funny things to me. I spent the fixture entertained, so at the end I decided to jump to the stands and give him a hug. Stopping penalties was a way to repay that faith.'

RAFA BENÍTEZ: 'We gave Pepe some information, but Sheringham changed his usual place, which was always a possibility. At the end, Reina saved three by his own intuition.'

PEPE REINA: 'I saved Zamora's spot-kick and that gave me confidence. 'I doubted where to go when Sheringham took the second penalty because of the information I was given. After that, I decided to go where my instinct told me. Then I was lucky, I also stopped Konchesky's and Anton Ferdinand's penalties, 3–1 to us in the shootout. It was a match that brought out the worst and the best in me. And I will keep both feelings. You learn from everything. Football is very generous – it takes away from you but it also gives back to you.'

PAKO AYESTARÁN: 'In Istanbul we went from bad to better, but we dominated the match more often. In Cardiff, we also came from behind, but with no control. We did win, but we had a feeling that maybe we didn't deserve to.'

PEPE REINA: 'In the changing rooms, champagne bottles were opened. People were pleased, thankful for how things turned out, relieved; we had the cup in our hands, we were taking private photos with it. And because of fans, the atmosphere, because of what this competition means, we had to feel proud.'

Rafa Benítez felt the team was far from the complete article, and with that frustrating sentiment, he joined the players in the changing room – compared to Istanbul it was a subdued one. Players boarded the coach after doing their press interviews. Nobody was singing, and faces showed relief rather than ecstasy. It did not feel as if Liverpool had just won the FA Cup. The coach was parked in a dim tunnel inside the stadium, not far from the exit. When the engine started up it was the only noise that reverberated into the darkness of the building. Then the vehicle drove out into the still bright evening sunlight, and was greeted by the celebrating fans. Their infectious mood transformed the glumness inside the coach; frowns changed to smiles. But for Rafa Benítez there was not much to honour yet. He reclined his head and started thinking about the following season and the ultimate target.

APPENDIX

European Cup Final Istanbul, 25 May 2005 (KO 21.45)

Milan 3 (3)–3 (0) (AET) Liverpool
Maldini (7), Crespo (39 and 44), Gerrard (54), Smicer (56), Alonso (59)
Liverpool win 3–2 on penalties

Milan: Dida, Cafu, Maldini, Stam, Nesta, Gattuso (Rui Costa, 112), Seedorf (Serginho, 86), Pirlo, Kaká, Shevchenko, Crespo (Tomasson, 85)
Subs not used: Abbiati, Kaladze, Costacurta, Dhorasoo
Liverpool: Dudek, Finnan (Hamann, 46) Traore, Hyypia, Carragher, Riise, Gerrard, Luis García, Xabi Alonso, Kewell (Smicer, 23), Baroš (Cissé, 85)
Subs not used: Carson, Josemi, Núñez, Biscan

Bookings: Baroš, Carragher (Liverpool)
Attendance: 65,000
Referee: Mejuto González (Spain)

Liverpool 2004–05 results and fixtures

European Cup	Graz AK	0–2	Liverpool	10–08–2004
English Premier	Tottenham	1–1	Liverpool	14–08–2004
English Premier	Liverpool	2–1	Man. City	21–08–2004
European Cup	Liverpool	0–1	Graz AK	24–08–2004
English Premier	Bolton	1–0	Liverpool	29–08–2004
English Premier	Liverpool	3–0	West Brom.	11–09–2004
European Cup	Liverpool	2–0	Monaco	15–09–2004

English Premier	Man. Utd	2–1	Liverpool	20–09–2004
English Premier	Liverpool	3–0	Norwich	25–09–2004
European Cup	Olympiakos	1–0	Liverpool	28–09–2004
English Premier	Chelsea	1–0	Liverpool	03–10–2004
English Premier	Fulham	2–4	Liverpool	16–10–2004
European Cup	Liverpool	0–0	Deportivo	19–10–2004
English Premier	Liverpool	2–0	Charlton	23–10–2004
English League Cup	Millwall	0–3	Liverpool	26–10–2004
English Premier	Blackburn	2–2	Liverpool	30–10–2004
European Cup	Deportivo	0–1	Liverpool	03–11–2004
English Premier	Liverpool	0–1	Birmingham	06–11–2004
English League Cup	Liverpool	2–0	Middlesbrough	10–11–2004
English Premier	Liverpool	3–2	C. Palace	13–11–2004
English Premier	Middlesbrough	2–0	Liverpool	20–11–2004
European Cup	Monaco	1–0	Liverpool	23–11–2004
English Premier	Liverpool	2–1	Arsenal	28–11–2004
English League Cup	Tottenham	1–1	Liverpool	01–12–2004
English Premier	Aston Villa	1–1	Liverpool	04–12–2004
European Cup	Liverpool	3–1	Olympiakos	08–12–2004
English Premier	Everton	1–0	Liverpool	11–12–2004
English Premier	Liverpool	1–1	Portsmouth	14–12–2004
English Premier	Liverpool	3–1	Newcastle	19–12–2004
English Premier	West Brom.	0–5	Liverpool	26–12–2004
English Premier	Liverpool	1–0	Southampton	28–12–2004
English Premier	Liverpool	0–1	Chelsea	01–01–2005
English Premier	Norwich	1–2	Liverpool	03–01–2005
English League Cup	Liverpool	1–0	Watford	11–01–2005
English Premier	Liverpool	0–1	Man. Utd	15–01–2005
English FA Cup	Burnley	1–0	Liverpool	18–01–2005
English Premier	Southampton	2–0	Liverpool	22–01–2005
English League Cup	Watford	0–1	Liverpool	25–01–2005
English Premier	Charlton	1–2	Liverpool	01–02–2005
English Premier	Liverpool	3–1	Fulham	05–02–2005
English Premier	Birmingham	2–0	Liverpool	12–02–2005
European Cup	Liverpool	3–1	B. Leverkusen	22–02–2005

English League Cup	Liverpool	2–3	Chelsea	27–02–2005
English Premier	Newcastle	1–0	Liverpool	05–03–2005
European Cup	B. Leverkusen	1–3	Liverpool	09–03–2005
English Premier	Liverpool	0–0	Blackburn	16–03–2005
English Premier	Liverpool	2–1	Everton	20–03–2005
English Premier	Liverpool	1–0	Bolton	02–04–2005
European Cup	Liverpool	2–1	Juventus	05–04–2005
English Premier	Man. City	1–0	Liverpool	09–04–2005
European Cup	Juventus	0–0	Liverpool	13–04–2005
English Premier	Liverpool	2–2	Tottenham	16–04–2005
English Premier	Portsmouth	1–2	Liverpool	20–04–2005
English Premier	C. Palace	1–0	Liverpool	23–04–2005
European Cup	Chelsea	0–0	Liverpool	27–04–2005
English Premier	Liverpool	1–1	Middlesbrough	30–04–2005
European Cup	Liverpool	1–0	Chelsea	03–05–2005
English Premier	Arsenal	3–1	Liverpool	08–05–2005
English Premier	Liverpool	2–1	Aston Villa	15–05–2005
European Cup	Milan	3–3	Liverpool	25–05–2005

Liverpool 2005–06 results and fixtures

European Cup	Liverpool	3–0	TNS	13–07–2005
European Cup	TNS	0–3	Liverpool	19–07–2005
European Cup	FBS Kaunas	1–3	Liverpool	26–07–2005
European Cup	Liverpool	2–0	FBK Kaunas	02–08–2005
European Cup	CSKA Sofia	1–3	Liverpool	10–08–2005
English Premier	Middlesbrough	0–0	Liverpool	13–08–2005
English Premier	Liverpool	1–0	Sunderland	20–08–2005
European Cup	Liverpool	0–1	CSKA Sofia	23–08–2005
UEFA Super Cup	Liverpool	3–1	CSKA Moscow	26–08–2005
English Premier	Tottenham	0–0	Liverpool	10–09–2005
European Cup	Real Betis	1–2	Liverpool	13–09–2005
English Premier	Liverpool	0–0	Man. Utd	18–09–2005
English Premier	Birmingham	2–2	Liverpool	24–09–2005
European Cup	Liverpool	0–0	Chelsea	28–09–2005

English Premier	Liverpool	1–4	Chelsea	02–10–2005
English Premier	Liverpool	1–0	Blackburn	15–10–2005
European Cup	Anderlecht	0–1	Liverpool	19–10–2005
English Premier	Fulham	2–0	Liverpool	22–10–2005
English League Cup	C. Palace	2–1	Liverpool	25–10–2005
English Premier	Liverpool	2–0	West Ham	29–10–2005
European Cup	Liverpool	3–0	Anderlecht	01–11–2005
English Premier	Aston Villa	0–2	Liverpool	05–11–2005
English Premier	Liverpool	3–0	Portsmouth	19–11–2005
European Cup	Liverpool	0–0	Real Betis	23–11–2005
English Premier	Man. City	0–1	Liverpool	26–11–2005
English Premier	Sunderland	0–2	Liverpool	30–11–2005
English Premier	Liverpool	3–0	Wigan	03–12–2005
European Cup	Chelsea	0–0	Liverpool	06–12–2005
English Premier	Liverpool	2–0	Middlesbrough	10–12–2005
FIFA Club World Championship	Saprissa	0–3	Liverpool	15–12–2005
FIFA Club World Championship	Liverpool	0–1	Sao Paulo	18–12–2005
English Premier	Liverpool	2–0	Newcastle	26–12–2005
English Premier	Everton	1–3	Liverpool	28–12–2005
English Premier	Liverpool	1–0	West Brom.	31–12–2005
English Premier	Bolton	2–2	Liverpool	02–01–2006
English FA Cup	Luton	3–5	Liverpool	07–01–2006
English Premier	Liverpool	1–0	Tottenham	14–01–2006
English Premier	Man. Utd	1–0	Liverpool	22–01–2006
English FA Cup	Portsmouth	1–2	Liverpool	29–01–2006
English Premier	Liverpool	1–1	Birmingham	01–02–2006
English Premier	Chelsea	2–0	Liverpool	05–02–2006
English Premier	Charlton	2–0	Liverpool	08–02–2006
English Premier	Wigan	0–1	Liverpool	11–02–2006
English Premier	Liverpool	1–0	Arsenal	14–02–2006
English FA Cup	Liverpool	1–0	Man. Utd	18–02–2006
European Cup	Benfica	1–0	Liverpool	21–02–2006
English Premier	Liverpool	1–0	Man. City	26–02–2006

English Premier	Liverpool	0–0	Charlton	04–03–2006
European Cup	Liverpool	0–2	Benfica	08–03–2006
English Premier	Arsenal	2–1	Liverpool	12–03–2006
English Premier	Liverpool	5–1	Fulham	15–03–2006
English Premier	Newcastle	1–3	Liverpool	19–03–2006
English FA Cup	Birmingham	0–7	Liverpool	21–03–2006
English Premier	Liverpool	3–1	Everton	25–03–2006
English Premier	West Brom.	0–2	Liverpool	01–04–2006
English Premier	Liverpool	1–0	Bolton	09–04–2006
English Premier	Blackburn	0–1	Liverpool	16–04–2006
English FA Cup	Chelsea	1–2	Liverpool	22–04–2006
English Premier	West Ham	1–2	Liverpool	26–04–2006
English Premier	Liverpool	3–1	Aston Villa	29–04–2006
English Premier	Portsmouth	1–3	Liverpool	07–05–2006
English FA Cup	Liverpool	3–3	West Ham	13–05–2006

INDEX

ACKNOWLEDGEMENTS

Thanks go to everyone who gave generously of their time to be interviewed for this book, particularly players and staff of Liverpool, past and present: Jamie Carragher, Xabi Alonso, Steven Gerrard, Pepe Reina, Luis Garcia, Didi Hamann, Jerzy Dudek, Vladimir Smicer, Djimi Traore, Paco Herrera, Pako Ayestarán, José Manuel Ochotorena, Sammy Lee, Phil Thompson, John Aldridge, Steve McManaman and Michael Robinson. And of course to Rafa Benítez and Rick Parry, who found time to recapitulate about that marvellous season and, in the case of Rafa, who sat with me 20 years later to look back at what that magical title meant to him, to the players and to the club. Thanks as well to Ian Cotton, the Liverpool press officer, and the rest of the press office for their continuous help. Plus Milan player Gennaro Gattuso who decided to break his silence for the book, referee Mejuto González and the fans Lee Martin, Matt Barragan, Paul Flanagan and Paul Tremarco, plus so many more that have shared what they did and they felt on the night of Istanbul.

Several people have been key to the efficient manufacture of the book, especially David Luxton, my agent, whose words, even the slightly critical ones, sound like encouragement; Alan Samson and Mark Rusher at Weidenfeld & Nicolson, whose enthusiasm earlier on and love for the game have made this possible and trusted me when I said I could write a book even thought I had never even tried it before; Tierney Witty who suggested to do a foreword for the new edition and has managed to get me to look forward to his comments as they are so precise, encouraging and useful; Graham Hunter whose faithful translation, comments and support helped shape the book; Gabriele Marcotti who helped with the editing in between heated conversations in Frankfurt; Sid Lowe who was in Istanbul and has read the whole thing with his Liverpool glasses as well as with his sharp intelligence; Peter Bennett, to whom I owe a couple of meals for his help; Chris Parle (and his mother), for whom summer 2005 will be for ever related to the book; Luis Miguel García Vega, who has learnt lots of English and whose comments were always spot on, and Begoña Bergés, to whom I promise to record the next interviews away from a restaurant!

For help with logistics, I am indebted to Brent Wilks who provided encouragement and sometimes even the entertainment. I am grateful to my newspaper, *AS*, who allowed me to disappear from my obligations for a couple of months, and to Daniel Yáñez for doing my work in the meantime. Thanks as well to Chris Bascombe for his guidance and support, as well as other journalists who offered great insight and help, especially Aurelio Capaldi (RAI – I owe you a huge favour!), Raphael Honigstein (*Süddeutsche Zeitung*), Eduardo Esteve (*Onda Cero*), Tony Barrett (Liverpool *Echo* at the time and is now press officer at the club), Giancarlo Galavotti (*Gazetta dello Sport*), Pierluigi Pardo (*Sky Italia*), and Dave Usher, who edits the wonderful fanzine *The Liverpool Way* and who kindly let me use some material from it.

Finally, thanks to devoted Liverpool fans Sandra and Pepe, their two daughters, as well as Sandra's mum, for spreading the word about the book and for the wonderful football table that I will swap for a free book or two. To Maribel Herruzo who is now family as well as my personal publisher, editor, therapist and so many more things. To Gustavo Balagué,who is finally allowed to read it, and Yolanda Balagué, for allowing me to leave her on her own in the pool of the Marrakech hotel while I finished it. And to William Glasswell who keeps showing me the support that I need especially when I feel like burning everything down.